Probation and the Policing of the Private Sphere in Britain, 1907–1962

History of Crime, Deviance and Punishment

Series Editor: Anne-Marie Kilday, Professor of Criminal History, Oxford Brookes University, UK

Editorial Board: Neil Davie, University of Lyon II, France
Johannes Dillinger, University of Maine, Germany
Wilbur Miller, State University of New York, USA
Marianna Muravyeva, University of Helsinki, Finland
David Nash, Oxford Brookes University, UK
Judith Rowbotham, Nottingham Trent University, UK

Academic interest in the history of crime and punishment has never been greater and the *History of Crime, Deviance and Punishment* series provides a home for the wealth of new research being produced. Individual volumes within the series cover topics related to the history of crime and punishment, from the later medieval to modern period and in both Europe and North America, and seek to demonstrate the importance of this subject in furthering understanding of the way in which various societies and cultures operate. When taken together, the works in the series will show the evolution of the nature of illegality and attitudes towards its perpetration over time and will offer their readers a rounded and coherent history of crime and punishment through the centuries. The series' broad chronological and geographical coverage encourages comparative historical analysis of crime history between countries and cultures.

Published:

Policing the Factory, Barry Godfrey
Crime and Poverty in 19th-Century England, Adrian Ager
Print Culture, Crime and Justice in Eighteenth-Century London, Richard Ward
Rehabilitation and Probation in England and Wales, 1900–1950, Raymond Gard
The Policing of Belfast 1870–1914, Mark Radford
Crime, Regulation and Control during the Blitz, Peter Adey, David J. Cox and Barry Godfrey
The Italian Prison in the Age of Positivism, 1861–1914, Mary Gibson
Life Courses of Young Convicts Transported to Van Diemen's Land, Emma D. Watkins
Fair and Unfair Trials in the British Isles, 1800–1940, eds. David Nash and Anne-Marie Kilday
Photographing Crime Scenes in Twentieth-Century London, Alexa Neale
Combating London's Criminal Class, Matthew Bach

Forthcoming:

Sex and Violence in 1920s Scotland, Louise Heren
Mothers, Criminal Insanity and the Asylum in Victorian England, Alison Pedley
Feminist Campaigns against Child Sexual Abuse, Daniel J. R. Grey
Crime and Criminal Justice in Early Modern Ireland, Coleman A. Dennehy
Male Suicide and Masculinity in 19th-century Britain, Lyndsay Galpin

Probation and the Policing of the Private Sphere in Britain, 1907–1962

Louise Settle

BLOOMSBURY ACADEMIC
LONDON • NEW YORK • OXFORD • NEW DELHI • SYDNEY

BLOOMSBURY ACADEMIC
Bloomsbury Publishing Plc
50 Bedford Square, London, WC1B 3DP, UK
1385 Broadway, New York, NY 10018, USA
29 Earlsfort Terrace, Dublin 2, Ireland

BLOOMSBURY, BLOOMSBURY ACADEMIC and the Diana logo
are trademarks of Bloomsbury Publishing Plc

First published in Great Britain 2022
This paperback edition published 2023

Copyright © Louise Settle, 2022

Louise Settle has asserted her right under the Copyright, Designs and Patents Act, 1988, to be identified as Author of this work.

For legal purposes the Acknowledgements on p. ix constitute an extension of this copyright page.

Cover design: Terry Woodley
Cover image © *Home Again*, 1884, Frederick McCubbin.
National Gallery of Victoria, Melbourne

All rights reserved. No part of this publication may be reproduced or transmitted in any form or by any means, electronic or mechanical, including photocopying, recording, or any information storage or retrieval system, without prior permission in writing from the publishers.

Bloomsbury Publishing Plc does not have any control over, or responsibility for, any third-party websites referred to or in this book. All internet addresses given in this book were correct at the time of going to press. The author and publisher regret any inconvenience caused if addresses have changed or sites have ceased to exist, but can accept no responsibility for any such changes.

A catalogue record for this book is available from the British Library.

Library of Congress Cataloging-in-Publication Data
Names: Settle, Louise, author.
Title: Probation and the policing of the private sphere in Britain, 1907-1967 / Louise Settle.
Description: 1 Edition. | New York, NY : Bloomsbury Academic, [2022] |
Series: History of crime, deviance and punishment | Includes bibliographical references and index.
Identifiers: LCCN 2021028692 (print) | LCCN 2021028693 (ebook) |
ISBN 9781350233454 (hardback) | ISBN 9781350233461 (pdf) | ISBN 9781350233478 (epub)
Subjects: LCSH: Probation–Great Britain–History–20th century. |
Law enforcement–Great Britain–History–20th century. |
Social control–Great Britain–History–20th century.
Classification: LCC HV9345.A5 S48 2022 (print) |
LCC HV9345.A5 (ebook) | DDC 364.6/30941–dc23
LC record available at https://lccn.loc.gov/2021028692
LC ebook record available at https://lccn.loc.gov/2021028693

ISBN:	HB:	978-1-3502-3345-4
	PB:	978-1-3502-3348-5
	ePDF:	978-1-3502-3346-1
	eBook:	978-1-3502-3347-8

Series: History of Crime, Deviance and Punishment

Typeset by Integra Sotware Services Pvt. Ltd.

To find out more about our authors and books visit www.bloomsbury.com and sign up for our newsletters.

For Lilja and Kip

Contents

List of tables	viii
Acknowledgements	ix
Introduction	1
1 Marriage menders: Probation and marriage reconciliation in England and Wales	29
2 Stopping domestic violence: Probation and wife assault	71
3 A safety net for the suicidal: Probation and attempted suicide in Britain, 1907–61	105
4 Probation and male sexual offences: Gross indecency, indecent assault and indecent exposure	131
5 Recusing 'fallen women': Prostitution and probation	173
6 Conclusions and reflections	207
Bibliography	225
Index	239

Tables

1.1	Manchester Probation Committee matrimonial cases	50
1.2	Liverpool Probation Committee matrimonial cases	51
1.3	Bristol Probation Committee matrimonial cases	51–2
2.1	Results of probation in cases of wife assault for the years 1909, 1917, 1918, 1919	92
3.1	Disposal of persons aged 21 and over summarily dealt with, according to criminal statistics, England and Wales, 1953	106

Acknowledgements

While undertaking the research for this book I have been very fortunate to have spent time as a researcher at three institutes for advanced study in Scotland and Finland. These wonderful academic environments have provided me with the rare opportunity to focus on research and given me the necessary time and funding to write this book. They have also allowed me to work alongside brilliant colleagues from a wide range of disciplines, whose advice and feedback have been invaluable. I would therefore like to thank all my friends and colleagues at the Institute for Advanced Studies in the Humanities in Edinburgh, the Institute for Advanced Social Research in Tampere and the Helsinki Collegium for Advanced Studies. I am also very grateful for my time as a researcher based at the Academy of Finland Centre of Excellence in The History of Experiences (HEX) based at Tampere University. I would especially like to thank Pirjo Markkola and my other colleagues at Tampere University for helping me to feel part of the academic community in my adopted home of Tampere.

I would like to give special thanks to the following people for their expert advice and feedback on various stages of draft chapters and for their help with editing and proofreading: Pertti Ahonen, Roger Davidson, Gayle Davis, Sofie Henriksen, Frances Houghton, Louise Jackson, Tuomas Laine-Frigren, Zsuzsanna Millei, Sophie Lockwood, Vince Settle and the anonymous reviewers at Bloomsbury. I would also like to give my thanks to the staff of the various archives and libraries I have visited across the UK.

Completing this book whilst becoming a mother and living through a pandemic has not been easy, so I would very much like to thank my friends and family for all their love, friendship, support and encouragement. There are too many to name them all individually, but particular thanks go to my parents Linda and Vince Settle, Pertti Ahonen, Frances Houghton, Leanne Nield, Ulla Oksanen and Hannah Parr.

Introduction

The laws of God, The laws of Man
The laws of God, the laws of man,
He may keep that will and can;
Not I: let God and man decree
Laws for themselves and not for me;
And if my ways are not as theirs
Let them mind their own affairs.
Their deeds I judge and much condemn,
Yet when did I make laws for them?
Please yourselves, say I, and they
Need only look the other way.
But no, they will not; they must still
Wrest their neighbour to their will,
And make me dance as they desire
With jail and gallows and hell-fire.
And how am I to face the odds
Of man's bedevilment and God's?
I, a stranger and afraid
In a world I never made.
They will be master, right or wrong;
Though both are foolish, both are strong.
And since, my soul, we cannot fly
To Saturn nor to Mercury,
Keep we must, if keep we can,
These foreign laws of God and man.

A. E. Houseman, 1922[1]

The above poem by A. E. Houseman was referred to in a report made in 1955 by a probation officer named Mr Riley.[2] At first glance it seems surprising that a probation officer would include a quotation from a poem which is critical of the law, when seemingly the point of probation was to try and encourage people to obey the law. Some may even go so far as to say that a probation officer's job was to 'wret thy neighbour to their will'. On further reflection, however, the reference to this poem does not seem quite so shocking when you consider that the origins of the probation service lay in the responses to criticisms made about the nineteenth- and early-twentieth-century British criminal justice system – particularly the ineffectiveness of fines and short prison sentences for reducing recidivism. While probation officers ultimately had to uphold the rule of law, there was a long tradition of them questioning the methods that were used to enforce that law. Rather than subjecting people to undue punishment, the aim of probation was to help people learn how to live according to 'the laws of God and man' by providing them with the necessary support and guidance so that they could reform their own behaviour. Moreover, befriending people who broke the law and trying to understand the reasons behind why they behaved in the way that they did were crucial elements in the process of rehabilitation. There was an appreciation, therefore, of the difficult personal and socio-economic circumstances which led some people to break the law and a sympathy for the stranger who was 'afraid in a world [he] never made'.

It is quite possible that the probation officer Mr Riley had no such thoughts about the nature of probation when he referenced this poem, and the reason for its inclusion in the report was not specified. Nevertheless, the contradictions inherent in his reference to such a subversive poem nicely highlight the complexities of the probation officer's role as both a law-enforcer and a social worker tasked with helping some of the most vulnerable in society. In the same 1955 report, Mr Riley made the following observations about the role of the probation service:

> According to leading psychologists of recent times the basic needs of man are given as love, significance and security. The modern trend of civilisation with vast factories and machines does not encourage love of work or pride of craftsmanship. Too often man is a mere number on a ticket punched night and morning and his significance is lost … he must go with the herd irrespective of his personal feelings or conscience … Family life too has undergone a peaceful revolution and often significance and love are not his even at home … There is then the need for an outside personal and human relationship – a relationship which can advise, assist, befriend, on these new problems. Here surely lies the role of the probation service in dealing with offenders – both juvenile and adult.[3]

Mr Riley understood that it was not possible for an individual officer to change the harsh realities and inequalities of an industrial capitalist society. However, they could help people to cope with the modern world by providing them with a much-needed 'personal human relationship'. Riley was not alone in this belief in the power of relationships – this emphasis on human relationships was a founding principle behind probation and its long-serving moto 'advise, assist, befriend'. And it was not only the relationship between the probationer and the probation officer that was important. Repairing the broken relationships between probationers and their families, and the relationship they had with themselves and society was, as we shall see, a crucial part of the rehabilitation process.

Aims and historiography

The 1907 Probation of Offenders Act stipulated that probation could be used in situations where the court thinks that:

> the charge is proven, but is of the opinion that, having regard to the character, antecedents, age, health, or mental condition of the person charged, or to the trivial nature of the offence, or to the extenuating circumstances under which the offence was committed, it is not expedient to inflict any punishment or any other than a nominal punishment, or that it is expedient to release the offender on probation.[4]

In situations where the person was charged before a court of summary justice, this meant the offender could be dismissed or discharged:

> Under the conditionality of his entering into a recognizances, with or without sureties, to be of good behaviour and to appear for conviction and sentence when called on at any time during such period, not exceeding three years, as may be specified in the order.[5]

In cases where the person was convicted of an indictable offence punishable by imprisonment there was no option for dismissal, but otherwise the conditions of discharge under recognizances were the same as for cases heard in the summary courts.

The Probation Act 1907 marked the official legislative starting point of probation as we understand it today. The origins story of how this act came to be, and the history of probation's subsequent development from that point on are well known. Authors such as Dorothy Bochel, Lol Burke, Raymond Gard, George Mair, Philip Priestley, Roger Statham, Maurice Vanstone, Philip Whitehead and William McWilliams have provided detailed accounts of probation theory, policy and practice in England and Wales during the twentieth century that explore the political, cultural and ideological influences which shaped the probation service's history.[6] Most of these studies exclude Scotland, but Christine Kelly and Fergus McNeil have begun to address this lacuna.[7] These histories have shown how probation developed from its beginnings as a religious mission predominantly run by Christian voluntary organizations, such as the Church of England Temperance Society, to a specific form of social work that was influenced by the 'diagnostic ideal'.[8] In short, as the service increasingly professionalized, more probation officers started to gain qualifications in social work and the influence of the new behavioural sciences, especially psychology, became more pronounced. However, as Maurice Vanstone and others have pointed out, religion continued to have an important influence over probation practice well into the mid-twentieth century.[9] While there have been several histories of probation which detail how these changes influenced policy and practice, this study takes a different approach. Rather than looking inward and tracing the factors which shaped probation's development, this study examines the influence that these developments had on the ways in which probation was used to police particular types of offences – especially those offences which occurred in the private sphere and/or involved interpersonal relationships.

By rehabilitating people at home, rather than sending them to prison, the rationale behind probation was that it could help individuals to reform their own behaviour in the long term. For this to work, officers needed access to the private sphere – both physically, in terms of entering the homes of people on probation, but also psychologically, in terms of trying to understand and influence the probationer's emotions and behaviour. This meant that probation officers were in a unique position to intervene in people's intimate private lives. Each chapter of the book, therefore, focuses on how probation was used to police a particular type of offence that occurred in the private sphere and/or involved interpersonal relationships: wife assault, attempted suicide, male sexual offences (gross indecency, indecent exposure and indecent assault) and female prostitution, along with a chapter on the work of probation officers involved in marriage reconciliation. The chapters examine the different methods that were used to try and rehabilitate individuals who were placed on probation for these offences, how successful these methods were for reducing recidivism, and what impact they had on probationers' lives.

Previous research on the intervention of the state into the private lives of citizens primarily focuses on women and children or does not prioritize the role of probation.[10] It has often been assumed, by historians and contempories alike, that state intervention in women and children's lives was considered more acceptable than intervention into the private lives of adult men.[11] However, probation offered a unique opportunity for the state to intervene in both men and women's emotional and domestic lives, albeit often with different aims and methods according to age, gender and class. By examining the diverse ways in which probation was used to intervene in the lives of both men and women, the book explores the short- and long-term consequences this intervention had for gender relations and the everyday lives of individuals and families.

The majority of adults convicted of first and/or minor offences came from working-class backgrounds, and this was reflected in the high number of working-class people placed on probation. However, probation could also be used as a way to avoid sending 'respectable' middle-class people to prison. The book explores how the high levels of discretion associated with the use of probation could enhance the role that notions of class and respectability played in the implementation of justice. Similarly, age was also an important factor in sentencing decisions. Probation was often seen as a sentence particularly well suited to 'young offenders' because they were considered less likely to have become 'hardened criminals' and therefore more susceptible to the guiding influence of probation officers. However, it was not only young people who were put on probation. Previous research on probation has tended to focus on 'young offenders', but this book explores what this intimate intervention into the private lives of adult citizens means for our understanding of the role of the state in policing the private sphere.

Probation and social control

A key method that was used to try and prevent probationers from reoffending was to insert conditions into the probation bond which the probationer had to follow during their period of probation. Aside from the obvious condition that they must not break the law, they could also be required to follow rules such as not drinking alcohol and to refrain from visiting certain places or associating with certain people. It was the probation officer's job to help ensure that these rules were followed. The probation officer's powers of surveillance, however, were somewhat limited given that people on probation were at large in the community and not confined to a prison cell. The probationer was required to report regularly to the probation officer, and the officer could check up on their charges by making enquires at their home or place of work, but the detection of any law-breaking activities was primarily a job for the police.

A probation officer's approach to reforming individuals was reliant on the notion that probationers wanted to reform their own behaviour and would develop the necessary self-control to do so. Probation was therefore intended for people who were assumed to be more likely to have the desire and potential for change, such as juveniles, petty offenders and first-time offenders. By providing advice and practical help, such as finding suitable accommodation and employment, the aim of probation was to provide people with the opportunity and motivation to follow the law. The primary role of the probation officer, therefore, was not to act as a gaoler but as a role model who would provide the necessary guidance, advice and encouragement for people while they developed self-control. Nonetheless, if probationers were caught breaking the rules of their bond, the probation officer was required to report this lapse to the judge, magistrate or Justice of the Peace (JP) who would then determine their new sentence.

This focus on encouraging people to change their own behaviour is often seen in the context of class-based social control – that the ruling elites were trying to impose their social and cultural ideologies onto working-class homes. Both Nikolas Rose and David Garland use probation as an example to demonstrate how the British state used more welfarist approaches to govern the lives of its citizens during the early twentieth century and to illustrate their concepts of the 'legal complex' and 'penal-welfare', respectively.[12] By allowing probation officers into their homes and agreeing to follow certain rules, probationers were spared punishment and instead given various forms of welfare support. This type of informal coercive power offered a cheaper, more effective way of 'normalising and correcting' people's 'problematic' behaviour. Maurice Vanstone also emphasizes probation's capacity for social control, describing it as a 'class-based activity that justified the social order' by setting the standards of what was considered good behaviour according to middle-class standards.[13] Similarly, Linda Mahood has shown how probation was used to police the family and to impose middle-class notions of respectable domesticity onto working-class homes.[14]

The above authors have all utilized the concept of policing as understood by Michel Foucault and Jacques Donzelot – policing not simply in the repressive sense, but as a method for governing society and controlling families through the use of expert knowledge, surveillance and informal power.[15] While these concepts are also used within this book, the nature of the discussion around power and social control can sometimes result in the portrayal of probation in an overly negative light. However, by looking in more detail at how probation was used in specific circumstances, the book argues that probation's propensity to impose social control via self-governance could have important benefits, especially in cases where it was used to protect people from crimes that occurred in the private sphere. If probation could be used to reform the behaviour of violent and abusive offenders, probation had the potential to be more effective than fines and short prison sentences in protecting vulnerable citizens in the long term. Moreover, the material and practical aid that probation officers gave to probationers who often had few alternative sources of support should not be dismissed as insignificant, especially in the period prior to the founding of the welfare state in 1945. The opportunities probation provided for helping people find new employment and housing, for example, could make real positive changes to people's lives. So too could the emotional support that probation officers provided. This book, therefore, uses new empirical research to explore the nuances of probation's role as, on the one hand, a form of social control, and on the other, a social work service designed to help and protect the most vulnerable in society, including the probationers themselves.

Probation and psychology

Raymond Gard has shown that by the late 1940s many aspects of probation officers' work resembled the methods of the new psychiatric social workers, particularly the way in which they relied on a casework approach that was based on making an individual assessment of each probationer and tailoring his/her supervision accordingly.[16] In particular, probation methods were strongly influenced by the work of the psychologist Cyril Burt, especially his book *The Juvenile Delinquent*, and by the teachings of the prominent psychologist Dr Adolf Meyer who called for the collection of detailed background information about the individual, a role that the probation officers often undertook.[17] The influence of humanistic psychologists on probation, especially the work of people such as Carl Rogers, can also be seen through probation officers' strong focus on trying to promote self-regulation.

One of the ways in which probation was intended to help people was by providing them with psychiatric treatment. In situations where it was thought necessary, the judge, magistrate or JP could stipulate in the probation bond that the probationer was required to undergo psychiatric treatment, either in an institution or as an outpatient. If a person agreed to be placed on probation with this condition of treatment, then they were technically volunteering to undergo treatment (even if the alternative to giving consent was prison). This meant that probationers could be required to undergo psychiatric treatment without necessitating that they be legally certified as insane and sectioned. On the one hand, this was beneficial for some probationers who were provided with access to the treatment they needed without being certified as 'insane'. Prior to the formation of the National Health Service in 1948, most people would not have been able to afford private psychiatric care and probation provided opportunities for free psychiatric therapy without necessarily having to be institutionalized. The fact that this approach did not require people to be officially labelled as 'insane' was particularly important because of the stigma surrounding insanity during the early-to-mid twentieth century.[18] Moreover, in cases where someone needed psychiatric care, but refused to take it – a situation that sometimes occurred after a person had attempted suicide, for example – this system could ensure people received the psychiatric treatment they needed. On the other hand, it enabled the forced psychiatric treatment of people who otherwise might not have needed or wanted psychiatric treatment – potentially causing serious psychological harm. This was especially problematic in situations where men who had been convicted of offences linked to homosexual behaviour between consenting adults were required to undergo various types of conversion therapies as part of their probation bond. The book explores these issues further and examines the role that probation played in the medicalization of certain offences or behaviours.

While the story of probation is largely one of increased professionalization, the book also analyses the role that Christianity continued to play throughout the whole period, especially the importance of probation's links to the Christian temperance movement. Alcohol was often blamed as being one of the main reasons why people broke the law and subsequently many probationers were required to abstain from alcohol during their period of probation. Abstinence, therefore, was often heralded as an important step on the way to rehabilitation. Even as more probation officers received training in social work methods, religious faith remained important for many officers and it continued to have an impact on their work. By examining the ways in which probation policy and practice were simultaneously shaped by religion and science, the book provides further evidence to support the argument that there was no linear progression of secularization in Britain during the early-to-mid twentieth century.[19]

Methods and sources

The book covers the first sixty years of the probation service's history because this period encapsulates the time in which probation was used most extensively to police the private sphere. This was a period of 'penal optimism' – a time in which there was a widely held belief in the 'rehabilitative ideal' and the reformative powers of probation.[20] The timeframe starts in 1907 when the Probation of Offenders Act was passed and ends in 1962 with the publication of the Morrison Report – a report which signified the 'high point of probation' in England and Wales, as described by Raymond Gard. The book ends as the big social and cultural upheavals of the 1960s began.[21] The reason for ending at a point prior to when this shift towards a more individualistic society fully got going is because the larger socio-economic, political and cultural changes that went along with this shift brought substantial changes to the probation services. For example, in 1967 the probation service in England and Wales officially began its involvement in parole, a development which kick-started a shift towards focusing on risk assessment and punishment in the community. Moreover, in 1968 The Social Work (Scotland) Act brought probation in Scotland within the social work services, a change that introduced even greater differences between practices in Scotland and those of England and Wales. The consequences of these post-1960 developments for the practice of probation have been well-studied elsewhere.[22] This, in part, provides another motive for focusing this research on the earlier period which, with the notable exception of Raymond Gard's book on probation in England and Wales from 1876 to 1962, has received much less attention.

The geographic scope of the project covers England, Scotland and Wales. The inclusion of Scotland here is significant given its separate legal system and relative neglect in the current historiography.[23] However, while there were some important differences between legislation and organizational practices in England/Wales and Scotland, there were also many similarities, especially given that many Scottish officers were initially sent for training in England. There were also several instances of policy exchange. For example, the Probation of Offenders (Scotland) Act 1931 was somewhat similar to the Criminal Justice Act 1925, as both acts aimed to increase the amount of salaried probation officers available to the court and both established the use of committees as a method for managing these probation officers. And the exchanges worked both ways. Chapter 5, for example, shows how the English and Welsh service adopted the Scottish approach of using probation to 'rescue' young women from prostitution and to deter them from soliciting on the street.

The structure of the services in both England/Wales and Scotland meant that local probation committees were in charge of the day-to-day running of local services. Local socio-economic differences were therefore very important, especially whether there was a strong tradition of religious missionaries volunteering in the area or whether there was easy access to institutions that provided training in social work or offered psychiatric treatments. For example, it was more likely that probation committees in large cities across the UK had closer connections with psychiatric clinics than committees in rural areas. This meant that probationers in cities with good psychiatric provisions were more likely to be sent for psychiatric treatments. Consequently, there could be more differences between probation services *within* the same country than there were *between* different countries. And it was not just a matter of a rural/urban divide. A good example of how probation committees within different cities in the same country could employ vastly different strategies can be seen when you compare Edinburgh and Glasgow during the first half of the twentieth century. Prior to the Probation of Offenders (Scotland) Act 1931 which banned the use of police officers acting as probation officers, Glasgow's probation service was mainly staffed by former police officers. After the 1931 Act, Glasgow replaced these police officers with new officers that were trained in social work methods. In Edinburgh, however, probation officers were mainly recruited from Christian voluntary organizations throughout the whole period up until the end of the Second World War.

The study uses probation records held at the National Archives in London and the National Records of Scotland in Edinburgh, alongside the records of local probation services held in archives across England, Wales and Scotland. To provide examples of practices in cities of varying sizes and socio-economic make-up, I have examined probation records from Bristol, Cardiff, Edinburgh, Glasgow, London, Liverpool, Manchester and Swansea. Depending on the surviving material at each local archive, these probation records include probation committee minutes, annual reports, probation registers, and various other miscellaneous letters and administration materials. The types of records available for each city are not like-for-like, which means it is difficult to carry out a systematic comparison. However, by including examples from across the country, the book shows how local and regional differences could be important in shaping the practical implantation of probation polices.

Another important type of source used in this study is the court records of individual cases or, more often, the newspaper coverage of these court cases. Many of the original court records have not been preserved or are not available for public access due to data protection legislation. Moreover, official court documents containing witness testimony were only generated and retained in the higher courts. The local newspaper reports, however, often provide a high level of detail about the court cases, including descriptions of the testimonies given by the defendant and other witnesses. Despite the potential problems associated with these sources, such as selective reporting by the press and the multiple mediated narratives contained in court records, if used carefully they are useful for providing more details about what happened in the courtroom.[24] Indeed, Adrian Bingham has shown how newspaper coverage of court cases during the early twentieth century was often highly accurate and reliable.[25] Another useful source is contemporary literature and the memoirs of probation officers which tell us more about the personalities, actions and motivations of individual probation officers. In addition to memoirs, I also use material from interviews that were conducted with retired probation officers in the 1990s. However, as is always true when using memoirs and oral testimony, it must be taken into consideration these are highly stylized narratives that have been written from a personal perspective, often with an agenda in mind.

One of the aims of this book is to explore the ways in which probation influenced the lives and experiences of probationers and to establish whether probation was successful in rehabilitating people. However, the majority of the sources available that could help us to answer these questions were not made by the probationers themselves and so they tell us more about the perceptions of the authorities who complied them than probationers' own experiences. Probation officers were mainly interested in recording information that was considered relevant to the court and the rehabilitation process, and so some officers may have chosen to leave out certain details if they thought that they were irrelevant or reflected badly on them or their charges. Similarly, probationers did not necessarily tell the officers everything about their lives and they could carefully construct narratives that they knew would satisfy the requirements and expectations of the probation officer. As is often the case with 'history from below', it is therefore difficult to hear the voices of the probationers themselves. However, by reading these records 'against the grain' we can at least begin to learn a little more about probationers' lives and their time on probation. For instance, by looking at probationers' actions, especially in cases which were deemed 'unsuccessful', we can learn more about probationers' everyday attempts to resist probation.[26] Moreover, these cases can show how probation officers were reliant on the cooperation of the probationers and their families. Probation officers had few means of knowing if the rules were being followed and probationers could lie or be selective with what they reported to the probation officer. The book explores this co-dependence and highlights the complexity of these power relations between probationer and probation officer.

Chapter outline

To highlight the importance of probation in shaping how authorities dealt with offences involving the domestic sphere, the book is arranged thematically with each chapter focusing on one type of offence, or in the case of marriage reconciliation, a service that the probation service provided. Each chapter of the book therefore adds to, and often complicates, historical knowledge about each of these topics. The chapters cover marriage reconciliation, wife assault, attempted suicide, female prostitution, and male sexual offences (including gross indecency, indecent assault and indecent exposure). These five topics were chosen because they all deal in some way with behaviour or activities that are usually considered 'private' and because they involved intimate relationships or interactions. The contribution that probation made to the policing of these particular crimes, and to the rehabilitation of those involved, is often overlooked. However, as we shall see, the use of probation in these cases could have long-lasting consequences for the individuals involved and for society more generally.

The first chapter after this introduction focuses on the probation service's involvement in marriage reconciliation. Probation officers had informally been providing advice and guidance to married couples since the service began. However, after the 1937 Matrimonial Summary Jurisdiction (Domestic Proceedings) Act was passed, probation officers were officially tasked with trying to reconcile couples who sought a separation order in English and Welsh courts (probation officers in Scotland never formally became involved in marriage reconciliation). Couples or individuals could go directly to a probation officer for advice and guidance, or they could be referred there by a magistrate. Before granting couples a separation order, the magistrate could require that they should go to see the probation officer with the hope that the couple could be helped to reconcile. One of the main ways in which probation officers tried to reconcile couples was by providing a space in which they could talk through their difficulties.

This chapter explores how these 'marriage mending' meetings functioned in England and Wales between 1937 and 1962 and examines the ways in which the methods probation officers used to reconcile couples were influenced by both traditional Christian ideologies about marriage and newer behavioural science theories. The chapter examines the extent to which the different types of practical and emotional help offered by the probation service were successful in helping couples 'fix' their marriage and reduce the number of separations. One of the justifications for the probation service's involvement in marriage reconciliation was that healthy, stable families played an essential part in ensuring the stability of the nation. By looking more closely at the justifications given for the probation service's involvement in marriage reconciliation, this chapter reveals more about contemporary concerns surrounding marriage and gender relations, as well as the relationship between citizens and the state.

Marriage reconciliation was not the only way in which probation officers became involved in married life. Probation was also used in situations where a man had been convicted of assaulting his wife. Chapter 2 focuses on these cases of domestic violence. During the late nineteenth and early twentieth centuries men convicted of wife assault were mainly given fines and short prison sentences, or they were 'bound over', forfeiting a sum of money as a security for good behaviour. The Probation of Offenders Act 1907, however, meant that men who were 'bound over' could also be placed under the supervision of a probation officer and required to follow certain conditions, such as not drinking alcohol. This meant that, in theory at least, probation officers could have more control over men's behaviour while they were on probation than previously was the case.

Probation was seen as preferable to a fine or prison sentence in many situations because it meant that the wife and family did not suffer from the loss of the breadwinner's earnings. Moreover, it was hoped that probation would have a positive influence over men's behaviour in the long term. At the very least, the husband was likely to refrain from violence during the period of probation, a period which ranged between one month and three years – a considerably longer period than the usual prison sentence for wife assault. However, contemporaries and historians alike have argued that releasing men on probation was merely a 'let off'. Not only was it ineffective in stopping domestic violence, it was also symptomatic of a more widespread acceptance of non-lethal domestic violence in Britain during the first half of the twentieth century. This chapter argues that, while probation may have resulted in some men being 'let off', this was not the overall intention. By trying to change men's behaviour in the domestic sphere, probation in these cases challenged men's authority in the home and offered women some tangible, practical help. This chapter examines how probation was implemented in practice and explores how successful it was in helping women and reducing male violence.

Chapter 3 moves away from looking at marital relationships to focus on how probation was used to help improve people's relationships with themselves. Prior to the 1961 Suicide Act, a person who attempted suicide in England and Wales could technically be charged with 'conspiracy to self-murder', a charge which carried a potential recommended sentence of up to two years' imprisonment.

However, it was much more common for cases to be dismissed, admonished, or for the person to be placed on probation, with or without supervision by a probation officer. In Scotland suicide was not illegal, but attempting suicide was often prosecuted under public order legislation, such as 'breach of the peace', and defendants were mainly admonished or placed on probation. This chapter examines the ways in which this system of probation functioned as a 'safety net' for suicidal people in Britain between 1907 and its legalization in 1961 by providing various types of material, social and psychological help.

If a suicidal individual was considered mentally ill, a condition could be included in the probation bond that required them to undergo psychiatric treatment (in a hospital or as an outpatient) without requiring them to be certified as insane. Probation, therefore, played an important, yet often overlooked, role in expanding the provision of psychiatric treatment to people who otherwise would not have received it. However, if psychiatric treatment was not deemed necessary, probation could instead be used to ensure the suicidal person had an appropriate friend or family member to care for them. When this was not possible, a probation officer would fill this role. The probation officer could also try to alleviate any practical problems that had contributed to the person's desire to commit suicide, such as unemployment and homelessness. The chapter explores how probation officers' approaches towards helping suicidal people were influenced by their exposure to different theories about social work and psychiatry, their interactions with individual probationers, and their backgrounds in religious philanthropy. In doing so, the chapter also tells us more about wider changes in attitudes towards insanity, suicide and its prevention.

Chapter 4 focuses on the use of probation in cases relating to three different types of male sexual offences: gross indecency between men, indecent assault and indecent exposure. During the period of this study (1907–62), a conviction for these offences could result in a prison sentence. However, by the 1940s these 'deviant' sexual practices were increasingly seen as being caused by a medical condition that could be cured. Probation was subsequently used as a method for requiring men to undergo the medical treatments that were meant to provide that cure. This could include hormone therapy, aversion therapy or psychoanalysis-based therapies. By asking whether probation was used as a 'let off', a 'cure' or a punishment, this chapter examines probation's role in the medicalization of male sexual offences and the policing of male sexuality. The high levels of discretionary power involved in the probation process meant that assumptions concerning a person's age, class and respectability were crucial in shaping the ways in which probation was used to rehabilitate men convicted of sexual offences. Similarly, this discretionary power meant that assumptions about the immorality of certain sexual practices were also important – assumptions that were often based on traditional Christian attitudes towards sex. The chapter explores how these factors influenced the implementation of probation policy and shaped men's experiences of probation. Finally, the chapter evaluates the extent to which the use of probation in these cases could be deemed as 'successful' in changing men's sexual behaviour.

After examining male sexual offences, Chapter 5 then turns to look at the most common form of female sexual activity that was criminalized during this period – solicitation for the purposes of prostitution. Whereas men placed on probation for sexual offences were increasingly given medical treatment to cure their 'deviant' sexual behaviour, women convicted of solicitation offences were more likely to be sent to a religious voluntary institution where they received moral guidance and domestic training to reform their 'immoral' behaviour. As was the case with male sexual offenders, the treatment of these women often depended on the judge, JP or magistrate's opinion about the nature of the offence and the 'character' of the 'offender', especially her age and previous conviction record. Using the records of local probation services and the court cases of individual women, the chapter explores how the implementation of this system developed throughout the early-to-mid twentieth century across England, Scotland and Wales and examines the influence it had on the women involved, including whether it was successful in helping them to exit prostitution.

The final chapter will summarize each of the previous chapters and bring all the main arguments together to provide an overall conclusion to the book. There will also be a short discussion about the relevance of these finding for contemporary policy debates surrounding probation and the criminal justice system.

Short overview of the history of probation in Britain

As previously stated, the general history of probation is well known and has already been outlined in several other studies.[27] However, to provide some background context for the following chapters, this short overview will provide a summary of the key events, laws and policy changes that are most relevant to this study.

The origins of the probation service in England and Wales have traditionally been traced to the mid-to-late-nineteenth-century work of the Church of

England Temperance Society (CETS) who began sending missionaries to Police Courts to try and encourage people to take the pledge of abstinence.[28] The story goes that in 1876 Frederic Rainer, a printer from Hertfordshire and member of CETS, became concerned about the lack of help available for people leaving the police courts and so he wrote to the CETS about the issue and included a donation of five shillings towards providing practical help for these people. The CETS responded to this by sending two missionaries to the Southwark Police Court. Subsequently these missionaries began to develop a system with the courts so that people who were charged with drunkenness were placed into the care of the missionary rather than being given a prison sentence. The idea was that the missionary would help them to stop drinking by providing them with support, advice and, if necessary, help them to find work and somewhere to live. These two missionaries are often seen as the first forerunners to probation officers.

In terms of legislation, the first act to specifically mention probation was the Probation of First Offenders Act 1887 which allowed courts to release defendants on their own recognizances, but they were required to reappear in court when called to do so. This gave courts across the country the opportunity to set up a system of releasing people into the care of missionaries. The 1887 Act was not just designed for use in cases of drunkenness, but in all cases where 'the youth, character, and antecedents of the offender' meant that the offender was suitable for, and could benefit from, being released under their own recognizances rather than being sent to prison.[29] The credit for the introduction of the Probation of First Offenders Act 1887 is often attributed to Howard Vincent, Tory MP for Sheffield Central and former head of Criminal Investigations Department (CID), who put forward the bill after being inspired by his trip to the United States. During that trip he visited Boston and learnt about the Massachusetts system of probation where people sentenced for minor offences could have that sentence deferred until a period of probation had elapsed. During this period the offender was placed under the supervision of a probation officer who ensured his good conduct. While the 1887 Probation of Time Offenders Act was clearly influenced by the Boston system, the 1887 Act did not include the requirement of supervision. That would have to wait until the next piece of significant legislation, The 1907 Probation of Offenders Act.[30]

The 1907 Probation of Offenders Act stipulated that a person could be released 'on probation' with or without sureties after the court had given regard to his 'character, antecedents, age, health or mental condition'.[31] In this sense it was very similar to the 1887 Act, but crucially, it now used the term 'on probation' and officially introduced the use of probation officers to supervise offenders. The Act required that a specific individual probation officer should be named in the court order. This meant that the individual relationship between the probationer and the probation officer was emphasized from the start. The Act did not specify who could qualify to act as a probation officer, but a government memorandum in 1908 stated that 'in all cases the officers should be persons of good education and having some knowledge of the industrial and social conditions of the locality'.[32] In most cases the probation officers appointed were the same missionaries who had already been carrying out supervision under the previous 1887 Act. In London the Home Office stipulated that they would pay for half of the probation officer's salary while CETS and other societies who employed missionaries would pay the other half. However, the newly appointed children's probation officers were paid for fully by the Home Office. Similar funding arrangements between local authorities and voluntary organizations were organized outside of London, although the exact details of these varied according to local practices.[33]

Many earlier histories of probation, such as Dorothy Bochel's 1976 study, cite the CETS Police Court Missionaries as the founders of probation and the motivating force behind the passing of the Probation of Offenders Act 1907.[34] However, Raymond Gard has argued that revisionist histories of probation given by Maurice Vanstone, George Mair and Lol Burke are more accurate in their emphasis on the origins of the 1907 Probation Act laying in the wider political and socio-economic conditions of the period.[35] They pinpoint late-nineteenth- and early-twentieth-century fears about increasing crime rates, degeneration and national efficiency as reasons for increased concern about the ineffectiveness of a criminal justice system based on fines and imprisonment which did little to stop reoffending. The need to find more effective ways to stop crime and reform the behaviour of people who broke the law was seen as being of national importance because the British Empire needed morally and psychically fit citizens. According to Mair and Burke, this was one of the main reasons why the government was receptive to new methods such as probation.[36] It was hoped that by preventing young or petty offenders from turning into habitual offenders this new approach would reduce the amount of 'human stock' lost to crime and degeneracy. Crucially, reducing the prison population would also save money.

These explanations for the origins of probation in England and Wales are well known, but a probation origin story that has often been overlooked is the early use of probation in Scotland. In Glasgow, the first probation officers were appointed in 1905, two years before the first ones were appointed in England.

According to a history of the Glasgow probation service which was published as part of the celebrations for the service's fiftieth anniversary in 1955, the service was established thanks to the efforts of Baillie John Bruce Murray who had studied the use of probation in North America and sought to establish a similar service in Glasgow in an effort to reduce the city's prison population.[37] Not only was Glasgow ahead of the trend, the decision to appoint police officers as paid probation officers in a professionally organized service was also unique. Dundee was also ahead of England in setting up a more comprehensive system of probation prior to 1907. The minutes of the special committee on 'Probation Guardianship of Criminal Offenders' held in Glasgow on 7 June 1905 described how at this point Dundee had already developed a system where they dismissed the offender with an admonition, delaying the pronounced sentence for a set period (usually six weeks) during which time the convicted person was set at liberty and put upon their good behaviour.[38] During this period, they were looked after by one of the assistants from various voluntary organizations who then wrote a report about the person's behaviour. Based on that report the JP decided if he/she was freed after the six weeks or sentenced for their original crime.

After the 1907 Act, the next important piece of legislation to influence probation policy was the Criminal Justice Administration Act 1914. This allowed for the probation bond to

> contain such additional conditions with respect to residence, abstention from intoxicating liquor, and any other matters, as the court may, having regard to the particular circumstances of the case, consider necessary for preventing a repetition of the same offence or the commission of other offences.[39]

The Act therefore gave judges and magistrates the power to require probationers to reside in particular locations and to follow certain conditions. This legislation is very important when we turn in later chapters to look at how probation was used in cases of attempted suicide and various sexual offences to require people to undergo medical treatment or reside in an institution.

The year 1914 is also notable for being the year that the First World War began. During the war there was increased concern about juvenile delinquency and probation was promoted as an important method for dealing with this problem. The war was also important for probation in the sense that it gave more widespread recognition to mental health problems, such as shell shock, and because previously healthy 'ordinary' men who suffered from shell shock received psychiatric treatment. This led to a general increase in the acceptance of psychiatry as being a legitimate and important field of scientific research, which smoothed the path for it to have more of an influence over probation as the service professionalized. Nonetheless, despite the slight increase in the influence that psychology had on probation during the 1920s, Maurice Vanstone and others have shown that it was still mainly the Christian missionaries who had the most influence over probation practice during this period, with 60 per cent of all probation officers being employed by voluntary societies in 1924.[40]

It was not until after the 1925 Criminal Justice Act was passed that the professionalization of probation got into full swing. The Act compelled all courts in England and Wales to have at least one salaried probation officer and the local authority could apply for a grant from the Home Office to cover half of the officer's salary. The Act also required local authorities to set up probation committees who would appoint and manage these officers and a new rule in 1926 required that probation officers should meet with probationers weekly for at least the first month. Many local courts tried (mostly unsuccessfully) to object to these requirements, primarily due to the increased cost (many preferred to use the free services of local voluntary organizations) or because they thought that the numbers placed on probation in their area did not warrant the services of a full-time officer. Several local authorities were also unhappy about the increased interference of the central government into local government matters. Despite these complaints, the new act was successful in its aim to increase the number of probation orders made, and according to Raymond Gard, 'by 1927 there were only sixteen petty sessional divisions with no paid probation officer'.[41]

The 1925 Criminal Justice Act was also the first piece of major probation legislation which did not apply to Scotland. Instead, the Probation of Offenders (Scotland) was passed in 1931 which was very similar in its aim to create a comprehensive set of local services by establishing probation committees in each local authority. As in England, each probation area was required to appoint at least one salaried probation officer. The debates leading up to the Act in Scotland were also similar to those in England and Wales. Several local councils, especially in rural areas, but also in larger cities such as Edinburgh, did not want to be forced to hire a salaried probation officer because they felt that the local voluntary organizations were already doing a sufficient job for very little expense, and they were reluctant to spend local tax money on hiring full-time salaried officers. They were also critical of creeping 'officialdom' and felt that the use of several part-time local voluntary workers would allow for closer relationships to develop between probation officer and probationer, rather than one full-time officer who was employed to visit probationers across the whole county.⁴² These disagreements continued for a long time and in many areas, such as Edinburgh, local committees managed to avoid hiring full-time paid officers until the mid-1940s. In this way, the influence of Christian voluntary organizations remained strong throughout the first half of the twentieth century in many areas of Scotland.

To ensure that the relationship between the probation officer and the probationer was one of friendship and trust, the 1931 Probation of Offenders (Scotland) Act also prohibited the use of former police officers to work as probation officers (this rule was particularly influential in Glasgow, a city which until then had mainly employed former police officers as probation officers). The Act also created the Central Probation Council to advise the Secretary of State for Scotland as to matters specifically pertaining to the probation context in Scotland. There was considerable emphasis on the uniqueness of the Scottish context, especially the different legal systems, which meant that most commentators were keen for Scotland to develop its own training schemes rather than send their new recruits to the Home Office course.

Most historians of probation agree that the 1930s can be described as a 'transitional phase' for the professionalization of probation across Britain.⁴³ As probation became more closely linked to social work, an increasing number of probation officers began to undertake social work diplomas at university or underwent training in the Home Office training scheme that was set up in 1930. However, many courts still relied on the services of missionaries and the amount of professionally trained officers at each court depended on the local conditions. For example, a survey in 1932 found that out of the 145 courts in England and Wales that replied to the survey, 17 stated that they were opposed to the Home Office training scheme.⁴⁴ The survey also showed that most courts were still appointing their own choice of probation officer, and often it was from the CETs. In London, this period is best described as one of 'dual control', with professionally trained social workers being employed in the juvenile courts, and CETS being employed in the adult courts.⁴⁵ Overall, this transitional phase meant that, while some officers were attending lectures on psychological methods at the Institute for the Scientific Treatment of Delinquency (ISTD) and working closely with child guidance clinics, others were mainly working with religious organizations, clubs and societies. Some were working with a mixture of all of these different organizations at the same time.

In 1936 a report made by the National Association of Probation Officers (an organization which was first established in 1912) criticized this system of dual control in England and Wales. The authors of the report instead wanted to make a more standardized system across England and Wales and ensure that all officers were fully trained in fields such as administration, industrial conditions, child guidance work, psychological methods, court practice and procedures. The report also recommended that officers should be centrally appointed and no longer attached to religious voluntary organizations. To implement these policies a new Probation Branch was set up at the Home Office and probation inspectors were appointed. The CETS and other voluntary organizations were unhappy with this development but were unable to stop the changes as probation now became a fully public service staffed by paid professionals. By 1945 these changes meant that there were two set routes to becoming a probation officer in England and Wales. Either you took a two-year diploma in social science followed by a three-month Home Office course, or you underwent twelve months of practical experience and a Home Office theoretical course which included education in psychology, probation casework, law, medicine and ethics. In Scotland, similar developments occurred as more officers increasingly undertook classes aimed at social science or social welfare diplomas and the Scottish Office set up training courses so that trainee probation officers could get training in Scotland.[46]

As Gard, McWilliams, Vanstone and others have shown, the 1940s and 1950s were a period in which the influence of psychology became more noticeable. There were two different approaches to psychology that influenced probation. The first one was a more traditional approach that was epitomized by the work of Cyril Burt and later W. Norwood East.[47] This approach saw criminal behaviour as being linked to exposure to a bad environment, either at home, in school or at work. These 'bad' environments failed to teach children and young adults how to control instinctive actions and how to direct emotions towards purposes which were socially useful. It was also acknowledged that other physical and mental conditions, such as low intelligence, could be blamed for causing delinquency. The second approach, which gained more prominence after the Second World War, was based on Freudian psychoanalysis. This approach relied on Freudian concepts about the emotions and the unconscious, blaming traumatic early childhood experiences for later criminal behaviour. Despite the theoretical differences between these two schools of psychological thought, both saw the early home environment and family relationships as crucial factors in causing delinquent behaviour.

The emphasis that was placed on the damaging consequences of a 'broken home' meant that the Second World War was seen as a particularly problematic period because of the damage it caused to the family unit. As fathers went abroad to fight, mothers were recruited for work on the home front, and children were evacuated to the countryside; the stability of the family was increasingly undermined. The Second World War was also a difficult time for the probation service because many officers were enlisted to fight and those left behind were given the increased responsibility of making domestic enquires for the army welfare service. There was also a large increase in the amount of matrimonial reconciliation work undertaken by the probation service because the disruption of war caused more marital breakdown. As we shall see in Chapter 1, this increase in the amount of matrimonial work continued well into the post-war period as more couples applied for separation orders and divorce.

After the war ended, the Criminal Justice Act 1948 and the Criminal Justice (Scotland) Act 1949 introduced residence orders for up to twelve months in an approved hostel or home, and allowed for the condition of mental treatment as an in- or outpatient at an approved institution (although, as we shall see in Chapter 3, this was already happening informally prior to this act).[48] They also led to the creation of case committees whose role was to review the work of individual probation officers. By the 1950s the influence of psychology had increased further, especially as criminology took hold as a more established field in Britain.[49] This meant that focusing on the motivations behind why people offended became more central, especially the need to learn more about the probationer's background, including their psychology and the relationship they had with their families. This was seen as crucial information for detecting the causes behind an individual's delinquent behaviour and for determining how best to cure them. This emphasis on the scientific assessment and treatment of offenders is why William McWilliams described this period as the height of the diagnostic ideal.[50] However, Williams also pointed out that the probation officer's new scientific methods of assessing offender's behaviour was in many cases just a glossed-over version of the older methods that were based on making moral judgements about probationers.

Not everyone, however, was happy about these developments and there were concerns raised by some probation officers that increased professionalization was leading to a loss of probation's 'Christian spirit'. For example, already in 1936 at the annual conference of the Sussex Branch of the National Association of Probation officers, a probation officer named Mr E. W. Watts gave a talk entitled 'The Religious Spirit in Probation', in which he claimed that 'in several parts of the country the probation service had become all the poorer because the religious spirit had been lost'.[51] To rectify this he proposed that probation officers should 'become spiritual advisers' while the 'authorities should be responsible for the financial side'.[52] Similarly, in 1947 a probation officer named Mr C. A.

Joyce gave a talk to the Kent Branch of the National Association of Probation Officers entitled 'dealing with the psychological aspect of crime' in which he argued that psychology was 'only in its experimental stages' and he pleaded with the magistrates

> not to accept it all at its face value. They must not be led into believing that all these 'isms' and 'ologies' can replace Christian ethics ... As a power religion was disappearing and a recent survey showed that only two boys out a total of 300 attended a place of worship after the age of 12.[53]

Despite these concerns, Christianity continued to play an important role in the probation service well into the 1950s, and in 1962 the findings of the Morrison Committee confirmed that probation officers in England and Wales continued to use a mix of old and new methods to reform offenders.[54] While the professional casework methods were stressed, providing practical material help was still seen as an important aspect of probation. As Gard has shown, probation therefore remained a site for 'the meeting of competing discourses from psychology and religion'.[55]

The Morrison Committee report was also important because, according to Gard, it marked the highpoint of the probation's standing and influence within the criminal justice system.[56] However, this high did not last long and by the 1970s changes within the probation service had begun to undermine the rehabilitative ideal. Most notably, in 1967 the probation service in England and Wales was required to take over the role of looking after prisoners released on parole in accordance with the 1967 Criminal Justice Act. This allowed for a shift towards probation being used as a method of punishment in the community. In Scotland, however, things took a different turn after the publication of the Kilbrandon Report in 1964 which, amongst other things, led to the integration of the criminal justice services in generic social work departments and the establishment of a welfare-based approach to the criminal justice system in Scotland.

The 1970s is seen by many historians as the point in which confidence in the probation service began to decline in England and Wales. Several studies, especially those which seek to understand the origins of recent probation policy trends, see the 1974 report by Robert Martinson as the moment when a 'nothing works' mentality began to take hold.[57] The report questioned the effectiveness of probation in reducing reoffending, and in time this started to undermine the rehabilitate ideal that had been so prominent in the previous sixty years. Despite this, there were some interesting developments, such as the introduction of probation-day hostels in 1973 and local projects to set up group therapy meetings for people convicted of sexual offences and domestic abuse.[58]

Nonetheless, the punitive thinking that had begun in the 1970s increased during the 1980s and 1990s, and in 1993 Home Secretary Michael Howard signalled his intention to continue this preference for punitive policies by declaring 'prison works', and removed the requirement that probation officers undergo professional training. In 2014 the Conservative government decided to partly privatize the probation service. Probation Trusts were abolished and the new National Probation Service (NPS) was set up. The NPS became part of the civil service and managed people deemed to be high risk. Those who were deemed low–medium risk were managed by twenty-one new privately owned community rehabilitation companies (CRCs). Many experts on probation warned the government that privatization would put the public at risk and that private companies would struggle to make high-enough profits for the plan to be sustainable. As predicted, the plan failed and in May 2019 it was announced that the majority of probation work would return to the National Probation Service.

Notes

1   A. E. Houseman, *Last Poems, XII: The Laws of God the Laws of Man* (1922).
2   The National Archives: HO 330/9 Probation and After Care Department: Criminal Statistics; Analysis of probation orders, 1946–59.
3   Ibid.
4   Probation of Offenders Act 1907(3 Edw. 7, c.25).
5   Ibid.
6   Sascha Auerbach, 'Beyond the Pale of Mercy: Victorian Penal Culture, Police Court Missionaries, and the Origins of Probation in England', *Law and History Review*, 33, 3 (2015), pp. 621–63; Dorothy Bochel, *Probation and After-Care: Its Development in England and Wales* (Scottish Academic Press, 1976); Raymond Gard, *Probation and Rehabilitation in England and Wales, 1876–1962* (Bloomsbury Academic, 2014); George Mair and Lol Burke, *Redemption, Rehabilitation and Risk Management: A History of Probation* (Routledge, 2012); Martin Page, *Crimefighters of London: A History of the Origins and Development of the Probation and Aftercare Service* (London Action Trust, 1972); Maurice Vanstone, *Supervising Offenders in the Community: A History of Probation Theory and Practice* (Ashgate, 2004); Philip Priestley and Maurice Vanstone (eds), *Offenders or Citizens? A Reader in Rehabilitation* (Willan, 2010); Philip Whitehead and Roger Statham, *The History of Probation: Politics, Power and Cultural Change 1876–2005* (Crayford, 2006);

William McWilliams, 'The Mission to the English Police Courts 1876–1936', *The Howard Journal of Criminal Justice*, 22, 1–3 (1983), pp. 129–47; William McWilliams, 'The Mission Transformed: Professionalisation of Probation between the Wars', *The Howard Journal of Criminal Justice*, 24, 4 (1985), pp. 7–274; William McWilliams, 'The English Probation System and the Diagnostic Ideal', *The Howard Journal of Criminal Justice*, 25, 4 (1986), pp. 241–60; William McWilliams, 'Probation, Pragmatism and Policy', *The Howard Journal of Criminal Justice*, 26, 2 (1987), pp. 97–121.

7   Christine Kelly, 'Probation Officers for Young Offenders in 1920's Scotland', *European Journal of Probation*, 9, 2 (2017), pp. 169–91; Fergus McNeill, 'Remembering Probation in Scotland', *Probation Journal*, 52, 1 (2005), pp. 23–38.

8   Williams was the first to use the term 'diagnostic ideal' in his series of articles in *The Howard Journal*, see above.

9   Vanstone, *Supervising Offenders in the Community, esp. chapters 3–5*.

10 Victor Bailey, *Delinquency and Citizenship: Reclaiming the Young Offender, 1914–48* (Clarendon Press, 1987); Pamela Cox, *Bad Girls in Britain, Gender, Justice and Welfare, 1900–1950* (Palgrave, 2003); Linda Mahood, *Policing Gender, Class and Family in Britain, 1800–1945* (Routledge, 1995); Stephanie Olsen, *Juvenile Nation: Youth, Emotions and the Making of the Modern British Citizen, 1880–1914* (Bloomsbury Academic, 2015); Linda Mahood and Barbara Littlewood, 'The "Vicious" Girl and the "Street-Corner" Boy: Sexuality and the Gendered Delinquent in the Scottish Child-Saving Movement, 1850–1940', *Journal of History of Sexuality*, 4, 4 (1994), pp. 549–78.

11 Linda Gordon, *Heroes of Their Own Lives: The Politics and History of Family Violence* (Viking, 1988).

12 David Garland, *Punishment and Welfare: A History of Penal Strategies* (Ashgate, 1985); David Garland, *The Culture of Control: Crime and Social Order in Contemporary Society* (Oxford University Press, 2001); Nikolas Rose, *Governing the Soul: The Shaping of the Private Self* (Routledge, 1990).

13 Vanstone, *Supervising Offenders in the Community*, p. 10.

14 Mahood, *Policing Gender, Class and Family*.

15 Jacques Donzelot, *The Policing of Families* (The Johns Hopkins University Press, 1997); Michel Foucault, *Discipline and Punish* (Harmondsworth, 1977); Foucault, *The History of Sexuality. Volume 1* (Penguin Books, 1990).

16 Gard, *Probation and Rehabilitation*, p. 86.

17 Ibid., p. 202; Cyril Burt, *The Young Delinquent* (London University Press, 1933).

18 For further discussion about the connection between insanity and social stigma, see, for example, Petteri Pietikainen, *Madness: A History* (Routledge, 2015); J. Woodhouse, 'Eugenics and the Feeble-Minded, the Parliamentary Debates of 1912–14', *History of Education*, 11 (1982), pp. 127–37; John Macnicol, 'Eugenics,

Medicine and Mental Deficiency: An Introduction', *Oxford Review of Education*, 9 (1983), pp. 177–81.
19 For more on the debates surrounding secularization, see, for example, Calum Brown, *The Death of Christian Britain: Understanding Secularisation, 1800–2000* (Routledge, 2001); J. C. D. Clark, 'Secularization and Modernisation: The Failure of the Grand Narrative', *The Historical Journal*, 55, 1 (2012), pp. 161–94; Hugh McLeod, *The Decline of Christendom in Western Europe 1750–2000* (Cambridge University Press, 2003); David Nash, 'Reconnecting Religion with Social and Cultural History: Secularization's Failure as a Master Narrative', *Cultural and Social History*, 1 (2004), pp. 302–25.
20 For more on the rehabilitative ideal, see, for example, Victor Bailey, *The Rise and Fall of the Rehabilitative Ideal, 1895–1970* (Routledge, 2019).
21 Marcus Collins (ed.), *The Permissive Society and Its Enemies: Sixties British Culture* (Rivers Oram Press, 2007).
22 Maurice Vanstone and Philip Priestley (eds), *Probation and Politics: Academic Reflections from Former Practitioners* (Palgrave Macmillan, 2019).
23 With the notable exceptions of Kelly, 'Probation Officers for Young Offenders in 1920's Scotland'; McNeill, 'Remembering Probation in Scotland'.
24 For a more detailed discussion about the potential methodological problems associated with using court records, see, for example, Stephen Robertson, 'What's Law Got to Do with It? Legal Records and Sexual Histories', *Journal of the History of Sexuality*, 14, 1/2 (2005), pp. 161–85.
25 Adrian Bingham, *Family Newspapers? Sex, Private Life, and the British Popular Press, 1918–1978* (Oxford University Press, 2009).
26 For further discussion on everyday resistance, see, for example, James Scott, *Weapons of the Weak: Everyday Forms of Peasant Resistance* (Yale University Press, 1985).
27 See above, footnote 2.
28 Auerbach, 'Beyond the Pale of Mercy'.
29 The Probation of First Offenders Act 1887 (50 & 51 Vict. c.25).
30 The Probation of Offenders Act 1907 (3 Edw. 7, c.25).
31 Ibid.
32 Home Office 1908: 5, as cited in Raymond Gard, *Probation and Rehabilitation in England and Wales, 1876–1962* (Bloomsbury Academic, 2014), p. 62.
33 Gard, *Rehabilitation and Probation*, p. 62.
34 Bochel, *Probation and After-Care*.
35 Gard, *Rehabilitation and Probation*, pp. 49–50.
36 Mair and Burke, *Redemption, Rehabilitation and Risk Management*, see chapters 1–2.
37 City of Glasgow Probation Area Committee, *Brief Survey of Fifty Years of the Probation Service of the City of Glasgow 1905–1955* (Glasgow Corporation, 1955).

38 National Records of Scotland (NRS), ED20/2: Minutes of the Special Committee on Probation Guardianship of Criminal Offenders, 7 June 1905.
39 Criminal Justice Administration Act, 1914 (4 & 5 Geo.5.), Section 8.2.
40 Nikolas Rose, *The Psychological Complex: Psychology, Politics and Society in England, 1869–1939* (Routledge, 1985), p. 147.
41 Gard, *Probation and Rehabilitation,* p. 114.
42 Hansard: HC Deb 2 March 1931 vol 249 cc107-39, 107.
43 Gard, *Rehabilitation and Probation*, p. 142.
44 Vanstone, *Supervising Offenders in the Community,* p. 73.
45 Ibid.
46 McNeill, 'Remembering Probation in Scotland', p. 29.
47 Burt, *The Young Delinquent*; W. Norwood East, *The Adolescent Criminal: A Medico-Sociological Study of 4,000 Male Adolescents* (J. & A. Churchill, 1942).
48 The Criminal Justice Act 1948 (11 & 12 Geo 6 c.58); The Criminal Justice (Scotland) Act 1949 (12, 13 & 14 Geo.6 c.94).
49 David Garland, 'Of Crimes and Criminals: The Development of Criminology in Britain', in M. Maguire et al. (eds), *The Oxford Handbook of Criminology*, 3rd edition (Oxford University Press, 2002).
50 William McWilliams, 'The English Probation System and the Diagnostic Ideal', *The Howard Journal of Criminal Justice*, 25, 4 (1986), pp. 241–60.
51 *The Mid-Sussex Times*, 20 October 1936, p. 1.
52 Ibid.
53 *Thanet Advertiser*, 4 April 1947, p. 6.
54 The Morison Report (Home Office, 1962).
55 Gard, *Rehabilitation and Probation in England*, p. 222.
56 Ibid., p. 1.
57 R. Martinson, 'What Works? Questions and Answers about Prison Reform', *The Public Interest*, 5 (1974), pp. 22–54; Vanstone, *Supervising Offenders in the Community,* p. 134.
58 Maurice Vanstone, 'A History of the Use of Groups in Probation Work: Part One – From "Clubbing the Unclubbables" to Therapeutic Intervention', *The Howard Journal of Crime and Justice*, 42, 1 (2003), pp. 69–86.

1

Marriage menders: Probation and marriage reconciliation in England and Wales

Much of his work lies with married people whom he seeks to rescue from the monsters of bad temper, jealousy, indifference and other failings, showing them they can only reach the highest form of married happiness by making their homes those in which mutual love and forbearance with one another reign supreme.[1]

The above quotation is taken from the memoir of Walter Stanton, who was a probation officer in Worcester during the 1930s. His assertion that much of his work revolved around repairing the emotional relationships of married couples implies that marriage reconciliation constituted a significant proportion of a probation officer's duties; yet, much of the existing historiography on probation does not discuss the significance of marriage reconciliation in any meaningful way. This is most likely because probation is more commonly associated with criminal law and the supervision of offenders, rather than civil law and marriage. However, this chapter will show how probation's social work role extended far beyond criminal law.

Probation officers had informally been involved in helping couples with marriage problems since the probation service began in 1907. However, in 1937 the Matrimonial Summary Jurisdiction (Domestic Proceedings) Act marked the beginning of the probation service's official role in marriage reconciliation in England and Wales. The Act did not apply to Scotland, and Scottish probation officers never officially became involved in marriage reconciliation (apart from a brief involvement during the Second World War). However, as we shall see in Chapter 2, Scottish probation officers did sometimes become involved in trying to reconcile couples in situations where the husband had been convicted of assaulting his wife. This chapter, however, will only focus on marriage reconciliation that happened in England and Wales between 1907 and 1962 and was not necessarily connected to domestic violence.

As was the case with all forms of social work, the ways in which marriage reconciliation services were practically implemented varied over time and from place to place. The methods probation officers used to try and reconcile couples, however, were particularly shaped by changing attitudes towards marriage and gender roles, and the varying level of influence that religious and secular theories about marriage and human relationships held at a given time or place. These different theories not only influenced the practice of probation but had tangible consequences for determining how 'successfully' couples were reconciled. This chapter explores how marriage reconciliation functioned in England and Wales between 1937 and 1962 and the extent to which the different types of practical and emotional advice that was given to couples helped them to successfully 'mend' their marriages. By doing so, the chapter will examine the role that the state played in regulating relationships in the private sphere and explore what this can tell us about marriage and gender relations in England and Wales during the early-to-mid twentieth century.

Rationales for reconciliation

In 1937 the Matrimonial Clauses Act extended the grounds for which a divorce could be sought in England and Wales. The 1937 Act amended the 1857 Matrimonial Clauses Act (England and Wales) which had stipulated that women had to prove that their husband had committed adultery and another offence such as cruelty, insanity, incest or sodomy, before a divorce could be granted.[2] Instead of proving two offences, the 1937 Act only required women to prove that their husband had committed one of these offences and it added 'unlawful desertion for two years or more' as another grounds for divorce. The passing of the Act raised concerns that there would be a sudden increase in the number of divorces and that the 'broken homes' which resulted from these divorces would undermine the stability of British society. Stable marriages were not just important for the individual family, but for society in general. An article in the *Eastbourne Herald* from March 1946 provides a good example of the widely held concerns about 'broken homes' during this period:

> It is not only the happiness of the man and wife which is at stake. Children are frequently involved, and for them a broken home may mean a lifetime of sorrow. Nor must the effect on the state be forgotten. Society as we know it is based upon the sanctity of the marriage tie, and anything that tends to weaken that tie is inimical to the wellbeing of the nation.[3]

A pamphlet by the Moral Welfare Council entitled 'The Threshold of Marriage' similarly described how the family was understood to be fundamental in ensuring a morally sound society:

> Various laws about marriage have been made regarding husbands' duties to maintain his wife and of parents to maintain their children. The reason why such laws have been made is that the state is deeply interested in the well-being of the family. The state wants children to be born and cared for because they will be the next generation of its citizens and nowhere are children so well cared for as in the family. Indeed, without family there would be no civilization.[4]

These sentiments were also shared by many probation officers and magistrates. For example, in October 1938 magistrate Lady Buxton gave a talk to the Probation Officers' Weekend Conference in Haywards Heath where she stated that 'everybody who was a magistrate would agree that matrimonial cases were the most important part of their work, because on the stability of marriage rested the whole social structure of our national life'.[5] In 1939 H. E. Norman, secretary for the National Association of Probation Officers, described how 'a nation anxious about its birth rate cannot afford to have children handicapped by upbringing in the atmosphere of unhappiness and insecurity of a home broken by matrimonial dissension'.[6] Similarly, in 1945 the Middlesex Probation Committee described how the importance of marriage reconciliation 'cannot be over emphasised ... [because] the security of the home depends upon it'.[7] In 1954 the Cardiff Probation Committee described in their annual report how 'the maintenance of the home life, particularly where children are involved, is obviously important for the well-being of the members of the family as well as for the community'.[8]

In addition to concerns about the general social consequences of 'broken homes', experts were increasingly linking the rise in divorce and separation rates with a rise in juvenile delinquency. In June 1938 Claud Mullins, a London magistrate who was a keen supporter of probation officers' work with married couples, wrote an article in *Probation* about 'The Matrimonial Work of the Courts'. In it he described how

> every student of juvenile delinquency has found that one of the principal causes lies in discord between parents ... The experts are unanimous – Cyril Burt, Healy, Bronner, Sheldon and Eleanor Glueck, and countless others whom I could cite, they have all shown from their own researches the serious dangers to children that lie in matrimonial discord.[9]

He further elaborated on this point in a 1943 article in *Probation* entitled 'Probation Officers and Post-war Problems' where he made reference to Cyril

Burt's findings in *The Young Delinquent* that '57.9 per cent of his delinquent children suffered from defective family relationships'.[10]

For many within the probation service, it appeared that there was a direct link between broken homes and the future delinquency of children who grew up in those homes. For example, the Liverpool Probation Committee Report in 1943 described how 'one of the main causes of juvenile delinquency has been found to be the interruption of normal family relationships, so it is hoped that successful conciliation work will have a considerable effect in reducing the number of juvenile offenders'.[11] Similarly, the 1953 Manchester Probation Committee Annual Report described how 'it is now generally accepted that there is an unhappy relationship between juvenile delinquency and matrimonial upset'.[12] Also in 1953, C. H. Stanley highlighted in *Probation* how 'problem and unhappy homes are a very serious factor when considering how it is that people do not seem able to cope with the difficulties and temptations of life'.[13] He continued to elaborate on this theme by explaining how 'in conciliation work the probation officer feels he is cutting at the roots of both juvenile delinquency and the adult crime which may follow'.[14] It was generally agreed, therefore, that marriage reconciliation played a crucial role in improving the well-being of society and reducing offending. Any concerns about the state's intervention into the private married lives of its citizens were consequently dismissed by referring to the impressive claim that this intervention could save marriages and thus reduce the delinquency and social problems associated with 'broken homes'.

It was within this context of concerns about 'broken homes' that the 1937 Matrimonial Summary Jurisdiction Act had recommended that probation officers be officially tasked with attempting marriage reconciliation with suitable couples who wanted to apply for a separation order. This recommendation came about primarily due to the 1936 Report of the Departmental Committee on the Social Services in Courts of Summary Jurisdiction which stated:

> Probation officers should be employed as conciliators in matrimonial cases, and to the subsequent statutory recognition of conciliation as one of the duties of the probation officer. In most areas the practice of entrusting this work to probation officers has now been established, and the officers have gained valuable experience in it.[15]

Matrimonial cases in this instance referred primarily to the separation and maintenance cases that were brought to the magistrates courts as a result of the Matrimonial Clauses Act 1878. This Act made it possible for women to obtain separation and maintenance orders from magistrates courts in cases of persistent cruelty and desertion (the latter being included as grounds for separation after an amendment to the Act in 1886).[16] The Act was intended to help women who wanted to leave their husbands but could not afford to go through the expensive divorce court process.

For a separation order to be granted, a summons first had to be issued by the magistrate. To get this summons the complainant could go directly to the magistrate who would decide if there were sufficient grounds to issue one. At this stage, the magistrate also had the option of adjourning the case for a short period so that he could refer the couple to a probation officer who would investigate their circumstances and establish if reconciliation was possible. This was one of the main ways in which probation officers became involved in reconciliation work. However, probation officers also became involved in reconciliation if the person who wanted a separation went directly to a probation officer for advice. At this point the officer could refer them to the magistrate or try to reconcile the couple themselves without necessarily involving the magistrate.

Reconciliation methods

The main role of the probation officer in the reconciliation process was to investigate the couple's relationship and home circumstances and provide appropriate advice and assistance. The exact methods used by probation officers differed between local probation areas and were dependent upon the approach adopted by individual officers. However, in general the aim of these interviews was to determine the cause of the domestic difficulties and help the couple find ways to remedy those problems. The probation officer would usually first interview each spouse separately and then together. This method was summarized in the report of the 1936 Departmental Committee on the Social Services in Courts of Summary Jurisdiction which described how both parties should be seen in order to 'gain full understanding of the causes of disharmony' and then the officer should 'think about what can be done'.[17] It was recommended that probation officers who worked with couples should 'let them talk about their grievances' and that it was important to 'gain their confidence and listen carefully'.[18] This approach was used by Probation Officer Jo Harris who in his memoir described how, when dealing with matrimonial cases, 'the probation officer should not just have one meeting, but needs to go to their home and really understand the background of the causes of the quarrels'.[19]

Similarly, in 1953 Hayden R. Llewellyn, the principal probation officer for Cardiff, described how

> matrimonial work makes great demands upon the probation officer, requiring patience, time and insight into each problem as a whole, as well as the ability to break down the problem and interpret it to both parties in such a way as to bring each to see and appreciate the other's point of view. This cannot be undertaken lightly, nor can the officer hope to conclude any case speedily ... [it takes] at least 3 meetings and usually many more over several months.[20]

Regarding the subjects that should be covered during the reconciliation meetings, a 1948 Home Office memorandum recommended that they 'discuss early days of married life' and ask questions such as 'how did this couple come together, why did they marry, what went wrong?'[21] It was also advised that 'sexual matters should be talked about, but don't embarrass'.[22]

The work of probation officers involved in marriage reconciliation was one of the earliest forms of state-funded marriage counselling in Britain. In the *Short History of the Bristol Probation Service* that was published in 1937, the author described how the Bristol probation officers 'often dealt with domestic problems which came into the office without reference to the court because, at the time, there were no other agencies around to cope – nothing like Marriage Guidance Council existed then'.[23] While the Marriage Guidance Council started operating locally on a voluntary basis in 1938, it was not until 1948 that the National Marriage Guidance Council (NMGC) was established and services were made available across the country. Moreover, the NMGC remained an independent body which retained its independent voluntary status (despite receiving some funding from the state). Jane Lewis has shown how the NMGC kept its independence because the government was reluctant to become directly involved in marriage guidance due to concerns about the possible negative opinion attached to heavy-handed government intervention in marriage.[24] However, by 1937 the probation service was already organized and funded on a local government level (with the exception of the London probation committee which was directly controlled by the Home Office). Probation officers' official involvement in marriage reconciliation in England and Wales from 1937 onwards shows that there *was* some support for state intervention into married life by the late 1930s, albeit via a less obvious route of locally funded probation services.

In many ways, the probation service provided a similar counselling service as the Marriage Guidance Council. However, there was a general understanding that the Marriage Guidance Council aimed to help couples prepare for married life and how to cope with its difficulties, whereas the probation service was there to provide help for couples who were already at the point of considering a separation. This rough division of labour was explained by David Mace, the secretary of the Marriage Guidance Council, who in 1947 wrote an article in *Probation* describing how

> the programme of marriage reconciliation falls naturally into two parts … what can be done in a preventative sense before the couple makes an approach to the court, and what can be done after they have approached the court.[25]

The Marriage Guidance Council was to focus on the former, and the probation service on the latter. However, his insistence that 'there need not be any overlapping or clashing of interest … there is enough work for us all to do' suggests that their caseloads were not necessarily always so neatly distributed.[26]

There was also an assumption held by some that the services of the Marriage Guidance Council were more likely to be utilized by middle-class couples, whereas the clients of probation officers tended to be from working-class backgrounds. For example, in 1939 H. E. Norman stated in *Probation* that most of the people who seek marriage conciliation meetings 'are the wives of manual workers or artisans', and in 1954, a former probation officer named Beatrice Pollard referred to this assumption when she noted that 'it is sometimes assumed that, in general, they [people who used probation officer's reconciliation services] rank lower socially than do those who seek help from marriage guidance agencies'.[27] However, Pollard also noted that there was little evidence for this assumption and that it was not necessarily one that was held by everyone. In her article she asked 'how widespread is the social difference sometimes observed?' and admitted that 'there is no reliable opinion covering the whole country on this topic'.[28]

A place to talk and listen

An important aim of marriage reconciliation was to provide couples with the opportunity to talk about their problems in a private setting with someone from outside of their usual family and friendship circles. This type of counselling fulfilled people's need for 'catharsis', something which Debora Cohen has shown was a necessary aspect of marriage counselling during the 1940s and 1950s. According to Cohen, couples during this period needed the 'process of emotional release following the outpouring of one's troubles' because there was much that 'could not be discussed at home. Problems festered for years, and silence or sniping substituted for communication. Unhappy husbands and wives could not talk to each other'.[29] Probation officers therefore provided an important counselling service for couples who struggled to communicate.

The importance of probation officers' role in helping to facilitate good communication was emphasized in various articles in *Probation*. For example, in 1933 H. E. Norman described how

> the contestants themselves so rarely understand the real causes of their own problems. The usual explanations offered to the court are poverty, extravagance, gambling, drunkenness, immorality, and jealousy, but these on skilful investigation will be found to be symptoms and not basic causes.[30]

Similarly, in a *Probation* article from 1956 C. H. Stanley stressed how

> it is a good thing to get them together, describe what an ideal marriage is like, and invite them to discuss how their marriage falls short of that ideal. This method gets things moving in a positive direction and avoids raking over the 'muck heap'.[31]

Probation officers working in different areas across the country also highlighted the importance of facilitating good communication in their everyday reconciliation practices. For example, in June 1937 a probation officer named Mr Sage gave a talk at the Northern Branch of the National Association of Probation where he described how 'a talk before they got to the court was of great value', because once it got to court 'each one wanted to "keep their end up" and did not like to give way'.[32] In March 1946, an Eastbourne probation officer described how couples just needed someone to talk to so that they could 'unburden themselves', and a report in the *Sheffield Daily Telegraph* in August 1950 credited the reduction in divorce being due to probation officers who, by talking with couples, stop 'any rash divorces that occur just after a small argument'.[33] Giving couples a chance to talk and be heard was also stressed by Probation Officer Joyce Rimmer in her interview for *Changing Lives* oral history book project. Joyce described how talking 'was the main thing … if you listened to them for half an hour that was the best thing you could do'.[34]

A good example of the importance placed on the use of talking as a reconciliation method can be seen in the report made about probation work undertaken during the Second World War. Probation officers from around the country were asked to send in reports about the social work that occurred in their region. The contributor for Sheffield described how the general policy adopted with voluntary and official cases has been to interview the wife first, then the husband, and if both are willing, to arrange a meeting between the two. I have often found that although reconciliation did not immediately take place, the meeting did help to pave the way for this at a later date by clearing up some of the differences between the couple and dispensing the bitterness which so often creeps into such cases.[35]

It was understood that an essential part of a probation officer's role was to listen and provide a safe space in which couples could talk through their problems together. For example, another contributor to the report on probation social work undertaken during the Second World War described how during the war,

> most wives welcome[d] the opportunity to tell their story, and the enquiry is seldom resented. In quite a number of cases confidence has been won and frequently both husband and wives will visit the probation officer time and time again for further help.[36]

The contribution by the Liverpool Probation Committee to the report highlighted the need for gaining people's confidence and not forcing their own concepts of morality onto couples. The Liverpool officer wrote how 'it was experienced that where the advice given could be accepted with confidence and without the feeling that the ordinary joys of life were being denied, then there was a reasonable opportunity of achieving success'.[37] The importance of creating an environment where people could talk in confidence came up again in the report of the Cardiff Probation Committee in 1948 which described how 'there is no chance of reconciliation unless the parties are able to talk with frankness to the probation officer and with complete confidence that what they say will not be disclosed'.[38]

The 1948 Home Office Memorandum on the Principles and Practice in the Work of Matrimonial Conciliation in Magistrates Courts also highlighted how listening was an important part of the reconciliation process.[39] The memorandum suggested that the officer needed to 'let people tell their story in their own way' and that the officer should 'give them time to do so'.[40] However, the officer was also warned not to let them 'ramble on indefinitely'.[41] While talking and listening were deemed crucial, there was a concern that probation officers should not take up too much of their time dedicated to this. For example, the Swansea Probation Committee minutes for September 1945 described how

> the committee discussed the practice which had arisen during the last few years, of persons casually visiting the probation office on matrimonial matters ... The committee felt that such unconstrained and excessively easy accessibility was

capable of abuse, and must inevitably result in many instances in a waste of time and was accordingly undesirable.[42]

The Swansea officers were clearly spending a lot of their time on matrimonial matters. The fact that people were 'casually visiting' the probation office on matrimonial matters suggests that the residents of Swansea felt confident that they could confide in the probation officers and that it was worthwhile to seek their advice.

Emotional support and mutual love

Another important function of marriage reconciliation meetings was to give people the opportunity to discuss their emotional needs. While it was well understood that violence, desertion and failing to support a wife financially were solid grounds for a separation, individuals might have needed help when trying to make demands for other things, such as more romance, intimacy or emotional support. For example, Walter Stanton described in his memoir how it was important for couples to provide each other with emotional support because 'trouble in relationships begin when either or both of the couple stop seeking to make each other happy'.[43] He also understood the importance of sexual intimacy and stressed that it was important that 'people are not ignorant of sexual matters' and should be provided with a proper education in such things.[44] Stanton in particular seemed sympathetic to the fact that people's needs within marriage might go beyond the material, and his belief in the importance of emotional fulfilment can be seen elsewhere in his writings. For example, he wrote how 'every home should have happiness where the sunshine of mutual love is a prominent feature', and pointed out that 'material needs are not everything'; men should 'also treat their wives to nice things like they did during courtship as it can make them feel a whole lot better and enable them to cope with their hard work'.[45] To illustrate his point he described an example of a situation where a young woman had asked him to talk with her husband because, although 'the husband was not unkind to her and provided everything for her, he did not take her out to the pictures or for walks anymore'.[46] Stanton agreed to talk with the husband and encourage him to treat his wife with more affection.

When discussing the causes of marital disharmony, Stanton blamed 'jealousies, incompatibility of temperament, bad temper, selfishness, need for give and take'.[47] He was even critical of patriarchal authority, saying that 'it has been found that trouble is sometimes caused by a husband adhering to the ancient Mid-Victorian idea that because he is the bread-winner and head of the house his wife must of necessity take a subordinate place'.[48] Stanton's ideas here reflect the concept of mutual love that, according to Marcus Collins, was at its height of popularity in Britain during the 1940s and 1950s.[49] Love was considered mutual in this context when it was based on an 'intimate equality between men and women', something which Stanton clearly promoted.[50] Nevertheless, while some probation officers appeared to be somewhat progressive in their beliefs about how 'mutual love' necessitated a certain level of equality between man and wife, most officers prior to the 1960s still agreed that couples should live according to traditional roles of 'homemaker' for women and 'bread winner' for men. Indeed, there was a strong belief that much of the marital disharmony they saw was caused by situations where couples could not, or would not, follow these traditional roles. For example, an article written by a probation officer in *The Scotsman* in March 1938 described how

> many of the adult cases are young men and women who have entered on the married state but with little preparation for, and less knowledge of, the demand upon which matrimony make upon each party to contract. For these the settling-down process is inevitably difficult, and quite frequently the wife assaults which appear in the city courts are but the result of faulty adjustment between man and wife. Probation can and does help these cases. Talks with an experienced probation officer help the young husband to realise his privileges and responsibilities, while the young wife can be aided in many ways in the art of homemaking.[51]

This preference for upholding traditional gender roles can be seen most starkly during, and directly after, the Second World War. The necessity for more women to become involved in work outside the home caused considerable concern amongst probation officers who were fearful of the negative consequences this disruption of traditional gender roles would have on society. An entry in the 1942 annual report for the Liverpool Probation Committee offers a useful summary of these concerns regarding women's increased presence in the public sphere:

> It is apparent that the war conditions have had a disturbing effect on family and home life of the community. There is ample evidence to support the belief that where married women have gone into war work some have become unsettled as a result of finding a wider interest and a temporary release from domestic ties. As a result they have tended to treat lightly their obligations towards their husbands and children. Some have sought greater liberty even to a consequent slackness of morals which has had regrettable effects on the family life.[52]

This emphasis on women's proper role as being in the home as wives and mothers continued to be supported by the probation service after the war and throughout the 1950s. It was not until the wider social changes of the 1960s and 1970s that most probation officers began to slowly change their beliefs about men and women's separate roles within marriage.[53] This discrepancy between theories of companionship and mutual love, and people's everyday experiences of marriage fits closely with the findings of wider studies on marriage by authors such as Marcus Collins, Alana Harris, Claire Langhamer, Simon Szreter and Kate Fisher, which have revealed the tensions that existed between the ideal of 'companionate marriage' and the realities of putting it into practice prior to the 1960s.[54]

Influence of religion and psychiatry

From the 1930s onwards probation increasingly professionalized as more probation officers undertook training in modern social work methods, including lessons on psychology, psychiatry and child guidance.[55] As Raymond Gard and others have shown, this type of training started to influence probation officers' everyday practices, and marriage reconciliation was no exception.[56] An example of this type of knowledge exchange can be seen in 1938, when probation officers attended a conference on marriage guidance which aimed to help officers to 'promote happy marriages and to repair those that have been wrecked'.[57] According to the Organizing Secretary, Mrs Hume, the first day was 'devoted to lectures by eminent medical men and psychologists on the social background of marriage, preparation for marriage and its psychological aspects'.[58] In addition to the conference, Mrs Hume also referred to 'numerous lectures in different parts of the country' on these topics.[59] The importance of the psychological approach was therefore being taught widely to probation officers across the country.

For officers who learnt about psychology and psychoanalysis, marriage reconciliating meetings could have provided an opportunity for them to introduce a psychoanalysis-inspired lay-person's version of 'talking therapy' into their reconciliation meetings with couples. An article in *Probation*, published in 1954 by C. H. Stanley, shows how by this point some officers were indeed engaging with psychoanalytical theories.[60] However, although he was supportive of this type of psychoanalytic 'treatment', he was sceptical about how feasible it was to provide everyone with this type of treatment, and he was keen to point out that other methods were equally valid.

I have recently shared the experience of some who are experimenting and perfecting the use of psychoanalytic theory in the relief of marital tensions. The success of these treatments is encouraging, but to assume they are the only valid treatments would be a desperate matter, for there is no sign that the number of those available with the necessary skills will ever match the volume of help needed. But the study of these techniques gives a most valuable insight into the relative value of the traditional methods of the probation service. We should remember that real love has a great therapeutic value.[61]

His statement also highlights the similarities between psychoanalytic methods and traditional probation methods. Certainly, one similarity between the two approaches was talking which, as we have seen, formed a central part of the reconciliation process. However, the extent to which the probation service's version of talking therapy actually resembled psychoanalysis is questionable. In this respect, Maurice Vanstone's description of how probation officers developed 'folk theories' in which 'psychoanalytical concepts were domesticated to make them more manageable in the probation context' is probably a more accurate description of how probation officers employed psychology in their reconciliation meetings.[62]

Not all officers, however, were so keen to engage with psychology. Just because officers were being taught about psychology, it did not necessarily mean that they all liked it or applied it. Although in general the influence of the behavioural sciences became more pronounced over time, there was not necessarily a straightforward or uniform progression. Whether individual officers engaged with these theories also depended on their individual background, education, opinions and preferences. Although some officers were already engaging with psychological theories during the 1930s, others continued to be influenced by more traditional Christian attitudes towards marriage well into the second half of the twentieth century and remained sceptical of psychiatry. A good example of this can be seen in the case of Mary Wilkinson, a probation officer in Bedfordshire between 1939 and 1972, who was critical of psychoanalysis throughout her career. When explaining her approach towards interviewing married couples she warned, 'whatever you do, don't dissect them, and don't start a psychoanalysis programme'.[63] At the end of the interview she professed, 'I couldn't live without my faith', and said that she was 'a great believer in prayer' when cases were proving particularly difficult. Mrs Wilkinson's preference for prayer over psychology provides a good example of why it is best to be cautious about assuming that increased professionalization necessarily went hand in hand with increased secularization.

In 1937, the Matrimonial Clauses Act stipulated that reconciliation work must be done by paid probation officers. This meant that it should not be left to Christian voluntary organizations, such as the Police Court Missionaries who had previously been involved in this type of work. However, this did not necessarily mean that people affiliated with Christian organizations stopped their involvement in marriage reconciliation altogether, far from it. For example, in 1937 the Liverpool Probation Committee described how

> for many years now the Liverpool justices have utilised the service of the police court missionaries in the work of conciliation. These missionaries are employed and paid by either the Church of England Police Court Mission, or the Catholic Aid Society. In some cases the representative of the women's police patrol have acted as conciliators. So far as Liverpool is concerned, the Act merely gives statutory authority for a practice which has been in operation for many years. It is, however, contemplated that the work shall be done by probation officers.[64]

While probation officers were to be employed to undertake marriage reconciliation work rather than police court missionaries, in practice little changed regarding the methods they used. In many situations the former police court missionaries merely changed their titles to become probation officers. This meant that, even though they were paid directly by the probation service rather than via the Church of England, the basic ideas underlying their role in reconciliation did not change dramatically at this point and the counselling work continued to be influenced by their Christian faith.

In 1940 the Liverpool Probation Committee annual report described how Mr John Davies, who had been 'for a number of years representing the church of England temperance society, and had devoted a great deal of time in connection with domestic proceedings and kindred matters', died and Mr Boulger, 'part-time officer for the Catholic Aid Society', retired.[65] This meant that the committee 'decided to transfer the conciliation work to the whole-time probation staff, with the assistance of Mr C. H. Done (a rep of the CETS) as a part-time officer'.[66] This move towards having only one part-time Church of England Temperance-affiliated probation officer involved in marriage reconciliation shows how the direct influence of religious organizations was beginning to wane by the 1940s, but it had not gone altogether. Even in 1949 the Liverpool Probation Committee still acknowledged the importance of missionary workers by giving 'thanks for the police court missionaries for their help with marriage reconciliation'.[67]

The transcript of an interview conducted with Probation Officer George Chesters demonstrates how religion also continued to influence marriage conciliation methods in Manchester during the 1940s, despite the move towards using officers trained in modern social work methods during this period. When detailing his time as an officer in Manchester, Hull and Stoke-on-Trent during the 1930s and 1940s, Chesters described how during the 1930s 'Manchester was still very religious', but 'after the training in the 1940s there was more focus on psychology and new jargon, but many didn't like this'.[68] Chesters also described how 'right up until 1944 when he went to Stoke-on-Trent the probation officers were really police court missionaries (they were full time probation officers but their salaries were paid to the mission)'.[69] That religion was still influential in Manchester during the 1940s (despite the new training and psychological jargon) can also be seen by the fact that in 1942 the Manchester committee decided they would continue to deal with reconciliation cases denominationally.[70] Even as the practice of using former police court missionaries declined by the 1950s, Christianity continued to influence many probation officers' attitudes towards marriage, and how best to save it. In many respects, therefore, the probation service's origins as a religious voluntary movement continued to influence the work of probation officers involved in marriage reconciliation well into the 1950s – a finding which fits with Callum Brown's argument that widespread secularization in Britain did not start until the 1960s when people started to question church teachings about marriage and sexuality.[71]

Legal aid and practical help

Aside from offering a type of talking therapy, another important function of marriage reconciliation work was to provide couples with legal advice and practical help. Probation officers were not qualified lawyers, but they were required to be 'well informed legally' and their training, coupled with experience in court, provided them with a good understanding of divorce law and matrimonial procedures.[72] For example, the Manchester Probation Committee report for 1946 described how there was a fresh course of lectures given by the Home Office Training Board for Manchester on topics such as 'law, matrimonial procedures … and reconciliation work in the courts'.[73]

This legal advice was especially valuable prior to the Legal Aid and Advice Act 1949 that gave free access to legal help for those unable to pay for a solicitor. Prior to this, working-class couples had limited access to legal advice and were often reliant on the services of the 'Poor Man's Lawyer' or charity from the court's poor law box, both of which were not always available in every court, especially in smaller towns or rural areas. Miss M. A. Roloff, a probation officer for Gateshead, acknowledged this fact in 1944 when she pointed out that 'many of the applicants cannot afford to be legally represented even with the fullest operation of Free Legal Aid and Poor Man's Lawyer Schemes'.[74] Probation officers therefore provided a much-needed service for working-class couples who required information about the legal requirements involved in gaining a divorce or a separation order. Even when legal advice was made more accessible after the 1949 Legal Aid and Advice Act, a probation officer's legal knowledge was still deemed beneficial. For example, an article in *Probation* in 1959 described how 'the probation officer may in many cases be regarded as a marriage councillor, but a councillor with additional training – he can attempt not only the conciliation but knows the legal alternatives'.[75]

Probation officers, however, were not qualified lawyers and it was feared by some that the appearance of having expert authority in legal matters could mislead couples. There were concerns that probation officers may, unintentionally or otherwise, overemphasize the difficulties associated with getting a separation order to encourage couples to try reconciliation. London Magistrate Claud Mullins voiced these concerns when he reminded probation officers that it was important that they did not become 'a barrier to the court'.[76] To illustrate this point, he told a cautionary tale about a police court missionary who had informed the people who she interviewed that 'God intended a husband and wife to live together and that they would not get a summons'.[77] This story reflected the concern that those officers who had a background in Christian missionary work may have been too enthusiastic about reconciling couples due to their belief in the sanctity of marriage. However, in 1944 an article in *Probation* by M. A. Roloff reminded readers that 'there must be no blocking of access to the magistrates', and she reassured them that 'instances of such denying are not unknown in the past, though happily they are very few'.[78] Nonetheless, even if some officers were reluctant to refer couples straight to the magistrate, individuals retained the right to apply to the magistrate for a summons regardless of the probation officer's opinion or advice.

In addition to providing legal advice, probation officers involved in marriage reconciliation also provided other types of practical help. For example, in 1936 the Departmental Committee on the Social Services in the Courts of Summary Justice Report suggested that officers provide couples help with 'the many practical sides of things' such as finding couples suitable housing and employment.[79] The report even suggested that this practical help could include 'convalescent holidays while the children are cared for which might help the wife cope'.[80] Officers could also help their clients to access funding from the poor box at the court (if the court had one). For example, in 1939 a survey given to probation officers found that '24 per cent of county officers are able to find legal aid for couples when necessary [and] 28 per cent of town officers do'.[81] Further examples of the type of practical help that was provided by officers can be seen in the transcripts of interviews undertaken by Alan Cohen between 1980 and 1981 with various social workers and probation officers who had worked in those fields as far back as the 1930s.[82] In an interview conducted with Mary Wilkinson, a probation officer in Bedfordshire between 1939 and 1972, Mary described a case in which she gave cooking advice to a woman whose husband was unhappy with her lack of culinary skills:

> Well I had a case where they were always quarrelling. I said 'Well what starts the quarrel?' She said, 'You know, Miss Wilkinson, he's a Yorkshire man and I can't make a Yorkshire pudding.' My father being a Yorkshire man, and my mother being from Lincolnshire, good cooks from there. So I said to the woman, 'When are you going to have dinner together?' And she told me. I said, 'I shall be out here 9 a.m.' I went 16 miles by car and I taught her how to make the mixture. Then I went visiting round their area and went back at the right time to put the pudding in. And that was the end of that trouble. It always started with Yorkshire puddings. Many, many of my women I've gone in and taught them how to cook. And it pays and it cements friendships, which are invaluable.[83]

The offer of cooking advice may sound trivial, but Mary had listened to the concerns of her client and helped her in a way she believed would make a difference. Moreover, her emphasis on cementing a friendship with her client highlights another key method for making the reconciliation process run more smoothly.

A particularly important service that probation officers could provide was to help couples find suitable housing. George Chesters, a probation officer who worked in various cities in northern England during the 1940s, described how he helped find people housing by putting 'pressure on housing committees to get some re-housed'.[84] While probation officers themselves did not have the authority to make decisions about who was allocated housing, their professional networks meant that they may have known the people who did, and in this way they were able to influence decisions in their clients' favour. The importance of helping couples find housing was considered especially pertinent during and shortly after the Second World War when housing shortages were understood to have had an exacerbating effect on marriage problems. For example, in the 1943 Liverpool Probation Committee annual report it was noted how during the war 'the housing shortage has very often hampered conciliation efforts', and in their 1944 report there was a description of how the 'shortage of houses is still a regrettable cause of much domestic strife. In some instances, young couples have been assisted to find other accommodation, and the results have been most satisfactory'.[85]

By finding couples housing the probation officer provided much-needed valuable practical help. Another important way that probation officers tried to help couples was by finding the husband employment. In a case from 1942, a Manchester probation officer described how she remedied the situation of a woman who applied for a summons against her husband for neglecting to maintain her by finding the husband 'a good job'.[86] The officer described how this practical help consequently 'kept them together' and that twelve months later they were 'extremely happy. He has refurnished the home. They often write expressing their gratitude for all that has been done for them'.[87] The Liverpool Probation Committee even kept a record of reconciliation cases in which employment had been found for the husband. For example, in 1944 it was reported that they had helped 250 people to find employment.[88]

Probation officers in these situations used their position of authority and their professional networks to get their clients the necessary practical help that they required. If probation officers themselves were not able to directly secure the housing or employment that was needed, they could refer them to other social work agencies or charities. In this way they acted as important gatekeepers to different types of practical aid. For example, the Liverpool Probation Committee minutes for 1944 described how they 'work closely with other agencies to assist the couple. Put people in touch with legal aid to help them with divorces'.[89] The Bristol Probation Committee 1938 report also mentioned how they sent cases to 'Women's Aid', and the 1948 Home Office Memorandum on the Principles and Practice in the Work of Matrimonial Conciliation in Magistrates Courts advised probation officers that when dealing with couples that had sexual problems, they 'should refer them to a minister or medical doctor'.[90]

Marriage reconciliation during the Second World War and beyond

The Second World War was a particularly busy time for probation officers engaged in reconciliation work. In addition to the increased workload due to the rise in marital problems caused by the disruption of war, the probation service was also asked to help with army welfare work. This work primarily involved investigating allegations that a wife had been unfaithful to her husband while he was serving in the army. Investigating these rumours was considered important for protecting soldiers' morale and ensuring that wives were not claiming welfare benefits fraudulently. In particular, there were concerns about promiscuity between British wives and American soldiers because the latter were thought to be especially attractive to British women due to their exotic appeal, high wages and 'Hollywood glamour'.[91] These fears were symbolic of wider anxieties about women's increased freedoms as they left the home to replace men in the workforce. In particular, there were concerns that this taste of freedom may encourage women to abandon their homes and families in pursuit of excitement and new opportunities, including sexual promiscuity while their husbands were away fighting.

Despite these well-documented fears, the report suggested that these concerns were often more imagined than real. The Summary of Probation Officers' Reports on Social Work during the War described how there were many 'allegations made to service men by ill-natured neighbours that wives were unfaithful or neglecting home and children. In many cases these allegations were unfounded'.[92] Instead, the commentator said they dealt more with 'complaints from wives that they were ill, unhappy, had bad accommodation, children problems, financial difficulties'.[93] Similarly, the London Thames probation officer who contributed to the report described how

> one has heard a great deal about the unfaithfulness of wives during the present war but it is interesting to note that out of the 177 cases investigated, 61 were simple estrangement. The marriage had perhaps never been happy … The wife realised she was much happier without him.[94]

Despite the concerns about the increased promiscuity of wives being largely unfounded, it was reported that the rise in the use of probation as a method for intervening in domestic problems increased the acceptability of this type of work. The Summary of the Probation Officers Reports on Social Work during the War described how 'it is found that married couples will now refer their matrimonial troubles to the probation officer at an earlier stage, after having found them helpful during wartime difficulties'.[95]

This increased enthusiasm for the probation service's involvement in marriage reconciliation that had occurred during the Second World War continued into the late 1940s and early 1950s, and by 1952 the number of marriage conciliation cases dealt with by probation officers was 76,716.[96] Crucially, the importance of the probation service's involvement in reconciliation was recognized by the

Denning Committee which had been set up in 1946 in response to the large increase in divorce petitions after the Second World War. The report asserted that 'the reconciliation of estranged parties to marriage is so important that the state itself should do all it can to assist reconciliation'.[97] The committee paid tribute to the excellent work done by the probation service in regard to conciliation work in the magistrates courts and recommended that they expand their activities into the divorce courts.

In 1956, the report of the Royal Commission on Marriage and Divorce similarly supported the institution of marriage and the need for the probation service's involvement in reconciliation. The report emphasized that allowing for an easier divorce procedure should not undermine the importance of marriage, and to ensure that this did not happen there should be 'a long-term policy of education, pre-marital instruction, marriage guidance and conciliation work'.[98] The report stipulated that it should be the state's role to 'give every encouragement to existing agencies, statutory or voluntary, engaged in individual reconciliation'.[99] The report also noted that there was considerable public support for reconciliation, something which could be seen by the fact that in 1954 there were '40,000 matrimonial cases dealt with in which both man and wife were seen by probation officers, and a further 36,000 cases in which only one party was seen'.[100] This moment perhaps marked the high point in enthusiasm for marriage reconciliation.

However, during this height of enthusiasm for marriage reconciliation new legislation had already been passed that would undermine the need for reconciliation. In 1949 the Legal Aid and Advice Act gave people with more modest means access to free professional legal advice. This meant people could go straight to a solicitor to get advice and initiate separation or divorce proceedings rather than having to seek the assistance of probation officers. During the second reading of the Legal Aid and Advice Bill in the House of Lords in June 1949, the Bishop of Norwich voiced the concern that 'anything that restricted or handicapped the work of reconciliation would be disastrous'.[101] There was nothing, he said, 'which so gravely threatened the moral fibre of the nation as the decline – almost disappearance – of belief in the life-long obligations of matrimony'.[102] The Lord Chancellor, however, while agreeing that 'marriage guidance work was very useful', stated that he was 'not willing that it should be a public service'.[103] The mood, therefore, was beginning to change and although support for marriage reconciliation continued throughout the 1950s, by the end of the decade this support was beginning to decline.

The wider social changes that occurred during the 1960s also played a crucial role in further reducing enthusiasm for marriage reconciliation as increasing secularization and individualism within society shifted public opinions away from accepting the need for state intervention into married life. Furthermore, in 1969 the Divorce Reform Act simplified divorce procedures which led to an increase in divorces and less need for separation orders or advice from probation officers. As divorce became more commonplace and the stigma attached to it lessened, so too did the fears about the social consequences of broken homes. Instead, there was a general shift in attitudes and an acceptance of the idea that a divorce was better for children than making them live in an unhappy home where the parents were arguing. For these reasons, the probation service saw their official work in marriage reconciliation reduce considerably during the 1960s.

How successful was marriage reconciliation?

So far we have seen the various ways in which reconciliation was intended to help couples 'mend' their marriages, but evaluating how 'successful' this service was in actually reducing the number of separations and divorces is more difficult. According to their own estimations, many officers believed that reconciliation *was* successful in reducing the number of separations. For example, in 1937 one probation officer at London's South Western police court claimed that 'over the past 12 months over 400 domestic squabbles have been referred to me and I have been happily able to terminate all but 30 of them'.[104] In Leeds, the Probation Committee claimed in 1936 that 'out of the 88 matrimonial cases that were adjourned by the Leeds magistrates that year, all but 8 were successfully reconciled by probation officers'.[105] In August 1950, the *Sheffield Daily Telegraph* reported that 'applications for divorce have reduced since the new court opened and thanks to the work of the probation service', and in 1954, the Cardiff Probation Committee reported that they were successful in reconciling couples in 64.6 per cent of cases.[106]

Some probation services also kept more detailed records of how many reconciliations they undertook and what proportion of them were deemed 'successful'. Tables 1.1–1.3 show these 'success' statistics for Manchester from 1939–40 and 1950–5; Bristol from 1937 and 1954 to 69; Liverpool, from 1938 to 1949.

Table 1.1 Manchester Probation Committee matrimonial cases[107]

	1939–1940	1942–1943	1943–1944	1945–1946	1947	1948	1950	1951	1952–1953	1954	1955
Total no. of reconciliation cases	1263	1237	1400	1315	1881	1864	1490	791	1376	1034	983
No. of cases 'successfully' reconciled	500						992	478	705	327	489
Referred by courts before summons							217	127	143	97	114
Referred by courts after summons							159	109	66	75	106
Referred by clerk to the justices							10	5	55	60	26
Direct application to probation officer							908	501	938	681	559
Referred by social agencies or police							196	49	174	121	178
Number of reconciliation interviews								5092		4838	

Table 1.2 Liverpool Probation Committee matrimonial cases[108]

Year	No. of interviews	No. of home visits	No. of reconciliations effected
1938	8468	1327	329
1939	6685	897	216
1940	5609	728	
1941	5411	576	281
1942	5522	55	306
1943	6393	536	314
1944	7179	594	324
1945	7796	546	356
1946	10,926	642	417
1947	9249	740	481
1948	8955	738	502
1949	7206	513	421

Table 1.3 Bristol Probation Committee matrimonial cases[109]

Year	Total no. of cases	No. successfully reconciled	Unsuccessful cases
1937	389	156 (40.1 per cent)	
1939	401		
1940	231		
1942	990		
1943	1114		
1944	1110		
1946	1667		
1947	1239		
1948	1192		
1950	967		
1954	405	162 (40 per cent)	243
1955	415	263 (63.4 per cent)	152
1956	346	176 (50.9 per cent)	170
1957	414	269 (65 per cent)	145

1958	311	151 (48.6 per cent)	160
1959	283	136 (48.1 per cent)	147
1960	245	152 (62 per cent)	93
1961	317	188 (59.3 per cent)	129
1962	208	123 (59.1 per cent)	85
1963	240	159 (66.25 per cent)	81
1964	160	93 (58.1 per cent)	67
1965	148	96 (64.9 per cent)	52
1966	105	61 (58 per cent)	44
1968	209	163 (78 per cent)	46
1969	182	147 (80.8 per cent)	35

Tables 1.1–1.3 show that Manchester, Liverpool and Bristol all dealt with large numbers of couples from the late 1930s until the mid-1950s. The exact numbers vary from year to year and from city to city, but overall, the widespread use of reconciliation services in these cities suggests that their services were considered useful by some; otherwise, people would not have gone to officers for advice and magistrates would not have referred couples to them. The Bristol records include data over a longer time period and the reduction in the number of cases after the mid-1950s suggests that, in Bristol at least, enthusiasm for reconciliation was beginning to decline by this point. Although that was not necessarily the case across the country, as the last available record for Manchester shows that in 1955 there were still 983 matrimonial cases in that city, 49.7 per cent of which were successfully reconciled.

The Manchester records are particularly useful because between 1950 and 1955 the Manchester Probation Committee recorded information about the ways in which reconciliation cases were referred to the probation service. Table 1.1 shows that in 1950, 60.9 per cent of all reconciliation cases were those in which the person had come directly to the probation officer, as opposed to being referred there by the police, magistrate or clerk to the justices. In 1951 this figure was 63.3 per cent, in 1952–3 it was 68.2 per cent, in 1954 it was 65.9 per cent and in 1955 it was 56.9 per cent. These statistics fit with the larger pattern outlined in a report by the National Council on Family Relations which stated that in about half of all matrimonial cases between 1950 and 1955 the couple had come directly to the probation officer.[110] Similarly, a report in *The Herald and News* from 1950 described how 'a good many hundreds of wives do wisely seek a probation officer's advice before the rift becomes too great to close'.[111] That people were coming forward to see the probation officers on their own accord suggests that the public had confidence in the service, and that going to visit the probation officer played an important role in the conciliation or separation process for many couples. Rather than being an unwarranted intervention into their private lives, the reconciliation services offered by probation officers were sought out by those who found these services useful.

Unfortunately, the majority of surviving probation records do not include statistics about how successful marriage reconciliation was, but the Manchester and Bristol Probation records do include some data about success rates.[112] In their self-assessment they equated 'success' with cases in which the couple did not divorce or separate and were still living together at the end of the process. This was a common evaluation criterion used by probation committees, although it is important to remember when comparing success rates that the exact definition of what constituted a 'successfully reconciled' case could vary between the local areas and this influenced the results of their calculations. Table 1.1 shows that in Manchester during the years 1939–40, 500 cases were described as 'successful' and this equated to 39.6 per cent of all matrimonial cases dealt with by the Manchester Probation Committee during that period. Regrettably, the Manchester Probation Committee stopped recording the number of successful cases after 1940 and did not resume the practice until 1950 when the number of successful cases was noted as 992, or 66.6 per cent of all the matrimonial cases dealt with. In 1951 the success rate figure was 60.4 per cent and in 1952–3 it was 51.2 per cent. The early 1950s was clearly a high point in the achievements of the Manchester probation service's reconciliation activities. However, in 1954 the success rate for Manchester dropped to 33.6 per cent, and although it rose to 49.7 per cent in 1955, the numbers after this did not reach the higher levels recorded earlier in the decade.[113]

Table 1.3 shows that Bristol had similar levels of success during this period, with a success rate usually ranging between 40 and 60 per cent. The highest success rate was in 1969 (80.8 per cent) and the lowest was in 1954 (40 per cent). There were no steady increases in the success rate, as the figures fluctuated throughout the period. For example, in 1957 the success rate was 65 per cent, but then in 1958 and 1959 the success rate dropped down to 48 per cent, only for it to then jump back up to 60 per cent in 1960. In 1968 and 1969 there was a considerable jump up to 78 per cent and 80.8 per cent. However, the total number of cases for the latter period is much smaller, which may have affected the averages. Despite these variations across time in both Manchester and

Bristol, the statistics suggest that the reconciliation efforts of probation officers in these cities were relatively successful. In some years Manchester and Bristol were reporting success rates of between 60 and 80 per cent and even when the success rate was at its lowest, 31.6 per cent in Manchester in 1954, this still represented a third of all cases.

Probation officers were often aware, however, that it was not always easy to evaluate or calculate how successful their efforts were via the type of statistical analysis described above. For example, in October 1950 Hayden Llewellyn, Cardiff's principal probation officer at that point, made the following comments in his report to the Cardiff probation committee:

> Judging by available figures there appears to be a more or less constant number of people each year whose marriages go awry and who seek the help of the probation officers either to end or mend them. He would be a brave man who dared to give figures of success and failure in the field of conciliation, but at least this can be said, that it is a wise provision that the attempt should be made in every possible case before the law is called into operation, and those who undertake these attempts know without the need for statistical proof that ... the time spent with distracted and distressed wives and husbands in helping them to sort out their difficulties is worthwhile in itself, as leading the individual to more harmonious living, even if it fails to bring about reconciliation; and at the highest there are many occasions when the real purpose of the work is achieved and a marriage saved.[114]

Llewellyn's statement shows how, even if it was not possible to accurately quantify success rates, probation officers' attempt to help the 'distracted and distressed' was a worthwhile undertaking. Although their efforts did not always result in successful reconciliation, they could at least help to ease people's problems and potentially 'save' a few marriages.

Other probation officers were equally aware of how difficult it was to affect long-term reconciliation. For example, in the address given at a probation officers weekend conference in Haywards Heath on 18 October 1938 the speaker, Mr Gervoise, described how 'conciliation was the most difficult of all the probation officers work ... among the qualities needed by the probation officers were tact, diplomacy, imagination, tolerance, a breadth of mind and freedom from pre-conceived ideas'.[115] He then pointed out that despite possessing these skills, 'nobody, even if he had the wisdom of Solomon, could effect a reconciliation in every case'.[116] Similarly, the 1948 annual report for the West Sussex Probation Committee shows how some probation officers were well aware of the limitations they faced. The report described how the difficult housing and shopping situation after the Second World War was 'making reconciliation difficult' and they 'didn't have enough time to work with [couples] properly'.[117] The report was critical of the high expectations placed upon probation officers, explaining how most 'marriage problems developed over many years, but officers were expected to reconcile these in 3 short meetings'.[118] Despite these difficulties, some did believe that reconciliation was helpful. For example, in 1944 Mrs M. A. Roloff claimed that 'where the officer tackles their problems with sympathy and understanding … he can and often does effect a reconciliation which may be permanent'.[119] Despite this uncertainly over the exact level of success probation officers had in helping couples to reconcile, it is clear that the reconciliation service offered by probation officers did provide a useful function for some couples, even if officers were not always able to prevent couples from separating.

Opinions of the couples

In 1948, an article by John Mogey entitled *Marriage and Family Living* described how people from across the country valued marriage reconciliation services because the probation officers gave them advice and helped them to voice their grievances. According to Mogey:

> Working class people in all parts of England have come to trust the probation officer with their matrimonial troubles, and much of this work involves going out to meet a reluctant partner. It is delicate work with humble people who for lack of a proper vocabulary cannot present their problems to the world. Many people now approach the probation officer who have no intention of going to court for a separation order.[120]

The above statement explains why John Mogey thought that visiting the probation officer was a popular method for working-class people, but it does not tell us much about the opinions of the couples themselves. Indeed, this reminds us why it is important to keep in mind that many of the articles and documents written about probation were done so from the perspective of probation officers and their supporters, and tell us little about probation from the perspective of the couples or how long reconciliation lasted.

The best way to establish how successful the reconciliation services were would be to hear from the couples themselves. Unfortunately, there are few available sources which recorded the opinions of these men and women. There are, however, a handful of sources which have references to the opinions of couples, albeit still mediated via documents created by probation officers. For example, in 1936 a probation officer for Bristol named A. E. Tyrer gave the following description of a successful reconciliation case:

> In the same street lived a young married couple who last summer hurled bitter jibes at each other across the court. The wife had summoned her husband for assault, and reconciliation seemed remote. The magistrates, however, had asked me to see what I could do. I had slowly gained their confidence and helped them to regain trust in each other, and now after some months I looked in again to see how they were getting on. I was invited as a friend and was offered a large cup of tea. 'Everything's alright,' was the mutual comment, and I came away with the satisfaction which constructive effort always brings.[121]

While the statement 'everything's alright' does not tell us in any depth how the couple felt about the reconciliation, the fact that the officer was able to gain their confidence and was greeted as a friend suggests that the couple were at least somewhat satisfied with the officer's involvement. In 1942 the Liverpool Probation Committee minutes referred to letters that had been sent by couples which expressed their gratitude for officers' help with their marital problems. Unfortunately, the letters have not survived but the report did describe how 'from letters received at various times it is evident that the work done in this direction [reconciliation] has been much appreciated'.[122]

The Manchester annual reports for 1942 and 1943 also include examples of couples who were apparently grateful for the reconciliation services provided by probation officers. However, the following two cases demonstrate how the circumstances in which this gratitude was expressed were not necessarily so straightforward. The two cases were described in the minutes as follows:

1) Mrs A who was pregnant, applied for a summons against her husband for his neglect to maintain her. He had a criminal record, was unemployed, gambling and deceiving her. Probation officer got him a good job, and kept them together. Child born but died in 6 weeks. It was a shock to both of them. They wanted to adopt a child, but PO advised against it because they were both young. Husband improved. In 12 months another child born. They are extremely happy. He has refurnished the home. They often write expressing their gratitude for all that has been done for them.[123]
2) Wife applied for summons on case of persistent cruelty – only married 18 months, one child, 9 months. She alleged husband knocked her about and told her to clear out. As a result of an intervention by the probation officer, she returned, but only remained one week – the case went before the justices and, on the suggestion of the probation officers, was adjourned for one

month. Probation officer interviewed couples and parents on both sides; was able to effect another reconciliation and a promise that in-laws would not interfere. On a recent visit husband and wife appeared quite happy – all smiles – and thanked probation officer for what she had done.[124]

These accounts show that the reconciliations effected by the probation officers were successful in terms of keeping the couples together and the couples appeared to be grateful for the involvement of the probation officer. However, the second example from Manchester details how a probation officer encouraged a woman to return to a man who had assaulted her. This raises some serious questions about just how 'helpful' this type of reconciliation really was. There was a risk that the desire to keep marriages together for the sake of the children could override the needs of individual women, even in cases where the husband was abusive. As we shall see in the following chapter on domestic violence, it was not uncommon for probation officers to encourage a woman to stay with her violent husband in the belief that the husband could be encouraged to reform his behaviour. In the above example the woman appeared to be happy with this resolution, and it is possible that the probation officer did help the couple to resolve their marital problems. However, it is not unfeasible that the 'smiles' referred to above were for the benefit of the probation officer, and without talking to the woman herself it is difficult to know how happy or long-lasting this marriage subsequently was.

An article in *The Gloucester Citizen* newspaper from September 1936 provides two further examples of cases where women were encouraged to reconcile with their husbands, despite having requested a separation order due to persistent cruelty.[125] The first case involved a woman named Rita M. from Gloucester who wanted a separation order from her husband due to his persistent cruelty. The Gloucester magistrate, however, instead decided to give the woman some unsolicited 'fatherly advice' by suggesting 'you young people talk over your differences quietly and come to a peaceful understanding'.[126] However, Rita told the magistrate:

> I have given my husband plenty of opportunity to behave as he should towards me … He has beaten me, and when his mother also beat me I thought it was time to leave him. I will never go back to him now.[127]

In reply to this description of abuse the magistrate dismissed the seriousness of the situation by telling Rita 'come, you must give and take when you are married … you must not be obstinate. You must try not to punish him for what his mother has done'.[128] To this Rita replied that 'she would not stand her mother-in-law's interference'.[129] Both the magistrate and Rita appeared to agree that it was the mother-in-law's behaviour that was the most unacceptable aspect of the situation, suggesting that a certain level of violence was seen as tolerable from a husband, but not from a mother-in-law. For this reason, the magistrate next chastised the husband, informing him that 'when he is married, a man should forsake his parents and cling to his wife'.[130] The fact that a mother was challenging the authority of a grown-up son appeared to be the magistrate's main concern, not that the husband was being violent towards his wife. To resolve the situation the magistrate decided that it would 'be advisable for the couple to talk over their troubles with the court probation officer'.[131] Rita, however, 'vigorously objected to any adjournment of the case for this purpose'.[132] The magistrate ignored this objection and instead proceeded to give them more unsolicited advice, despite Rita protesting that 'they would never patch it up'.[133] The magistrate condescendingly pronounced that the couple were

> not wise in their own interests in not trying to come together again. The clerk has given you sound advice. He and the members of the bench have had much longer experience of life than you have, and we know that little things happen sometimes which are unfortunate. We want you to do your best to settle your differences and to give you the opportunity to do this we shall adjourn the case for a fortnight, during which time the husband will pay £1 a week. In the meantime, we hope you will agree to see the probation officer and discuss your troubles with him.[134]

The second case that is referred to in the article is that of another woman from Gloucester named Annie G. who had also requested a separation order due to persistent cruelty. When asked by the clerk if she would consent to an adjournment for a fortnight to enable efforts to be made to effect a reconciliation, Annie 'expressed herself opposed to the course' because 'I summoned my husband four years ago for the same thing and it was then adjourned some time … I don't want to go back to him'.[135] Despite these objections, the bench 'decided to adjourn the case for a fortnight, during which time, the chairman remarked, the husband would pay 30/- a week and efforts would be made by the probation officer to see if their differences could not be settled'.[136]

These two cases provide good examples of the possible downside of using probation officers to try and reconcile couples. The magistrate in both cases ignored the wishes of the women and put them in potential danger by requiring them to see a probation officer before they could be granted a separation order. However, if we follow these cases further, it becomes clear that despite the magistrate's insistence that reconciliation be attempted, the probation officer realized that reconciliation was not a feasible option. Two weeks later another article in *The Gloucester Citizen* described how the two couples came back to the court and that the probation officer told the court he 'had to confess that his efforts had not had the desired effect'.[137] The probation officer explained how in the case of Annie G. 'he thought there was no hope of reconciliation to be found … I believe in the interests of both parties a separation order is the only thing'.[138] The probation officer here seemed much more in touch with the realities of this woman's life and more sympathetic to her request for a separation order than the magistrate had been. The opportunity he had during the two weeks' adjournment to talk with the couple and make a 'social investigation' into their home life probably played a role in this. A probation officer's involvement in the reconciliation process, therefore, could actually help people to gain a separation order in some situations, rather than block access to it, as was feared by some.

Nonetheless, the potential dangers associated with trying to reconcile couples in situations involving domestic violence did not go unnoticed. In 1946, the report of the Denning Committee, which had been set up in response to the large increase in divorce petitions after the Second World War, officially addressed the problems associated with trying to reconcile couples in cases where the wife wanted to separate due to 'alleged cruelty'. The report stated that in these cases

> reconciliation does not take place unless and until mutual trust and confidence are restored. It is not to be expected that the parties can ever recapture the mutual devotion which existed when they were first married, but their relationship must be restored, by mutual consent, to a settled rhythm in which the past offences, if not forgotten, at least no longer rankle and embitter their daily lives. Then and not till then, are the offence condoned.[139]

It was clearly intended, therefore, that reconciliation should only be encouraged in situations where violence no longer occurred and both husband and wife wanted to be reconciled. Indeed, it was generally understood that it was not only in situations where violence had occurred that reconciliation might not be appropriate. Already in 1936 the Departmental Committee on the Social Services in Courts of Summary Jurisdiction clearly stated that 'there is only point in conciliation if affection still remains' and 'everyone must be told they have the right to state their case to the court if they so desire'.[140] This view was shared by a Derby probation officer in 1948 who described how 'sometimes reconciliation in a matrimonial dispute is out of the question – if the home is so unhappy, for instance, that the children will never get a chance to grow up in decent surrounding'.[141]

In 1948, a Home Office memorandum tried to address concerns about the potential pitfalls of intervening in people's private lives and the dangers associated with probation officers using their position of authority to impose their own values onto those who they tried to reconcile. The report warned probation officers that the purpose of seeing the husband was to 'get his point of view, not to give him a good talking to'.[142] The report further stipulated that

> the conciliator must show that he brings an unbiased mind to the problems, and seeks to find what will be to the most lasting benefit, not only of the wife or the husband, but of the whole family unit, including the children.[143]

Probation officers 'on the ground' also recognized the dangers of heavy-handed intervention. For example, C. H. Stanley was keen to point out how

> I am no way concerned as to who is right or wrong, but rather as to whether I can help them discover what is wrong, and help them put it right. I must be careful to prevent one of them using me as a stick with which to beat the other.[144]

He further explained how 'conciliation is not a matter of giving good advice. It does not help for us to understand their problems, if we cannot communicate that understanding in a way which enables them to understand themselves and each other'.[145]

This awareness about the dangers associated with trying to reconcile couples can also be seen in the transcript of an interview conducted with a probation officer named Mr Chesters. He described how

> It used to be that we nearly did more matrimonial work than we did probation work. It was fairly much the thing that people should live together, whether they liked the idea or not! I remember having quite a set to with a clerk who said that it was the probation officer's duty to reconcile these people whether they wanted to be reconciled or not, because the magistrates had said so. They'd adjourned it for you to obtain their reconciliation, the possibility of a reconciliation, but they didn't say possibility. What he meant was he just wanted it out of the way so he wouldn't have to waste time hearing it in court. But it was also – and I had a theory that the magistrates who were the most unhappy in their marriage were the ones who were so interested in trying to get people together. Like – I've got to suffer, so why shouldn't you?[146]

Chesters placed the blame for couples being forcibly required to undergo reconciliation squarely on the shoulders of the magistrates. His theory of unhappily married magistrates seeking revenge sounds a little farfetched, but his statement does highlight how the probation officers were not responsible for deciding who should be referred to them for reconciliation.

The principal probation officer for Cardiff, Hayden R. Llewellyn, also admitted that there could be some potential dangers associated with marriage reconciliation if it was used as a 'barrier to the court' and resulted in couples being forced to reconcile. He explained how

> the applicant is seen first by the probation officer, and he listens to her story and arranges to see the husband, or, if she wishes to apply for a summons, assists her in making her application. The latter method usually reduced the number of applicants seeing the magistrates, and ensures the probation officer might be tempted to advise the applicant on the merits of her case, and perhaps to tell her that she has no grounds for summons, an applicant who comes to court wanting to take process, may thus be deterred from seeing the magistrates, who alone should decide whether she has a prima facie case. It is necessary for the probation officer who is engaged in work of conciliation to recognise that his position as a conciliator is different from that which he occupied in relation to probationers or to applicants who come of their own accord seeking his help. The parties to matrimonial disputes are adults, and for the most part they approach the court because they desire to obtain relief from a situation which appears to them intolerable. Anything like forced conciliation may not only appear to them to be depriving them of their legal rights but also may in the end only aggravate the situation. Successful conciliation can only be arrived at by consent and co-operation of both parties.[147]

Llewellyn was clearly aware of the potential pitfalls associated with marriage reconciliation, but he also outlined the ways in which these dangers could be avoided, namely ensuring that there was consent and cooperation between the officer and the couple. He was keen to emphasize that the people who had come of their own accord to ask for advice were adults and therefore their consent was needed, and their will should be respected. He further explained how 'the object is not to extend any outside pressure upon the parties to bring them together again, but to facilitate this by explaining the point of view of one to the other with their consent and co-operation'.[148]

Llewellyn was similarly perceptive about the causes of domestic strife and cautious about the methods that should be used to resolve them. He explained how

> The 'social' causes leading to the rupture of an intimate personal relationship are more obscure and admit less easily a solution. The following are only suggestions, and no attempt has been made to list them in order of importance or frequency; in the majority of cases there is a multiplicity of elements which cause the break down, with what seems at first the root cause, is very often

only the precipitating factor. We find 1. Economic problems, 2. Bad housing (including overcrowding), 3. Tension from inter-family relationships (in-law trouble), 4. Sexual maladjustment, 5. Mixed marriage (this refers to racial, religious or intellectual factors) 6. Incompatibility – very often deficiencies of character, lack of preparation and/or desire for marriage and its responsibilities. These factors are seldom apparent at the outset of the case and the situation is only clarified after the case has been thoroughly investigated. Such investigation fans onto the following pattern: 1. Fact finding. 2 evaluation of the facts. 3. Diagnosis followed by. 4 treatment … the task of matrimonial reconciliation is an onerous one requiring patience and resilience in those undertaking it. Each problem is unique and the officer must therefore approach it with an open mind and a sympathetic interest in the problem.[149]

Llewellyn's diverse list of factors that could cause marital disharmony, and his advice that there was often a 'multiplicity' of emotional, cultural, social and economic causes, some of which may mask other underlying causes, demonstrates a good understanding of the complexity of marriage problems. His insistence that 'each problem is unique' and requires 'an open mind and a sympathetic interest' suggests that he also had a good appreciation for how difficult it could be to help couples solve their problems.[150] Nonetheless, he seemed optimistic that a probation officer who had the necessary 'patience and resilience' could be successful if he 'thoroughly investigated' each case.[151] Even though this may only be one man's idealistic hopes about how reconciliation should work, it at least gives us an idea of how some probation officers tried to conduct their marriage reconciliation meetings, even if all probation officers did not always live up to these expectations.

Conclusion

While the importance of reconciliation work has often been overlooked in previous histories of probation, this chapter has shown how reconciliation work formed a central part of probation officers' duties. Their services were well-used by both the courts who referred couples to them and the considerable number of people who went directly to probation officers for advice on their own accord. Moreover, the involvement of probation officers in marriage reconciliation demonstrates that there was a strong appetite for, and acceptance of, state intervention in the private sphere of married life, especially during the 1940s and 1950s.

The chapter has shown how the conciliation methods that probation officers used were influenced by traditional Christian understanding of marriage and gender roles, but also by new psychological theories about relationships as more officers undertook training which included classes about the behavioural sciences. The impact that this mixture of influences had on reconciliation methods can be seen most clearly by the fact that probation officers often promoted notions of mutual love and equality, while at the same time advising couples that men and women's roles in marriage should be separate but equal. Indeed, it was not until the wider social changes of the 1960s that challenges to this separate sphere ideology became more pronounced.

By creating a safe place in which couples could talk about their marital problems, marriage reconciliation meetings provided couples with an early version of state-funded marriage counselling. Listening to people's difficulties and letting them talk through their issues together formed a central aspect of how probation officers diagnosed relationship problems and found solutions. It was not all talk, however. Probation officers also provided practical solutions to problems such as unemployment and homelessness by finding people jobs and new homes. When they were unable to do this themselves, they utilized their extensive networks to put people in contact with various social, legal, medical, welfare and charity organizations who could help them. In these ways marriage reconciliation services offered couples both practical and emotional help.

The extent to which this practical and emotional help resulted in long-term successful reconciliation, however, is much harder to establish. The statistics compiled by the probation committees generally showed that they were able to successfully reconcile a fair percentage of couples that they worked with. However, these statistics have to be treated with caution given that it was in the interest of probation officers to show that their efforts had been successful. Moreover, the definition of what constituted a successful reconciliation was often based on whether the couple pursued separation proceedings or decided to continue living with each other. These statistics, therefore, only show whether probation officers were able to reduce the number of separations in the short-term, and not whether they were successful in helping couples to solve their marital problems in the long term. It is equally difficult to know how the couples themselves felt about the usefulness of the reconciliation services. Despite there being some references to couples being grateful for the work done by probation officers, this evidence was mainly found within the probation service's own records and should also be treated with caution. To learn how successful probation was in repairing relationships in the long term would need further oral history research to gain insights about people's experiences of reconciliation and how it impacted their lives.

Finally, the chapter also highlights the potential dangers associated with probation officer's involvement in marriage reconciliation. Most concerningly, there was a danger that officers could be so focused on ensuring that couples stayed together that they encouraged couples with serious problems to stay together, including in situations where the presence of domestic violence made this dangerous. An individual had the right to go straight to the magistrate for a summons and could bypass the probation officer altogether, and many did. However, for an individual who was unsure about whether they wanted a separation order or not, the influence of a professional advising them to try reconciliation may have persuaded some people not to apply for an order when it may have been the safer or more desirable option. The consequences of this desire to reconcile couples, even in situations where there was violence, will be explored further in the following chapter.

Notes

1. Walter Stanton, *Sidelights on Police Court Mission Work* (Worchester, 1935), pp. 15–16.
2. The 1857 Matrimonial Clauses Act (20 & 21 Vict. c.85.)
3. *The Eastbourne Herald*, 16 March 1946, p. 8.
4. West Glamorgan Archives P/60/CW/152: The Moral Welfare Council, *The Threshold of Marriage*.
5. *The Mid Sussex Reporter*, 18 October 1938, p. 12.
6. H. E. Norman, 'Matrimonial Conciliation', *Probation*, 3, 4 (1939), pp. 59–60.
7. National Archives, H45/19505: Summary of Probation Officers' Reports on Social Work during the War: Contribution from Middlesex.
8. Glamorgan Archives, PSCBO/60/5: Cardiff Probation Committee Minutes, Annual Report 1954.
9. Claud Mullins, 'The Matrimonial Work of the Courts', *Probation*, 3, 1 (1938), pp. 4–7.
10. Claud Mullins, 'Probation Officers and Post- War Problems', *Probation*, 4, 5 (1943), p. 58–9.
11. Liverpool City Archives, 347 MAG/1/6: Liverpool Probation Committee Annual Report 1943.
12. Manchester City Archives, GB127.M117/3/5: Manchester Probation Committee Minutes, Annual Report, 1953.

13 C. H. Stanley, 'The Probation Officer and Conciliation', *Probation*, 8, 1 (1956), pp. 3–5.
14 Ibid.
15 National Records of Scotland (NRS) ED20/130: The Report of the Departmental Committee on the Social Services in Courts of Summary Jurisdiction, 1936.
16 The Matrimonial Clauses Act 1878 (41 & 42 Vict. c.19).
17 NRS, ED20/130: The Report of the Departmental Committee on the Social Services in Courts of Summary Jurisdiction, 1936.
18 Ibid.
19 Jo Harris, *Probation: A Sheaf of Memories* (R. F. Robinson, 1937).
20 Glamorgan Archives: Q/A/M/7/2/1 Cardiff Probation Committee Agendas, Officers Reports and Related Papers, 1936–56.
21 NRS, ED20/130: Home Office Memorandum on the Principles and Practice in the Work of Matrimonial Conciliation in Magistrates Courts, 1948.
22 Ibid.
23 Bristol Archives, Pamphlet/1383: Missionaries to Managers. Memories of the Probation Service in the Bristol Area, 1907–87.
24 Jane Lewis, *Whom God Hath Joined Together: Work of Marriage Guidance* (Routledge, 1991).
25 David R. Mace, 'A Marriage Welfare Service', *Probation*, 5, 8 (1947), p. 86.
26 Ibid.
27 Norman, 'Matrimonial Conciliation', p. 60; Beatrice E. Pollard, 'Research in Matrimonial Work', *Probation*, 7, 5 (1954), p. 51.
28 Ibid.
29 Debora Cohen, *Family Secrets, the Things We Tried to Hide* (Penguin, 2014), p. 218.
30 H. E. Norman, 'Family Unity and Probation', *Probation*, 1, 14 (1933), pp. 213–6.
31 C. H. Stanley, 'The Probation Officer and Conciliation', *Probation*, 8, 1 (1956), p. 6.
32 *Northern Daily Mail*, Monday 11 June 1934, p. 2.
33 *Eastbourne Herald*, 16 March 1946, p. 8; *Sheffield Daily Telegraph*, 10 August 1950, p. 3.
34 Joyce Rimmer, *Changing Lives, An Oral History of Probation* (NAPO), p. 50.
35 Ibid.
36 National Archives: H45/19505: Summary of Probation Officers' Reports on Social Work during the War.
37 Ibid.
38 Glamorgan Archives: Q/A/M/7/2/1: Cardiff Probation Committee Agendas, Officers Reports and Related Papers 1936–56, Cardiff Probation Committee Annual Report 1948.
39 NRS, ED20/130: Matrimonial Conciliation by Probation Officers 1949–1950: Home Office Memorandum on the Principles and Practice in the Work of Matrimonial Conciliation in Magistrates Courts, 1948.

40 Ibid.
41 Ibid.
42 West Glamorgan Archives: S/TC4/Probation/1: Probation Committee Minutes, 29 September 1945.
43 Stanton, *Sidelights on Police Court Mission Work*, see Chapter 3.
44 Ibid.
45 Ibid.
46 Ibid.
47 Ibid.
48 Ibid.
49 Marcus Collins, *Modern Love: An Intimate History of Men and Women in Twentieth Century Britain* (Atlantic Books, 2003).
50 Ibid., p. 4.
51 *The Scotsman,* 24 March 1938, p. 9.
52 Liverpool City Archives, 347 MAG/1/6: Liverpool Probation Committee Annual Report, 1943.
53 Jill Annison, 'Delving into the Probation Journal: Portrayals of Women Probation Officers and Women Offenders', *Probation Journal*, 56, 4 (2009), pp. 435–50; Jill Annison, 'A Gendered Review of Change within the Probation Service', *The Howard Journal of Criminal Justice*, 46, 2 (2007), pp. 145–61.
54 See for example, Collins, *Modern Love*; Lucy Delap, Ben Griffin and Abigail Wills (eds), *The Politics of Domestic Authority in Britain since 1800* (Palgrave Macmillian, 2009); Kate Fisher and Simon Szreter, *Sex before the Sexual Revolution: Intimate Life in England 1918-1963* (Cambridge University Press, 2010); Claire Langhamer, *The English in Love: The Intimate Story of an Emotional Revolution* (Oxford University Press, 2013).
55 For a more detailed discussion on the professionalization of probation and the influence of psychology, see, for example, Maurice Vanstone, *Supervising Offenders in the Community: A History of Probation Theory and Practice* (Ashgate, 2004) (particularly Chapters 3 and 4).
56 Gard, *Rehabilitation and Probation* (particularly Chapters 3 and 4).
57 *The Sunderland Echo and Shipping Gazette*, 17 September 1938, p. 7.
58 Ibid.
59 Ibid.
60 C. H. Stanley, 'The Probation Officer and Conciliation', *Probation*, 8, 1 (1956), p. 4.
61 Ibid.
62 Vanstone, *Supervising Offenders in the Community*, pp. 114–19.
63 Modern Records Centre, University of Warwick, WISEArchive, The Cohen Interviews, Interview No. 23 Mary Wilkinson, edited by Tim Cook and Harry Marsh.

64 Liverpool City Archives, 347 MAG/1/6: Liverpool Probation Committee Minutes, Annual Report, 1937.
65 Liverpool City Archives, 347 MAG/1/6: Liverpool Probation Committee Annual Report, 1940.
66 Ibid.
67 Liverpool City Archives, 347 MAG/1/6: Liverpool Probation Committee Annual Report, 1949.
68 Modern Records Centre, University of Warwick, WISEArchive, The Cohen Interviews, Interview No. 6: George Chesters.
69 Ibid.
70 Manchester City Archives, GB127.M117/3/5: Manchester Probation Committee Minutes, Annual Reports for 1942–3.
71 Calum Brown, *The Death of Christian Britain: Understanding Secularisation 1800–2000* (Routledge, 2001).
72 NRS, ED20/130: Home Office Memorandum on the Principles and Practice in the Work of Matrimonial Conciliation in Magistrates Courts, 1948.
73 Manchester City Archives, GB127.M117/3/5: Manchester Probation Committee Minutes, Annual Report, 1946.
74 M. A. Roloff, 'Matrimonial Courts: How Can the Probation Officer Best Help?' *Probation*, 4, 7 (1944), pp. 82–5, p. 83.
75 Beatrice Pollard 'The Distinctive Nature of Probation Work', *Probation*, 9, 2 (1959), pp. 22–4.
76 Claud Mullins, *Wife vs Husband in the Courts* (London, 1935), p. 38.
77 Ibid.
78 Roloff, 'Matrimonial Courts', p. 83.
79 Report of the Departmental Committee on the Social Services in Courts of Summary Jurisdiction, Parliamentary Papers 8 (1935–36) (Cmd. 5122).
80 Ibid.
81 A. J. Westbury, 'Questionnaire Survey into Reconciliation Work', *Probation*, 3, 4 (1939), p. 61.
82 Modern Records Centre, University of Warwick, WISEArchive, The Cohen Interviews: Conversations with 26 Social Work Pioneers.
83 Modern Records Centre, University of Warwick, WISEArchive, The Cohen Interviews, Interview No. 23, Mary Wilkinson.
84 Modern Records Centre, University of Warwick, WISEArchive, The Cohen Interviews, Interview No. 6, George Chesters.
85 Liverpool City Archives, 347 MAG/1/6: Liverpool Probation Committee Annual Report 1943 and 1944.
86 Manchester City Archives, GB127.M117/3/5: Manchester Probation Committee Minutes, 1942.

87 Ibid.
88 Liverpool City Archives, 347 MAG/1/6: Liverpool Probation Committee Annual Report, 1944.
89 Ibid.
90 Bristol Archives, Jmag/adm/4/2: Bristol Probation Committee Minutes, Bristol Probation Committee Quarterly Report for Period Ending, 30 September 1938; NRS, ED20/130: Matrimonial Conciliation by Probation Officers 1949–1950: Home Office Memorandum on the Principles and Practice in the Work of Matrimonial Conciliation in Magistrates Courts, 1948.
91 Sonya O. Rose, 'Girls and GIs: Race, Sex, and Diplomacy in Second World War Britain', *The International History Review*, 19, 1 (1997), pp. 146–60.
92 National Archives, H45/19505: Summary of Probation Officers' Reports on Social Work during the War.
93 Ibid.
94 Ibid.
95 Ibid.
96 Beatrice E. Pollard, 'Research in Matrimonial Work', *Probation*, 7, 5 (1954), p. 51.
97 Final Report of the Committee on Procedure in Matrimonial Causes (The Denning Committee) (Cmd. 7024), 1947.
98 Beatrice Pollard, 'Marriage and Divorce: Report of the Royal Commission', *Probation*, 8, 2 (1956), pp. 27–30.
99 Ibid.
100 Ibid.
101 *The Western Morning News*, 28 June 1949, p. 5.
102 Ibid.
103 Ibid.
104 London Metropolitan Archives, PS/SWE/ COL: London South Western Police Court, Newspaper Cuttings Collection.
105 *Leeds Mercury*, 23 January 1926, p. 9.
106 *Sheffield Daily Telegraph*, 10 August 1950, p. 3: Glamorgan Archives: PSCBO/60/5: Cardiff Probation Committee Minutes, Annual Report 1950.
107 Manchester City Archives, GB127.M117/3/5: Manchester Probation Committee Minutes, data collected from the annual reports for the years 1939–55.
108 Manchester City Archives, GB127.M117/3/5: Manchester Probation Committee Minutes, data collected from the annual reports for the years 1938–49.
109 Bristol Archives, Jmag/adm/4/2: Probation Committee Minutes Bristol Probation Committee, data taken from the years 1937–69.
110 John Mogey, 'Marriage Counselling and Family Life Education in England', *Marriage and Family Living*, 23, 2 (1961), pp. 146–54.
111 *The Herald and News*, 29 December 1950, p. 4.

112 *Leeds Mercury*, 23 January 1926, p. 9.
113 Ibid.
114 Glamorgan Archives, Q/A/M/7/2/1 Probation Committee Agenda, Officers' Reports and Related Papers 1936–56, Report from 20 October 1950.
115 *The Mid-Sussex Times*, 18 October 1938, p. 12.
116 Ibid.
117 *The Herald*, 9 January 1948, p. 9.
118 Ibid.
119 Roloff, 'Matrimonial Courts', p. 83.
120 Mogey, 'Marriage Counselling and Family Life Education in England', p. 147.
121 A. E. Tyrer, 'A Probation Officer at Work', *Probation*, 2, 4 (1936), p. 58.
122 Liverpool City Archives, 347 MAG/1/6: Liverpool Probation Committee Annual Report, 1942.
123 Manchester City Archives, GB127.M117/3/5: Manchester Probation Committee Minutes, Annual Reports for 1942–3.
124 Manchester City Archives, GB127.M117/3/5: Manchester Probation Committee Minutes, Annual Reports, for 1943–4.
125 *The Gloucester Citizen*, 8 September 1936, p. 6.
126 Ibid.
127 Ibid.
128 Ibid.
129 Ibid.
130 Ibid.
131 Ibid.
132 Ibid.
133 Ibid.
134 Ibid.
135 Ibid.
136 Ibid.
137 *The Gloucester Citizen*, 22 September 1936, p. 1.
138 Ibid.
139 Cmd. 7024: Final Report of the Committee on Procedure in Matrimonial Causes (The Denning Committee), 1947.
140 NRS, ED20/130: The Report of the Departmental Committee on the Social Services in Courts of Summary Jurisdiction, 1936.
141 *Derby Evening Telegraph*, 14 January 1948, p. 3.
142 Ibid.
143 NRS, ED20/130: Home Office Memorandum on the Principles and Practice in the Work of Matrimonial Conciliation in Magistrates Courts, 1948.
144 C. H. Stanley, 'The Probation Officer and Conciliation', *Probation*, 8, 1 (1956), p. 5.

145 Ibid.
146 Modern Records Centre, University of Warwick, WISEArchive, The Cohen Interviews, Interview No. 6 George Chesters.
147 Glamorgan Archives, Q/A/M/7/2/1: Cardiff Probation Committee Agenda, Probation Officers' Reports and Related Papers 1936–56, Report from 26 June 1950.
148 Ibid., Letter from 22 April 1953.
149 Ibid.
150 Ibid
151 Ibid.

2

Stopping domestic violence: Probation and wife assault

Sir, could you send the man (who was here a little over a year ago) as soon as possible. My husband is drinking again and neglecting his work. I think he is off his head this morning with the drink and I am frightened to stay in the house with him. I have left him twice already and I think as the lawyer said, he requires to be put in a home till the drink is taken out of his system. I have six young children, the youngest 3 months old. He must not know it was I who reported it or he will kill me in the state he is in. Please do something for me, I need someone to help me, I cannot live like this.[1]

The above letter, written by Mrs F. and sent to the Scottish National Society for Prevention of Cruelty to Children (SNSPCC), was given as evidence during the trial of Mr F. at Edinburgh Police Court on 13 May 1915 for 'breach of the peace'. During the trial Mrs F. described how her husband had 'ordered me to go for more whisky. I was somewhat unwilling to do so, and he commenced to shout and swear, raised his hand and threated to strike me'.[2] The police officer further described how Mr F. had 'frighten[ed] his wife, who ran to the police station'.[3] Mr F. was subsequently convicted for threatening to assault his wife and sentenced to twelve months' probation under the supervision of a probation officer.

The above case highlights some of the difficulties faced by women who wanted to escape domestic violence but were reluctant to involve the police and instead sought various other avenues for help. In this instance Mrs F. first turned to the SNSPCC and a lawyer, with the hope of getting her husband into a reformatory where he might recover from his intemperance. However, when faced with the threat of imminent violence, she turned to the police for protection. Mr F. was not sent to a reformatory but was instead placed on probation with the condition that he must not consume alcohol. The use of probation to force men to stop drinking was a common method that was used to reduce male violence during the first half of the twentieth century. This chapter examines the ways in which the probation service's complex history, influenced by its roots in both the Christian temperance movement and the fields of social work and psychology, shaped the methods that were used by probation officers to reform violent men's behaviour and to improve families' emotional and material well-being. While there have been many excellent studies of domestic abuse in nineteenth-century Britain, this is less true for the early-to-mid twentieth century, and with the exception of Annmarie Hughes' study of Scotland, none have focused on probation.[4] By examining national and local probation records alongside a selection of court cases of men placed on probation for wife assault, this chapter explores the ways in which probation was used as a practical method for intervening in cases of domestic violence in Britain during the first half of the twentieth century and examines the extent to which these methods were helpful in protecting women like Mrs F.

A 'civilizing process' or a 'let off'?

Central to early studies of domestic violence was the concept of the 'civilizing process', as described by Norbert Elias.[5] According to this theory, societies' attitudes towards violence started to change in the eighteenth century, resulting in a decreasing tolerance of violence, a trend which continued throughout the nineteenth century and resulted in increasingly harsh legal penalties for violent crimes.[6] Accompanying these changes was a less tolerant attitude towards domestic violence, as concepts of manliness changed from those of violent masculinity to ones of self-restraint and paternalism.[7] Walter Stanton, a probation officer in Warwick during the early twentieth century, echoed a similar belief in his memoir:

> It used to be quite common to see a married woman with black eyes on the streets – it was not looked upon with as much abhorrence as it is today – now less wife beating is happening. What has brought about the change? The work of the police court mission across the country and the passing of the married woman's separation act in 1895. More importantly it is the spread of education and its civilizing effect – a new type of manhood that sees his wife as a help mate and comrade – her rightful place.[8]

Stanton rather confidently credited education, the law and the Police Court Missionaries (the forerunners of probation officers) with the reduction in domestic violence and its non-acceptance in society. This claim somewhat exaggerated the extent to which domestic abuse had declined and over-simplified the complex pattern of how and why behaviours and attitudes had changed. As we shall see in the remainder of the chapter, probation's role in the policing of domestic violence in Britain during the early twentieth century was much more nuanced than Stanton claimed.

Recent research on the history of domestic violence has problematized the notion of the civilizing process. James Hammerton's study of divorce in nineteenth-century Britain has shown how patriarchal ideology co-existed with the ideal of the companionate marriage, meaning that there was never universal condemnation of domestic violence.[9] Hammerton shows how magistrates' preference for reconciling couples, rather than convicting the male perpetrators of violence, was one of the reasons behind low rates of conviction for domestic abuse during the nineteenth century. As we have seen in the previous chapter on marriage reconciliation, the probation service was also heavily invested in trying to reconcile couples, and they continued this work into the mid-twentieth century. But what did this preference for reconciliation mean when it came to placing men on probation who had been convicted of violence against their wives? The remainder of this chapter will explore this question further.

Ann-Marie Hughes has also criticized the civilizing process theory by questioning the extent to which ideas about masculinity had actually changed by the early twentieth century, especially in working-class communities in Scotland. Hughes argues that there was still a certain level of acceptance of domestic violence in popular culture, as seen through the newspaper reporting of such incidents.[10] Hughes shows how women were often blamed for their husbands' abusive behaviour, with men regularly defending themselves by claiming that they had been driven to violence because their wives were 'nagging shrews', bad house keepers or immoral drunks.[11] Hughes's argument that popular culture and the courtroom reflected a certain level of acceptance of domestic violence in Scottish society is convincing and, as we shall see throughout this chapter, examples of men justifying their violence as a result of their wives' poor behaviour can also be seen in the reports about wife assault cases which resulted in men being placed on probation.

However, Hughes's secondary argument that probation was a way to 'let off' men by adding yet another layer before they could be sent to prison is less substantiated. There were certainly some instances where probation was used as a 'let off', particularly in cases where the magistrate or Justice of the Peace (JP) was sympathetic towards a man considered to have been unfairly provoked into acting violently. This was especially problematic if it meant that women felt less compelled to report abuse because they doubted that their accusation would be taken seriously and result in a prison sentence. However, this was not the intended aim of probation, and those magistrates and JPs who used it in such a way did not fully appreciate the mission of probation, as seen by its practitioners and supporters. The dismissal of probation as merely a way for courts to ignore or condone domestic abuse misses the nuances of probation's complex role as, on the one hand, a more intrusive way to police men's private behaviour in the interests of the family and the state and, on the other hand, a practical social service that offered some help for women who had few alternative options.

Why probation?

Before the introduction of probation, the main sentences given in cases of wife assault during the late nineteenth and early twentieth centuries were fines and short prison sentences. Another common method was to 'bind over' the offender, allowing him to return home after forfeiting a sum of money as a security for good behaviour. Prior to the 1907 Probation Act, this method did not involve men being placed under supervision, but the 1907 Act made it possible for the accused to be placed under the supervision of a probation officer or some other suitable person for a maximum period of three years.[12] The probation bond could also stipulate that the probationer must follow certain conditions, such as remaining in employment or abstaining from consuming alcohol. Considering that poverty and intemperance were regarded as key contributing factors to domestic violence, these conditions were deemed particularly pertinent for helping to reduce violence.

The use of probation in cases of domestic violence was often seen as preferable to fines and short prison sentences because it meant that the man was likely to refrain from further violence during the period of the bond, usually between six to twenty-four months, a considerably longer period than that which he would have spent in prison (usually fewer than sixty days and rarely more than one year). If men could be encouraged to reform their violent behaviour and abstain from alcohol, this was seen as a better option than fines or short prison sentences because it had the potential to stop the man's violent behaviour in the long term, while also avoiding the family suffering from the loss of the main breadwinner's income. Today some might be sceptical about the likelihood that being placed on probation could lead to real long-term change in men's behaviour; however, it was exactly this faith in the potential of probation to genuinely reform people's behaviour that had led to the establishment of the service in 1907. Even if probation officers realized that they would not always be able to achieve long-term reformative transformations of men's behaviour, it was clear that fines and prison sentences were even less likely to achieve this aim. Indeed, it was feared that sending a man to prison could actually make the situation worse for the wife after his release.

An approach which kept the husband in employment was especially welcomed by local authorities because it meant that the family would not become a 'burden' on the local tax payers' rates. This economic reasoning sounds cynical. However, if a woman was concerned that reporting abuse could result in her family losing the husband's income, knowledge that her husband was likely to be placed on probation rather than fined or sent to prison may have encouraged her to report abuse rather than suffer in silence. An example of this logic can be seen in an article about Dundee's use of an early version of probation as a method for dealing with wife assaults in 1905:

> The plan has been of signal benefit in cases of wife-beating. If an offender in a case of this description is sent into prison for a first offence, he, if in employment, is almost certain to lose his work, and his wife and children are often left in a state of miserable destitution, necessitating an application being made to the parish council for relief, involving in some cases the breaking up of the home. When in such circumstances the husband comes out of prison, and has no work to go to, he is apt to lose heart and to go from bad to worse. Where the accused is punished by fine, with the alternative of imprisonment, the wife has often to sell or put in pawn or pledge some of the family clothing or other household goods to pay the fine, and thus the poor wife who has suffered violence at the hands of her husband has to suffer further punishment by being deprived of necessary household articles.[13]

A similar concern was voiced in the Corporation of Glasgow Special Committee on Probation of Offenders Report in 1919, which described how 'in too many cases, heavy fines, when imposed, create hardship and distress in homes where everything is sacrificed to avoid the imprisonment or secure the release of the bread-winner at the earliest moment' and therefore 'fines, if paid, only punish the wife and children'.[14] The report continued by detailing how, instead of sending 'wife-beaters' to prison, they have been placed on probation 'with fairly encouraging results'.[15]

These concerns about the economic plight of women whose husbands were imprisoned highlight how women's economic dependence on men meant that women, particularly those with young children, often had few alternatives other than to continue living with violent men. This was especially true prior to the welfare state. However, even after the introduction of the Family Allowance Act 1945 and the National Assistance Act 1948 made it more economically feasible for a woman to leave her husband, there were still other reasons why a woman might not leave. Aside from the obvious emotional reasons why a woman might want to stay with her husband, as we have seen in the previous chapter, there were strong societal pressures that emphasized the importance of keeping families together for the sake of the children. An approach towards domestic violence which prioritized trying to reform men's behaviour in the long term, therefore, had the potential to be more effective at protecting women from violence than fines or short prison sentences. However, this approach was dependent upon men being willing and able to change their behaviour, which, as we shall see, was not always possible.

Enforcing sobriety

During the period of their probation bond, men were required to be of 'good behaviour' and not commit any more offences, including violence towards their wives. However, the magistrate or JP could stipulate in the probation bond that other conditions must also be followed, the nature of which depended on the induvial case. While ultimately it was the magistrate or JP who decided what conditions should be made, they could ask the probation officer to undertake 'a social investigation' of the defendant's home circumstances to help inform their decision. In this context, the probation officer could provide recommendations, one of the most common of which was to include an abstinence order.

Given the probation service's origins within the temperance movement, it is not surprising that many officers recommended abstinence orders due to the long-standing belief that drink was one of the main causes of domestic violence. This belief was still going strong in 1948 when the Liverpool Probation Committee's Annual Report described how 'there has been abundant proof that one of the main causes of domestic unhappiness has been drink'.[16] Men who had a drinking problem were seen as particularly good candidates for probation because it was believed that once they were forced to 'sober up', the main cause of their violent behaviour would be removed. However, unlike in the nineteenth century when Police Court Missionaries could only rely on their moral authority to persuade men to sign the pledge of abstinence voluntarily, the probation officer now had the power of the law to force men to stop drinking. If men broke the conditions of their probation order, they could be sent to prison. Probation, therefore, gave legal authority to Christian temperance missionary work that had been ongoing since the nineteenth century.

Examples of men being placed on probation for wife assault and required to refrain from drinking alcohol can be found in court and probation records across Britain throughout the period under study. For example, in July 1908 Mr C. was convicted of maliciously wounding his wife at Ilminster. The magistrate decided that he would

> bind him over under the Probation of Offenders Act for 18 months in his own recognisances, with certain conditions, one of which would be that he should abstain from intoxicating liquor. Mr Edmunds, the probation officer, would look after him and report to the court from time to time.[17]

In September 1917, Mr T. was charged at Edinburgh Police Court with uttering 'threats of personal violence' towards his wife, whilst drunk, which put her in 'a state of fear and alarm'.[18] Mrs T's witness statement described how her husband

> came home the worse of drink. I asked him if he wanted his tea when he commenced to curse and swear and use filthy language ... saying he would cut my throat. He then took out a knife, went over to the bed and ripped up a pillow with it and said that is what he would do to me. He continued making a disturbance until about 2am when I sent for the police and gave him in charge.[19]

Mr T. was subsequently placed on probation and required to abstain from alcohol. This case is also a good example of how probation could be used to deal with men who had not yet been convicted of violence but had threatened it. At the Essex Quarter Sessions in September 1931, a thirty-four-year-old labourer named Mr F. pleaded guilty to common assault towards his wife. During the trial, it was alleged that on 'coming home at night quarrelsome after a little drink, the defendant started knocking his wife about'.[20] However, the defence argued that 'apart from drink, the accused was a good hard-working husband'.[21] The chairman stated that 'the Bench felt that the man's position was due to drink', and it was decided that the defendant should be bound over for two years on the condition that 'he should abstain from alcoholic liquor during that period, and should not enter a public house'.[22] In a case from London in 1953, alcohol was also blamed for the husband's behaviour. The probation officer described how Mr A., who was convicted for assaulting his wife with a broken banister rail, usually did not get drunk, but on this occasion 'unfortunately he had been drinking a lot of bitter beer which did not agree with him and this was the outcome'.[23]

Unfortunately, most of the surviving probation records do not provide systematic data about whether a man who was placed on probation for assaulting his wife was given an abstinence order. One city that did keep some useful statistics on this was Glasgow. Here there are records available for the years 1909, 1917, 1918 and 1919 that include information about the number of men who were placed on probation for wife assault and were required to abstain from alcohol.[24] These statistics show that whereas in 1909, 73 per cent of such men were given an abstinence order, in 1917 the corresponding figure was 40 per cent, in 1918 it was 33 per cent and in 1919 24 per cent. These numbers suggest that the use of abstinence orders was initially fairly common but had dropped significantly by 1917. This could reflect the fact that the influence of the probation service's connection to the temperance movement was fading over time. Nevertheless, despite the gradual decline in the numbers of men required to abstain from alcohol, even at its lowest point the figure still represented almost a quarter of all the men on probation for wife assault. The lack of statistical data makes it impossible to know how representative this sample is for other areas across the country and for different time periods, including what impact the First World War played in distorting the figures. Indeed, the likelihood that the First World War had an impact on domestic violence prosecutions is reflected in the Judicial Statistics of Scotland Report for the year 1915 which showed that there was a significant drop in persons proceeded against for 'wife assault' because of 'the absence of so many men on active service'.[25] Nonetheless, qualitative assessment of the wife assault cases that appeared sporadically in probation records and newspaper reports shows that abstinence orders continued to be used relatively frequently across the country during the whole period.

It was not only probation officers who saw the connection between alcohol and domestic violence. The connection between alcohol and domestic violence had been a long-standing topic since at least the nineteenth century and there were many instances of women complaining about their husbands' drinking causing violence. For example, in April 1914 Mr C. N. was found guilty of assaulting his wife, and during the trial at the Bath Police Court the wife described how 'drink was the cause of the trouble'.[26] Another witness in the case also described how 'when the defendant was an abstainer he went on alright', and Mr O. Restarick (the Police Court Missionary) suggested that Mr C. N. should sign the pledge and be placed on probation. Mr C. N. agreed to this and the magistrate sentenced him to twelve months' probation, with 'a condition being that he should not take intoxicants during this period'.[27] Interestingly, Mrs C. N. also agreed to take the pledge in order to support her husband in his efforts after another witness in the case described how 'it was likely to upset the defendant if he found alcohol being consumed in the house'.[28] At the same time, the witness was keen to point out that 'he made no suggestion whatsoever against Mrs C. N. She was a hard-working woman and only a moderate drinker'.[29]

Four further cases from Edinburgh provide additional examples of how women often blamed alcohol for their husbands' violence. The first case is that of Mr W., who was placed on probation for twelve months in 1909 for striking his wife 'on the face several times with [his] fists to the effusion of blood'.[30] Mrs W. described in her witness testimony how 'I have been subjected to similar treatment at the hands of accused on many occasions. Almost every time he gets drunk, about once a week, he creates a disturbance and assaults me.'[31] Mr W. was placed on probation for twelve months under the supervision of a probation officer and required to abstain from alcohol. In the second case, Mr S. was convicted of wife assault in June 1919.[32] Again, Mrs S. described alcohol consumption as the cause behind her husband's violent behaviour. During the trial Mrs S. explained that 'when my husband, accused, gets drink he goes mad and I'm much afraid of him. He had been drinking all day on Monday'.[33] In the third case, Mr P. was convicted for assaulting his wife in June 1922 while she was in an advanced state of pregnancy. Mrs P. described how

> life has not been happy in consequence of the accused taking drink, assaulting me and also keeping company with other women … About 9.45 am on date in question I asked the accused for money to purchase shoes for our baby. He refused and became very abusive and with his fist struck me a blow on the top of my head … I am six months pregnant, I am in a very nervous condition. I complained at Pleasance police station.[34]

After Mr P. confessed, he was placed on probation for twelve months and was required to abstain from intoxicating liquor. In the fourth case, Mr M. was convicted of breach of the peace in Edinburgh in January 1935 for putting his wife in a 'state of fear and alarm' after he threatened to kill her with a revolver.[35] In the witness testimony the wife stated that 'she noticed he had been drinking', and the explanation of the case given by the probation officer described how 'since the war, the accused has suffered from neurasthenia and, on taking drink, becomes very disorderly'.[36] He was placed on probation for twelve months, but there was no mention of an abstinence order.

The fact that the women in these cases thought that their husbands' drinking was the reason why the violence occurred suggests that there was some truth behind the assumption that alcohol and domestic violence were linked. A probation condition that required men to abstain from alcohol may, therefore, have been appreciated by women if it stopped their husbands from getting drunk and acting violently. Whereas in the nineteenth century women could only hope that men might take the pledge of abstinence voluntarily, these men had to abstain from alcohol or risk being sent to prison. In this way, the missionary spirit of the temperance movement gained legal authority through its historical link to the probation service. The women in these cases, however, also emphasized other factors that they believed had contributed to the violence, such as their husbands seeing other women or arguments over money. There was a danger, therefore, that the probation service's preoccupation with alcohol could draw attention away from the other causes behind why men were acting violently. Nonetheless, despite this focus on abstinence as a solution to stopping violence, probation officers did also try to resolve some of the other issues that were contributing to domestic violence, and they were willing to intervene in men's private lives in order to do so.

Policing men's private lives

One of the most interesting aspects of adult men being placed on probation for domestic abuse was the potential scope it provided for policing men's behaviour in the private sphere. This type of intervention in men's private lives has been seen by contemporaries and historians as something that was considered less acceptable than the intervention into the private lives of women and children. Linda Gordon, for example, has argued that in the areas of the domestic sphere and gender relations, it was primarily women who were the focus of attention and the ones who were required to change their behaviour.[37] Gordon has shown how social workers in Boston, Massachusetts, wanted families to stay together and therefore used their influence to try to make women change their behaviour so as not to antagonize men. The previous chapter has shown how probation officers also wanted to keep the 'traditional' nuclear family together and promoted the accompanying gender norms. However, when it came to policing domestic violence, it was the men who had been convicted of assault who were expected to change their behaviour in line with the conditions of the probation order. Rather than functioning as a 'let off', probation potentially allowed for a much more intrusive intervention into men's private domestic lives than a fine or a short prison sentence. Probation in these situations therefore challenged the perception that men had the right to act however they pleased in their own homes.

In addition to enforcing abstinence, there were other ways in which probation officers could intervene in men's private lives. For example, in Bath during March 1925, Mr S. was convicted of assaulting his wife and was placed on probation for twelve months. An article about the case in the *Bath Chronicle and Weekly Gazette* described how 'a number of special conditions were imposed, the principal being that he would not ill-treat his wife or children, or wilfully break any of the furniture'.[38] In another case from Bath, this time in 1916 and involving a man described as 'Austrian or German', the judge specifically stipulated that the man's behaviour was 'unjustifiable' and 'heartless'.[39] On passing the sentence of twelve months' probation he stipulated that the defendant must 'abstain from all intoxicating liquor, and behave properly towards his wife'.[40] In Nottingham during July 1914, Mr S. A. was convicted of unlawfully wounding his wife with a poker and placed on probation for twelve months. The magistrate stated that he was anxious to see if the accused and his wife could live happily together, and he told Mr S. A.: 'We suggest you give your wife more money'.[41] The latter comment was referring to the fact that Mrs S. A. had told the probation officer that she was only receiving £2.10s out of the husband's £5 15s a week wages to keep the family.[42]

Intervening in men's financial matters was particularly common, especially when the man was not living up to his role as the 'bread-winner', because being able to sufficiently provide for one's family was seen as an essential element of respectable masculinity.[43] For example, in May 1928, Mr H. J. was found guilty of assaulting his wife. According to the *Bath Chronicle and Herald*, the wife told the court that 'her husband was a gardener, but was out of work. He received 18s a week from the Guardians, and gave her 16s out of it which she had to provide food for the family and pay 5s a week rent'.[44] This was not considered to be an adequate amount for a family of four, and the wife described how the violence had occurred because 'she had no money to get tea for him and he struck her once with his fist'.[45] After having a private conversation with the probation officer Mr Harding, the judge decided to place Mr H. J. on probation, stipulating that 'he must keep away from bad companions and Mr Harding would try and get him work'.[46] By helping men to find work and encouraging them to give their wives a bigger share of their earnings, probation officers hoped to lessen the financial difficulties that were contributing to couples' marital problems. However, although this type of intervention may have been helpful in some situations, it did little to address the underlying socio-economic inequalities that lead to these families' precarious financial situations and caused women to be economically dependent upon men.

Another common justification for probation officers' interventions into men's private lives was the argument that the couple needed help to improve their relationship. For example, in March 1932 Mr J. S. was found guilty by Dundee Police Court of assaulting his wife by 'striking her a blow on the head with his fist'.[47] He was placed on probation for six months and the JP explained that he took this decision because 'his feeling was that there had been bad blood on both sides. By giving accused a chance he hoped a better state of affairs would be brought about in the home'.[48] In another example, the *Motherwell Times* reported a case from July 1932 in which a 'fine-haired, likeable-looking man' was charged with assaulting his wife in their home by 'catching hold of her by the arms, pushing her, and causing her head to strike against the wall'.[49] After hearing the evidence, the Fiscal Depute said that

> it was apparent that accused had received a good deal of provocation. The couple had been married eleven years, but meantime at least they were not getting on very well. They were not living very happily together, there being frequent disagreements.[50]

The judge consequently asked the accused 'to go home and try to come to terms with his wife', stipulating that the 'probation officer was to visit the home in the interval in an endeavour to improve the estranged relations between husband and wife'.[51]

Under this mandate of trying to improve relationships, probation officers learnt more about the intimate details of men's everyday lives. A good example of how this knowledge could then be used to make judgements about men's behaviour and prescribe how they should subsequently change their behaviour can be seen in another case reported in the *Motherwell Times* from September 1928. The article, entitled 'Young Hubby, Wife and the Divy', described how

> the probation officer (Mr James H Pugh) has been asked to undertake the role of philosopher, friend, and adviser to a young married couple who, to say the least of it, are not shining examples of a loving married pair. On the contrary, the husband gave the wife a "clout" on the forehead the other day, while she, on her part, struck him on the elbow with a hair-brush (taking care, of course, to let him have the hard end of the brush). The young couple live in a working-class district of the town, and, after hearing their respective stories at the police court on Saturday, when the husband was charged with assault, there was no doubt but that it was a suitable case for probation. The couple had been living in 'trouble street' for some months, and the climax arose on the question of the husband's claim to have an extra packet of fags out of the "divy". He wants money for fags, money for fish and chips, money to go to the pictures, all out of the divy, exclaims the wife plaintive. In answer to these requests of her husband for the means to satisfy his little petty pleasures, the young wife, intent on nobler and

deeper things, the sacred calling of motherhood, answered significantly that she would need all the divy for something she was expecting … Questioned by the fiscal-depute, accused admitted that his wife kept the house clean and tidy, and that she was always in when he came home for his meals … the FD remarked that, while the evidence went to show that the husband was technically guilty of assault, still there wasn't much in it, and the parties, he thought, could be brought together with the help of their good friend, Mr Pugh. If the husband would realize that he had duties to perform as well as duties to accept, things would work out much better. A promise was obtained from the husband that he would endeavor to mend his ways and do the right thing by his wife.[52]

In this case, the probation officer was tasked with being a 'philosopher, friend, and adviser' to the young couple, and both the husband and wife were seen as partly responsible for their domestic troubles. However, despite both committing acts of violence, it was the husband who was portrayed less favourably and told to 'mend his ways'. The Fiscal Depute was critical of the husband going out late at night and wasting his money, and so he requested that the probation officer help him to realize his duties and 'do right by his wife'.[53] That the wife was expecting a child was seen as an important reason why the family's money should be spent on milk rather than cigarettes. Although it was acknowledged that both the husband and wife were at fault, it was the husband who was primarily required to change his behaviour to be more in line with the demands of the wife and the needs of his family. This case, therefore, provides a good example of how probation could be used to intervene in a man's daily activities, habits and spending choices and was not merely a 'let off'.

Intervention into men's private lives was seen as especially warranted in cases where the husband failed to persuade the court that he had been provoked by the errant behaviour of his wife. For example, in July 1925 Mr G. P. was placed on probation for two years by Bath Magistrates for assaulting his wife, on condition that he 'lives apart from his wife, keeps away from her, and does not molest her'.[54] It was stated that the quarrel arose when he wished to give the cat some milk, and the wife objected because it would mean that there was not enough milk left for the baby.[55] The prioritizing of a cat over the needs of the baby was certainly not seen as acceptable behaviour for a good husband and father. A similarly dim view was taken of Mr R. G. who was charged with assaulting his wife in Essex during October 1925. According to the *Essex Newsman*, Mr R. G.'s defence was that he had been provoked into violence because his wife had 'not drawn the bedroom curtains'.[56] This was not accepted as a justifiable reason for violence, and the probation officer in the case described the defendant as 'a man of ungovernable temper' and warned the court that 'it was not safe for this wife to be with him. She was a good wife'.[57] The probation officer then recommended that a separation order be granted. While competing notions about masculinity meant that non-lethal violent behaviour was still sometimes seen as acceptable in certain circumstances, these cases highlight how the boundaries of those acceptable circumstances were growing narrower as men were increasingly expected to conform to more domesticated concepts of masculinity.

The intervention into men's private lives was justified in the above cases by their failure to live up to acceptable standards of masculine behaviour. However, this did not mean that women's behaviour was not also under scrutiny. It was still important that a wife demonstrated that she upheld good domestic standards, because this meant it was less likely that the husband would be able to justify his violent behaviour through claiming he had been provoked. For example, in October 1917 Mr E. was convicted of assaulting his wife and daughter at Edinburgh Police Court and placed under the supervision of a probation officer for twenty-four months. During the trial Mrs E. defended her reputation by describing how she had her husband's tea 'ready waiting for him', in contrast to her husband, who was 'very much addicted to drink'.[58] The women in these cases tried to ally themselves with the priorities of probation officers who wanted to ensure that homes were safe and healthy environments for children to be raised. However, if the wife was unable to prove her 'good character', this could influence both the probation officer's and the magistrate's perception of the case, which in turn could influence sentencing. In the context of probation, this could influence whether the husband was placed under the supervision of a probation officer and given specific conditions to follow or 'let off' without supervision. The following two cases from the Edinburgh Police Court provide examples of how judgements about the character of both the defendant and the victim, especially whether their behaviour lived up to traditional notions of appropriate gender roles, could influence the type of conditions that were included in the probation bond.

The first case is that of Mr G. S., a Private in the Royal Scots, who was convicted of wife assault at Edinburgh Police Court on 1 November 1918 and placed on probation for twelve months, but with no supervision. The charge stated that he had 'butted her on the mouth to the effusion of blood, and did strike her with [his] fists'.[59] Mrs J. S.'s witness testimony described how the 'accused cursed and swore and told me to take my bastard child out of the house and I was afraid of him, I ran out of the house and called the police'. The police witness then stated how accused when charged denied the charge and stated that whenever he entered the house his wife rushed to him asking where he had been, and without any provocation struck him one blow on the forehead with her fist and then ran out of the house. Accused says that his wife gave birth to a child about 6 weeks ago and he is not the father.[60]

The second case is that of Mr D. C., who was convicted of wife assault at Edinburgh Police Court on 5 August 1929 and placed on probation for twelve months under the supervision of a probation officer. The witness testimony of Mrs M. C. described how

> about 12.30 pm the accused dressed himself as if he was going out ... apparently, he thought I was going to accompany him, whereupon he caught hold of me round the throat with both hands, and forced me backwards over his knee, saying he would prevent me from going out. I screamed, and he let me go and I fell to the floor ... I am in an advanced state of pregnancy.[61]

The wives in these two cases are portrayed quite differently. Mrs J. S. allegedly committed adultery while her husband was fighting in the war, and she was also accused of being violent. Mrs M. C., however, was not described as behaving in a manner that might have provoked her husband, and she was sympathetically portrayed as particularly vulnerable due to being in 'an advanced state of pregnancy'. It is likely that the different portrayals of the two wives were a factor behind why Mr D. C. was placed on probation for twelve months under the supervision of a probation officer, whereas Mr G. S. was not placed under supervision. The transgression of accepted gender roles could therefore potentially influence whether or not probation was used as a 'let off'.

There were also situations in which both husband and wife did not live up to expected gender standards. An example of this can be seen in another case from Edinburgh. In May 1919, Mr B. was placed on probation for twelve months under the supervision of a probation officer and with the condition that he would abstain from alcohol. During the trial at Edinburgh Police Court, Mrs B. described how

> accused, since he came home from the army and while in drink, is always in the habit of assaulting me. About 9.50pm on this date accused came home the worse of drink and cursed and swore and commenced making reference to my conduct during his absence in the army, with the result that he struck me 2 or 3 blows on my face with his fist whereby my right eyebrow was cut and bleeding. I then called the police and gave accused in charge.[62]

In addition to the witness statement, there was also a report made by the SNSPCC, which described how

> the father in this case was a prisoner of war, he returned early in 1919 but found two illegitimate children, twins, in the home. On 5 March a complaint was made at the shelter and on enquiry it was found that Mrs B. has been put out of the house by her husband who threatened to cut her throat. Mrs B. stated that she has been to Dr Williamson as she considered her husband out of his mind. The children at this time were found to be healthy but very dirty and poorly clad. Since then the conditions have been most unsatisfactory as the man and wife are constantly quarrelling and in consequence the children have suffered.[63]

The fact that the SNSPCC report about Mrs B.'s adultery and the birth of two illegitimate children, both of whom were described as 'dirty and poorly clad', was included as necessary evidence for the court suggests that the wife's failure to live up to gendered expectations of good motherly behaviour was taken into consideration as a possible justification for the husband's violence. However, Mr B. was described as 'out of his mind' in the report, and his violence was attributed to alcohol. Given the belief that alcohol was a key factor behind domestic violence, Mr B. was deemed a good candidate for probation, with the addition of an abstinence order. This case highlights how the failure to live up to gender role expectations could be used as evidence to support the case of either the victim or the defendant. Clearly, the behaviour of both the man and woman was under scrutiny in these cases, and both were expected to change in order to improve the relationship and make further violence less likely.

However, it was not necessarily only the behaviour of the husband and wife that determined if a man was placed on probation or what level of supervision was imposed on him. These decisions could depend on many different factors. Aside from the merits of an individual case, the choice of which men should be placed under supervision and given particular conditions to follow was often dependent on local variations, especially the attitude of the judge, magistrate or JP and the availability of probation officers. In locations where there were not enough probation officers, it was less likely men would be placed under supervision. Even if there were officers available, some judges, magistrates and justices were generally less enthusiastic about the use of probation with supervision for adults because they believed that supervision should mainly be reserved for young offenders. The high level of discretion available to judges, magistrates and justices when making sentencing decisions about probation therefore meant that practices could vary significantly, and this ultimately had a major impact on how successfully probation could be used to change men's behaviour.

Practical and financial help

As we have seen, poverty and unemployment were often cited as contributing factors behind why men became violent. By helping offenders find employment, suitable housing and other forms of practical help, probation officers endeavoured to help alleviate some of the problems that could lead to violence. Several of the local probation committees had their own sources of funding to provide welfare support, such as the Manchester Probation Committee, which began its own 'social welfare fund' from charitable donations in 1932 and continued to provide support well into the 1950s. This support could include donations of money to those deemed 'deserving', along with food and clothing to those most in need.[64] Similarly, the Cardiff Probation Committee had 'funds at its disposal for the provisions of boots, clothing etc.' through its own voluntary committee. Local probation committees that did not have their own specific funds could instead apply for money from the magistrates or police court 'poor box' on behalf of their probationers. For example, the Liverpool Probation Committee report of 1930 described how 'clothing, food, railway fares etc. have been provided for 205 cases by grants from the police court poor box as well as by donations'.[65] Probation officers also worked closely with various social welfare agencies and acted as 'gate keepers' to different sources of charity, welfare services and financial help.

However, although this type of practical and financial aid may have been helpful for many families, it was subject to the proviso that they cooperate with the demands of the probation officers. In this respect, the provision of financial aid could be seen as being part of a wider class-based project to control and discipline working-class families, as described by David Garland, Linda Mahood and others.[66] By encouraging the poor to internalize middle-class notions of morality, working-class families were encouraged to accept individual responsibility for their circumstances rather than blaming wider political or socio-economic inequalities for contributing to their difficulties. The records do show that the people placed on probation for domestic violence were mainly from working-class backgrounds. For example, the probation register for Glasgow shows that the men convicted for wife assault were primarily listed as being employed in typically manual occupations of varying skill levels, such as labourers, dock workers, miners, iron workers, shipwrights and carpenters.[67] There were very few middle-class men placed on probation for wife assault, possibly reflecting the fact that it was generally less likely that middle-class men would be brought to court and found guilty in the first place. However, just because these working-class families may have welcomed welfare support, it did not necessarily mean that they listened to advice from probation officers or internalized their ideologies. As Jennifer Davies and George Behlmer have shown in the context of the police court, while these courts were popular with working-class complainants because of their philanthropic associations, this does not 'constitute proof that the disciplinary goal of a ruling elite had been achieved, or that the poor had learned to internalize the rule of law as defined by the rich'.[68]

Nonetheless, the probation literature from this period suggests that probation officers were aware of the potential problems that could stem from their position of authority over working-class families. For example, the minutes of the Scottish Catholic Probation Officers Association from November 1926 included a description of how the visiting of probationers' homes 'should not be overdone and should be tactful'.[69] Similarly, the rules laid down during the tenth meeting of the Probation Training Board in July 1939 described how 'care should be taken to make sure the probationer does not feel they have too many people keeping an eye on him'.[70] Moreover, probation officers tried to ensure that their middle-class status did not undermine their ability to engage meaningfully with people from working-class backgrounds, and the probation rules placed much emphasis on the need for officers to have a good understanding of working-class life so as not to be judgmental or offer impractical advice.

The impact of the welfare state and psychiatry

The introduction of the welfare state and social housing legislation after the Second World War made it slightly more feasible for women to support themselves and their children without necessarily needing a male breadwinner.[71] The fact that the Family Allowance Act 1945 allowed for child benefits to be given directly to mothers was particularly significant in this regard.[72] Although single motherhood was still not an easy prospect, the availability of more financial support for single mothers partly undermined the argument that men should be placed on probation rather than sent to prison because women relied on their husband's income to survive. Despite this, probation continued to be used in situations where men had assaulted their wives in the hope that this approach would keep families together. For example, in December 1946 Mr S. was placed on probation for twelve months after pleading guilty at Sussex Assizes court to assaulting his wife and causing actual bodily harm. According to the *Worthing Herald*, the judge advised Mr S.: 'Don't rashly break up your married life. Don't forget you have responsibilities. You know being married is not only getting married.'[73] Despite the husband's violence, the judge still prioritized keeping the family together. Clearly there were reasons other than financial incentives for why the probation service and women themselves still prioritized keeping families together.

Thanks in part to the influence of the child guidance movement and new behavioural sciences, such as psychology and psychiatry, there was a growing acceptance that fathers played an important emotional role within the family, especially in child development. This gave renewed support for the old argument that couples should stay together for the sake of the children. However, at the same time as the role of the father in children's lives was starting to become more appreciated, it was also becoming generally accepted that a violent and dysfunctional relationship between parents would lead to an unhealthy emotional home environment, which in turn could lead to children becoming juvenile delinquents and future criminals. For example, the Manchester Probation Committee's Annual report for 1953 described how

> It is now generally accepted that there is an unhappy relationship between juvenile delinquency and matrimonial upset: a child's happiness is the gift of the parents. The happiness of a married couple, on the other hand, is not fortuitous, it is a plant to be cultivated and cherished, but how many people seem to be ignorant of the elementary laws of this kind of husbandry![74]

It was important, therefore, to ensure that children lived in an emotionally stable home environment. In some instances, that aim was best served by sending the husband to prison and letting the couple separate. However, in other cases it was hoped that probation could be used to reform men's behaviour, stop violence and improve the home environment without the husband having to go to prison or the parents separating. A tall order – and one that, as we shall see, was not easily achieved.

The desire to keep families together was not always enough to justify the use of a probation, however, especially in situations where the man was a repeat offender or had used excessive violence. A case from Airdrie in January 1954 provides a good example of this. Mr J. S. was convicted of assaulting his wife and sentenced to six months in prison. According to the *Aberdeen Evening Express*, Mr J. S.'s defence lawyer asked for the defendant to be placed on probation.[75] In support of this request, he told the JP that the couple had moved into a new house recently and were working hard to establish a home. He continued to justify his request by explaining how 'Mr J. S. came into court with a good character – not a blemish on it – and if he was sent to prison it would just be additional punishment to Mrs J. S.'[76] However, unlike in the previous case of Mr S., where the Sussex magistrate prioritized keeping the family together, in this case the JP decided that he could not put J. S. on probation. He told the court that he had considered probation because 'in cases of wife assault one must always consider the effect on the afterlife of the couple'.[77] However, he could not put this man on probation because

> of all the cases of wife assault that I have heard in this court this one is undoubtedly by far the most serious. It is by far the most deliberate and cold blooded, and the repeated way in which you assaulted your wife makes it by far the most brutal – a brutality that, to my mind, was almost unbelievable.[78]

The JP therefore sentenced Mr J. S. to six months in prison.

The importance of keeping families together was clearly not enough to justify keeping a very violent offender out of prison. The sentence of six months was somewhat longer than the usual length of sentence given in wife assault cases during the first half of the twentieth century (often less than sixty days). However, given that the JP said it was the worst case he had ever dealt with, six months in prison does not seem especially long. What is more, the *Aberdeen Evening Express* reported how Mrs J. S. had originally not wanted to report the crime and that she wanted to continue living with her husband, despite his threat that he would kill her if she told the police about his violence towards her. When asked why she was not afraid to live with him, she replied: 'I don't need to be frightened ... he has deeply repented what he has done.'[79] Given Mrs J. S.'s apparent readiness to forgive her husband, it is likely that Mr J. S. returned home to his wife after he served his six months prison sentence. This scenario was not uncommon and reminds us why, in addition to longer prison sentences, the use of probation to rehabilitate men could play an important role in reducing violence.

The above examples are also interesting for what they tell us about the use of psychiatric treatment for men convicted of assaulting their wives. In the case of Mr S. from Sussex, who pleaded guilty to causing actual bodily harm against his wife in December 1946, it was reported that Mr S. had told a police officer that 'when I get depressed I get the urge to strangle other women. I hate women and want to strangle them'.[80] Despite that rather alarming admission, Mr S. was not required to undergo any psychiatric assessment or treatment. Instead, Mr S.'s own assessment that he 'did not think he needed special treatment' was apparently enough for the judge to decide that a referral was not necessary.[81]

In the example of Mr J. S., who was sentenced to six months imprisonment in January 1954 for assaulting his wife, he too was not required to undergo any psychiatric treatment despite the fact that the viciousness of the crime had raised suspicions about his mental health. According to the *Aberdeen Evening Express* Mr J. S. had been

> obsessed by jealous thoughts, [and had] assaulted his wife so brutally and viciously that a doctor who afterwards examined her injuries exclaimed that he had never seen anyone beaten up in such a fashion ... Because of the peculiar viciousness of the assault [J.S] was examined to his mental state after he had been taken into custody but there was no evidence as to any upset.[82]

That Mr J. S. was sent for a psychiatric assessment suggests that by the 1950s the psychiatric health of male perpetrators of domestic violence was beginning to be taken into consideration in some situations. Nonetheless, the fact that Mr J. S. was still not required to undergo any psychiatric treatment highlights how the actual use of psychiatric treatment remained rare at this point. As we will see in the next two chapters, requiring people to undergo psychiatric treatment as condition of their bond was more common in cases of attempted suicide and male sexual offences. However, none of the records that I have consulted in relation to wife assault referred to men receiving psychiatric treatment to 'cure' their violent behaviour. However, the lack of statistical data about the type of conditions given to men placed on probation for wife assault means it is difficult to know with certainty how many men may have been required to undergo psychiatric treatment during this period.

How successful was probation?

Despite a probation order making it possible to intervene in men's domestic lives, the level of success probation officers had in monitoring and supervising men's behaviour varied significantly. As we have seen, not all men were placed under supervision or given conditions to follow. Even in situations where men were closely supervised, officers were not always successful in stopping them from breaking the conditions of their bond or committing further acts of violence. So, just how successful was probation as a method of dealing with domestic violence in practice?

Unfortunately, most probation committees did not keep records which broke down success rates according to a particular crime. Glasgow was one of the only

Table 2.1 Results of probation in cases of wife assault for the years 1909, 1917, 1918, 1919[83]

Year	Bad	Fair	Unsatisfactory	Satisfactory	Improved	Good	Unknown	Total
1909	4	3	3	15		6	6	37
1917	5	5	2	30		1		43
1918	1	2	2	11	3	13		32
1919	7	4	4	50	3	12	5	85

cities that made these distinctions and that also has some surviving records. Table 2.1 shows the success rates for wife assault cases for the years that are available: 1909, 1917, 1918 and 1919.

It is not clear from the records what the criteria were for determining whether someone's behaviour was considered bad, fair, unsatisfactory, improved or good. However, when all of the 'positive' results are added together (fair, satisfactory, improved and good), the 'success' rate in 1909 was 65 per cent, in 1917 84 per cent, in 1918 90 per cent and in 1919 81 per cent. According to these figures, which were based on probation officers' own assessments, the Glasgow probation service appeared to have had a relatively high success rate in reforming men's behaviour, at least during the period of their probation order. However, the vast majority of those positive results fell into the category of 'satisfactory', rather than good, so their success was not exactly resounding. Unfortunately, the lack of similar records for the rest of the period or for probation committees in different locations means that it is difficult to know whether these results were representative of other cities and whether this 'success' continued later in the period.

Aside from the lack of surviving records, success statistics as reported by the probation service are also inadequate in other ways. Firstly, they are based on the probation officers' own opinions about men's behaviour, and their judgement may have been influenced by a desire to show that they had successfully reformed the men under their supervision. Secondly, the men may have been able to hide transgressions from their probation officers. Thirdly, the reports only tell us about men's behaviour during the probation period and reveal very little about how successful these methods were for reforming men's behaviour in the long term. Even if officers were able to stop men from committing violence during the period of the probation bond, it is difficult to know the extent to which probation was successful in encouraging long-term changes in men's behaviour because the probation service did not keep records about subsequent rates of recidivism. Once the probation bond had expired and the threat of being observed breaking the bond had ceased, there was less incentive to uphold newly reformed behaviour. This problem was highlighted by Govan Police Superintendent Mackinnon in 1919 who described how 'a few cases of wife assault came under the notice of the police here where the offenders abstained from liquor during the probation period, but immediately afterwards resorted to drink and violence again'.[84] Indeed, the difficultly of trying to get people to abstain from alcohol was well understood. For example, in 1932 probation officer Grace Harrison bemoaned the fact that while it only took a 'stroke of a pen' for a magistrate to insert an abstinence order, even the 'angels in heaven would probably find an absorbing task in enforcing it'.[85]

The fact that there are cases in which men who had been placed on probation went on to commit further violence against their wives after the sentence had ended shows that probation did not necessarily offer a reliable long-term 'cure' for violent behaviour. The case of twenty-seven-year-old Mr G., who was convicted of wife assault at Edinburgh Police Court in January 1928, provides a good example of this. In her witness testimony Mrs G. described how

> the accused is my husband and he is presently on a probation bond for having previously assaulted me. I am in advanced stage of pregnancy. About 4am on Sunday 1 January 1928 accused came into the house. He was drunk. He immediately locked the door, put on the light and stuck me on the left cheek with his clenched fist. I then went down on my knees to protect my body but he pulled me up on to my feet and struck me on the face. He then pushed me on to the sofa and stuck me on the face again. ... he said it was only done while under the influence of drink and asked me to forgive him ... I desire the accused prosecuted for his conduct towards me.[86]

Mr G. was convicted of wife assault and was placed on probation for six months under the supervision of a probation officer. However, Mr G. had previously been convicted of breach of the peace on 31 October 1927 for assaulting his wife and put under a caution with a £2 security or a twenty-day prison sentence. He was still on probation when he committed the offence described above. Therefore, not only did probation fail to stop him from being violent to his wife in the long run; it even failed to stop him from committing violence during his probation period. Probation similarly failed to stop violence in another case from 1927 of 'a young husband who had been on probation for wife assault'.[87] The Motherwell JP presiding over the case bemoaned the fact that 'unfortunately, probation in this case had not at first been successful, as during his term of probation the young man had assaulted his wife again'.[88] Unlike in a prison setting, probation officers were unable to closely monitor men's behaviour at all times, and they were reliant on men being able and willing to control their own behaviour. If the husband was unable or unwilling to do this, the wife remained vulnerable to further abuse.

In the above case of Mr G., the wife made a point of informing the court that her husband was already on probation and that she wanted him 'prosecuted'.[89] In this instance, Mr G. was reported for his violent behaviour, but this did not necessarily happen in all situations, especially if the wife did not want her husband to be sent to prison for breaching his bond. Despite Mrs G.'s dissatisfaction with probation, her husband was again placed on probation, although on this occasion he was put under supervision. This decision demonstrates the faith (misplaced or otherwise) that the probation service put in its officers' ability to have a positive influence on the offenders. The fact that Mr G.'s wife was pregnant, that the family already had two other young children and that the husband was recorded as being drunk during the attack meant that, in the eyes of the probation service, this man was still a good candidate for probation. Instead of him being sent to prison, which would have caused considerable financial distress to the young family and a 'burden' on the taxpayers, the hope was that under the good guidance of a supervising probation officer, Mr G. would stop the drinking which was thought to be causing his violent behaviour. Whether the probation officer was ultimately successful in reforming Mr G. is unclear, however, as there are no more references to him in the records. Despite this, the case is useful for highlighting how in some situations keeping families together, despite the danger this posed to women, could be seen as more important than sending men like Mr G. to prison.

Nevertheless, in cases where it was clear that the man had broken his bond and that probation was not working, the threat that he would be sent to prison was not necessarily an empty one. In January 1912 Mr T. J. appeared before Bath City Police Court for failing to observe the conditions of a probation bond which required him 'not to enter a public house (except for the purpose of performing his duties), or to take intoxicating liquor for a period of three years'.[90] The *Bath Chronical and Weekly Gazette* included a description of the trial testimony and it is worth quoting here in full:

> It was now alleged against him that on January 1st of this year he had entered a public house and partaken of intoxicants … P.S. Hembury deposed to seeing the defendant come out of a public house on January 1st. He asked the defendant if he were not on probation, and received the reply, 'Yes, sir; but look it over this time. You know what time of year it is.' Witness rejoined, 'Yes, and a very bad

start, too.' The landlady of the public house said she often employed defendant to do work for her, but there was no occasion for him to enter the bar. She was unaware that the defendant had been put on probation, the conditions which had been already referred to, and sometimes allowed him half a pint of beer in addition to his wages. The occasion on which the witness saw the defendant he had been treated by a friend who had invited him into the bar. Mr O. Restwick, the police court missionary and probation officer, stated that in 1909 defendant was put on probation for 12 months, and kept this probation fairly well. On Jan. 4th, he again made an appearance at that court and was then charged with assaulting his wife. Mr John told the defendant that the last occasion on which he appeared before that court he had been warned of the consequences, if he repeated the offence.[91]

The breach of the probation bond by drinking alcohol in this case was taken seriously, and Mr T. J. was subsequently sentenced to one-month's hard labour. However, the fact that it took another instance of assault before he was sent to prison supports the argument that probation could add another layer to the justice system before men were sent to prison, as described by Annmarie Hughes.[92]

However, while long prison sentences would have been much more preferable than probation for ensuring women's safety, the more common alternative to probation during the early-to-mid twentieth century was a fine or short prison sentence, and in many situations men only went to prison if they failed to pay their fine. For example, in June 1927 Mr R. R. was convicted at Stratford Petty Sessions Court of assaulting his wife. During the trial Mrs R. described how

> her husband came home about 11.30pm. He was dissatisfied with his supper, and he knocked [her] down in the passage and kicked her. When she got up he hit her in the face several times, blackening her eyes.[93]

This was the third time she had brought him to court, and this time he was fined £2 and 9s, or, in default of payment, one month in prison.[94] The fact that this was his third appearance in court for assaulting her shows that the threat of a fine or a short prison sentence did little to deter him from further violence.

Fines and short prison sentences were not necessarily very helpful in stopping male violence, but it could be argued that a prison sentence at least signified that the offence was being taken seriously and it may have served as a useful deterrent. It also meant that the wife was safe from violence during the period her husband was imprisoned. However, this power of protection and deterrence was somewhat undermined by the fact that most sentences were relatively short. Even in cases that were noted for being especially violent, the prison sentence could still be very short. For example, in January 1927 Mr J. Y. was convicted of wife assault at Edinburgh Police Court. A probation officer who had investigated the case said, 'It was about as bad a case as could possibly be.'[95] An expert witness, Professor Harvey Littlejohn, told the court that 'Y.'s wife, a slight woman, was covered all over with bruises, probably the marks of previous assaults.'[96] Despite this, Mr J. Y. was only sentenced to thirty days' imprisonment. During the same month that year Mr J. R. only received a sixty-days prison sentence at Edinburgh Police Court after pleading guilty to 'striking his wife on the face with his fist', despite the fact that he had seven previous conviction for similar violent offences.[97] These sentences seem woefully inadequate for such violent crimes, especially as it was made clear in both cases that the men were repeat offenders. Although the women were protected for thirty and sixty days, respectively, once their husbands were released from prison, there was nothing to stop them from returning home and committing more abuse. What is more, the likelihood that men would get a longer sentence did not necessarily increase over time either. For example, in March 1961 a thirty-seven-year-old man from Motherwell was sentenced to only fourteen days' imprisonment after pleading guilty to the charge of assaulting his wife, despite having two previous convictions for assault.[98]

Women's opinions

Due to the type of sources available it is difficult to know how the victims of domestic violence felt about men being placed on probation, rather than fined or imprisoned. However, there is some evidence that reveals a little more about women's opinions. The Preston and Rossendale Probation Committee minutes sometimes included information about the opinion of the wife to help determine whether the probation period had been a success, and in some of these cases women did appear to be satisfied with the results. For example, in the probation committee minutes for January 1953 there was a reference to the case of Mr T., who was put on probation for assaulting his wife. The case notes described how he was

> doing quite well. Working steadily. Another baby in the family. Wife is pleased with husband's behaviour since birth of his child. Wife works evening shifts. Husband now practically teetotal, and has made a real improvement.[99]

This example of the wife being 'pleased' that her husband had improved his behaviour suggests that some cases did result in successful reformation and that women's well-being was being taken into account, at least so far as it was important in ensuring overall family happiness.

As we have seen, probation officers were keen to keep families together, even if it meant accepting that some level of violence may occur. However, it was not only probation officers and social workers who felt like this. The women themselves sometimes voiced a similar preference. The economic realities of life for single women, especially mothers during the period prior to the introduction of the welfare state, meant that separation was often not feasible or desirable. For example, in January 1933 Mr H., a retired soldier, was arrested for assaulting his wife and charged with aggravated assault.[100] During the trial it became apparent that he had struck his wife on the head with a hammer after discovering she was having an affair. However, there was some reluctance on the part of the judge and Mr H.'s wife for him to be convicted because it would have meant the loss of his army pension although he had two young children to support. The report about the case in *The Western Gazette* described how his wife 'asked the judge to take a lenient view for the sake of the children' and that 'her husband, she agreed, had a good deal to forgive'.[101] The judge then asked her 'do you feel safe to live with your husband?' and she replied 'I do'.[102] To confirm that this was what the wife wanted, the probation officer told the court how 'the parties met at his house with the children to discuss their affairs. He understood that they could now live together happily'.[103]

Women may also not have wanted their husbands to be sent to prison for other practical or emotional reasons. For example, in 1908 Mr R. P. was placed on probation in Sheffield for assaulting his wife and causing her bodily harm. *The Sheffield Daily Telegraph* described how the husband was 'a man of good character' and that he had 'two children, of whom he seemed very fond'.[104] Mrs P. was reported to have said that 'the prisoner was a good husband and father, and his employer declared he was a good workman and an even-tempered man'.[105] Clearly, nobody in this situation wanted the husband to be sent to prison. In the case of Mr F. from Essex in 1931 that was mentioned earlier in relation to his assault upon his wife whilst intoxicated, Mrs F. was apparently anxious that her husband did not go to prison and told the court that she 'desired to have her husband back' and that 'apart from the drink he was a good hard-working husband'.[106] Mr F.'s defence lawyer also produced a letter written to Mr F. during the time he was in prison awaiting trial. In this letter 'every line mentioned her affectionate feeling she had for him'.[107] In cases like these, it is possible to see probation acting as a middle ground for women because it offered the potential for their husbands to be reformed without having to split up the family. Even though probation officers may not have always been successful in encouraging men to reform their behaviour, probation at least offered the potential that men could be rehabilitated in the long term.

Conclusion

This chapter has shown how probation was not intended as a 'let off' for men who committed violence against their wives, but as a more long-term approach to stopping domestic violence by making the private sphere a safer space. Rather than necessarily being a way to condone men's violent behaviour, the aim was to impose ideas of abstinence and self-restraint onto men in the hope that they would reform their own behaviour. In this respect, the probation service was continuing the 'civilizing mission' started in the nineteenth century by the Police Court Missionaries and temperance advocates. However, whereas the Christian missionaries could only hope to persuade men to take the pledge and to reform their behaviour voluntarily, probation officers now had the legal authority to enforce abstinence and good behaviour.

The chapter has shown how men's behaviour was increasingly scrutinized in the courtroom and that probation extended that surveillance into men's private lives. Probation allowed for intimate intervention into men's daily lives, including their spending and drinking habits and the relationship they had with their wives. While the task of creating a happy domestic environment was seen as the responsibility of both spouses, ultimately it was the man who was legally obliged to change his behaviour, and the aim of probation was to help him to do so. In comparison with fines and short prison sentences, probation provided a more practical way to deal with domestic violence that had the potential to stop violence in the long term, even if that potential was not always realized. In the period prior to the welfare state, when most working-class families were dependent upon the male bread winner's earnings, probation was a useful solution for women who wanted to keep their family together and were reluctant to report abuse if it meant the breadwinner would be imprisoned.

However, the focus on abstinence and the rehabilitation of individual men turned attention away from underlying class and gender inequalities that made women so economically dependent on men and thus more vulnerable to abuse. Even after the Family Allowance Act 1945 and the National Assistance Act 1948 made it financially more feasible for women to leave abusive men, the emphasis on trying to reform men so that families could stay together 'for the sake of the children' placed women in danger if probation failed to stop men from being violent. This latter point is important because, despite the increased intervention into men's private lives that probation facilitated, probation alone was not necessarily very successful in stopping domestic violence in the long term. The supervision of men was not always thorough, especially as not all men were given supervision or abstinence orders and it was very unlikely that they were required to undergo psychiatric therapy. What is more, men being provoked by women's 'improper' behaviour was still sometimes seen as a justifiable reason to use probation as a way to 'let off' men who had supposedly been unfairly provoked. Finally, and most crucially, the success of probation relied on the willingness of the man to change his own behaviour – something which was not always so forthcoming.

Notes

1 Edinburgh City Archives (ECA): Edinburgh Police Court Records, 13 May 1915.
2 Ibid.
3 Ibid.
4 Pat Ayers and Jan Lambertz, 'Marriage Relations, Money and Domestic Violence in Working-Class Liverpool, 1919–39', in Jane Lewis (ed.), *Labour and Love: Women's Experience of Home and Family 1850–1940* (Blackwell, 1986); Annmarie Hughes, 'The "Non-Criminal" Class: Wife-Beating in Scotland (c. 1800–1949)', *Crime History & Society*, 14, 2 (2010), pp. 31–54; James Hammerton, *Cruelty and Companionship: Conflict in Nineteenth Century Married Life* (Routledge, 1992); Shani D'Cruze, *Crimes of Outrage: Sex, Violence and Victorian Working Women* (Northern Illinois University Press, 1998); Maeve E. Doggett, *Marriage, Wife-Beating and the Law in Victorian England* (University of South Carolina Press, 1993); Nancy Tomes, 'A "torrent of abuse": Crimes of Violence between Working-Class Men and Women in London, 1840–1875', *Journal of Social History*, 11 (1978), pp. 328–45; Margaret Hunt, 'Wife-Beating, Domesticity and Women's Independence in Eighteenth and Nineteenth Century London', *Gender and History*, 4 (1992), pp. 10–33.
5 Norbert Elias, *The Civilizing Process: The History of Manners* (Urizen Books, 1978).
6 Peter King, 'Punishing Assault: The Transformation of Attitudes in the English Courts', *Journal of Interdisciplinary History*, 27 (1996), pp. 43–74.
7 Martin Weiner, *Men of Blood: Violence, Manliness, and Criminal Justice in Victorian England* (Cambridge University Press, 2004); John Carter Wood, *Violence and Crime in Nineteenth-Century England: The Shadow of Our Refinement* (Routledge, 2004).

8   Walter Stanton, *Sidelights on Police Court Mission Work* (Worcester, 1935), p. 61.
9   Hammerton, *Cruelty and Companionship*.
10 Annmarie Hughes, 'The "Non-Criminal" Class: Wife-beating in Scotland (c. 1800–1949)', *Crime History & Society*, 14, 2 (2010), pp. 31–54.
11 Ibid., p. 41.
12 Probation of Offenders Act 1907 (3 Edw. 7, c.25).
13 National Records of Scotland (NRS) ED20/3: Probation of Offenders Draft Bill, 1906: Newspaper Cutting from *Dundee Country and Municipal Record*, 20 June 1905.
14 Glasgow City Archives, D.tc 14/2/15: Reports of the Corporation of Glasgow 1919–1920 vol. 9: Report by the Special Committee on Probation of Offenders and Recommendation as Approved by the Corporation. Evidence by Joseph Paul Probation Officer for Mary Hill division, p. 82.
15 Ibid.
16 Liverpool City Archives, 347 MAG/1/6: Liverpool Probation Committee Annual Report, 1948.
17 *Western Daily Press*, 2 July 1908, p. 5.
18 ECA: Edinburgh Police Court Records, 30 September 1917.
19 Ibid.
20 *The Essex Newsman*, 12 September 1931, p. 3.
21 Ibid.
22 Ibid.
23 *West London Observer*, 20 February 1953, p. 7.
24 National Records of Scotland (NRS), ED20/432–464: Glasgow Probation Officers' Returns for the Years 1909, 1917, 1918, 1919.
25 Edinburgh: HMSO, 1917.
26 *Bath Chronicle and Weekly Gazette*, 11 April 1914, p. 10.
27 Ibid.
28 Ibid.
29 Ibid.
30 ECA: Edinburgh Police Court Records, 11 December 1909.
31 Ibid.
32 ECA: Edinburgh Police Court Records, 3 June 1919.
33 Ibid.
34 ECA: Edinburgh Police Court Records, 22 August 1922.
35 ECA: Edinburgh Police Court Records, 11 January 1935.
36 Ibid.
37 Linda Gordon, *Heroes of Their Own Lives: The Politics and History of Family Violence* (Viking, 1988).
38 *Bath Chronicle and Weekly Gazette*, 7 March 1925, p. 9.

39 *Bath Chronicle and Weekly Gazette*, 15 January 1916, p. 8.
40 Ibid.
41 *Nottingham Evening Post*, 12 July 1914, p. 1.
42 Ibid.
43 See, for example, Martin Francis, 'The Domestication of the Male? Recent Research on Nineteenth and Twentieth-Century British Masculinity', *History Workshop Journal*, 45, 3 (2002), pp. 637–52; Stephan Brooke, 'Gender and Working-Class Identity in Britain during the 1950s', *Journal of Social History*, 35 (2001), pp. 773–95.
44 *Bath Chronicle and Weekly Gazette*, 19 May 1928, p. 19.
45 Ibid.
46 Ibid.
47 *The Dundee Evening Telegraph*, 23 March 1932, p. 7.
48 Ibid.
49 *Motherwell Times*, 29 July 1932, p. 3.
50 Ibid.
51 Ibid.
52 *Motherwell Times*, 28 September 1928, p. 2. N.B. The term 'divy' refers to the sum of money that was kept aside to pay for household necessities.
53 Ibid.
54 *Bath Chronicle and Weekly Gazette*, 18 July 1925, p. 5
55 Ibid.
56 *Essex Newsman*, 13 November 1926, p. 2.
57 Ibid.
58 ECA: Edinburgh Police Court, October 1917.
59 ECA: Edinburgh Police Court Records, 1 November 1918.
60 Ibid.
61 ECA: Edinburgh Police Court Records, 5 August 1929.
62 ECA: Edinburgh Police Court Records, May 1919.
63 Ibid.
64 Manchester City Archives, Extract from Minutes of the 10th Meetings of the Probation Training Board, 14 July 1939.
65 Liverpool City Archives, 347 MAG/1/6: Liverpool Probation Committee Annual Report, 1930.
66 David Garland, *Punishment and Welfare: A History of Penal Strategies* (Ashgate, 1985); Linda Mahood, *Policing Gender, Class and Family in Britain, 1800–1945* (Routledge, 1995).
67 NRS, ED20/432–464: Glasgow Probation Officers' Returns for the years 1909, 1917, 1918, 1919.
68 George Behlmer, 'Summary Justice and Working-Class Marriage in England, 1870–1940', *Law and History Review*, 12, 2 (1994), pp. 229–75, p. 235; Jennifer Davis,

'A Poor Man's System of Justice: The London Police Courts in the Second Half of the Nineteenth Century', *Historical Journal*, 27 (1984), pp. 309–35.

69 Scottish Catholic Archives, SCA/DE/120/4: Minutes of the Scottish Catholic Probation Officers Association, 1926.
70 National Archives, H45/19505: 10th Meetings of the Probation Training Board, July 1939.
71 Pat Thane and Tanya Evans, *Sinners? Scroungers? Saints? Unmarried Motherhood in Twentieth-Century England* (Oxford University Press, 2012).
72 The Family Allowances Act 1945 (8 & 9 Geo. VI c.41).
73 *The Worthing Herald,* 14 December 1946, p. 15.
74 Manchester City Archives, GB127.M117/3/5: Manchester Probation Committee Annual Report, 1953.
75 *Aberdeen Evening Express,* 12 January 1954, p. 1.
76 Ibid.
77 Ibid.
78 Ibid.
79 Ibid.
80 *The Worthing Herald,* 14 December 1946, p. 15.
81 Ibid.
82 *Aberdeen Evening Express,* 12 January 1954, p. 1.
83 NRS, ED20/432–464: Glasgow Probation Officers' Returns for the Years 1909, 1917, 1918, 1919.
84 Glasgow City Archives, D.tc 14/2/15: Reports of the Corporation of Glasgow 1919–1920, vol. 9: Report by the Special Committee on Probation of Offenders and Recommendation as Approved by the Corporation on 14 August 1919.
85 Grace Harrison, 'The Case Load of the Probation Officer', *Probation*, 1, 13 (1932), pp. 201–2.
86 ECA: Edinburgh Police Court Records, 4 January 1928.
87 *Motherwell Times,* 9 September 1927, p. 2.
88 Ibid.
89 Ibid.
90 *Bath Chronical and Weekly Gazette,* 20 January 1912, p. 11.
91 Ibid.
92 Hughes, 'The Non-Criminal Class'.
93 *Barking, East Ham & Ilford Advertiser,* 28 June 1902, p. 1.
94 Ibid.
95 *The Scotsman,* 6 January 1927, p. 5.
96 Ibid.
97 Ibid.
98 *Wishaw Press,* 31 March 1961, p. 18.

99 Lancashire Archives, PSPr/4/2: Preston Probation Committee Minutes, 5 January 1953.
100 *The Western Gazette*, 27 January 1933, p. 10.
101 Ibid
102 Ibid.
103 Ibid.
104 *The Sheffield Daily Telegraph*, 6 October 1908, p. 5.
105 Ibid.
106 *The Essex Newsman*, 12 September 1931, p. 3.
107 Ibid.

3

A safety net for the suicidal: Probation and attempted suicide in Britain, 1907–61

The machinery of the criminal law ... has in recent years been used not to secure a prison sentence but to ensure that the unfortunate sufferer obtains the treatment required. There is a fear in some quarters that if we remove the existing responsibilities and duties of the police in this regard some of those who in the past have attempted suicide and who because of police intervention have had the appropriate treatment, will not get it.[1]

In 1961, the Suicide Act decriminalized suicide in England and Wales.[2] In the parliamentary debates leading up to this Act, one of the main arguments against decriminalization was the fact that the law functioned as a 'safety net' to protect those people who had attempted suicide and were in danger of making further attempts on their own lives. One of the key ways in which that safety net was implemented was to place people who had attempted suicide on probation so that they could be provided with emotional and practical support and/or psychiatric therapy. This chapter examines how the system, which was influenced by both scientific and lay attitudes towards insanity and suicide, functioned as a safety net for suicidal people in Britain between 1907 and 1961.

There have been many studies of the long-term changes in attitudes towards suicide, including the legal, physical and religious consequences for the body, soul and property of the deceased and their family.[3] However, with the exception of Chris Millar's recent study of self-harm, much less is known about what happened to those who were unsuccessful in their attempts to end their lives.[4] This is particularly true when considering the role that the law played in helping suicidal people during the twentieth century in Britain. Individuals who attempted suicide and were subsequently certified as insane could be sectioned and forced to receive psychiatric treatment in an insane asylum under the 1890 Lunacy Act.[5] However, the majority of people who attempted suicide were not diagnosed as insane, and it was this section of the population who were placed on probation for their own protection. Utilizing Elizabeth Lunbeck's notion of the 'nearly normal', a term used to describe those people who were thought to have 'minor' or 'temporary' mental health conditions rather than those who were certifiably 'insane', this chapter will explore how probation allowed for 'nearly normal' people to receive various forms of psychiatric treatment in and outside of hospital.[6] In this way, probation therefore played an important role in widening the social scope of psychiatric knowledge and practice in early-to-mid twentieth-century Britain.

Attempted suicide and the law

Prior to the 1961 Suicide Act, attempted suicide could technically be tried at the Assize and Quarter Sessions courts under the charge of 'conspiracy to self-murder'. However, the 1925 Criminal Justice Act allowed for attempted suicide to be tried summarily, resulting in the majority of these cases being tried in lower magistrates courts with lesser sentencing powers.[7] While a prison sentence was still given in some situations (with two years being the recommended maximum), it was much more common for cases to be dismissed, or for the accused to be admonished or placed on probation, with or without supervision by a probation officer.[8] This trend can be seen in the England and Wales Criminal Statistics for 1953 relating to the disposal of attempted suicide cases 'known to the police'. Table 3.1 shows that 62.6 per cent of all persons aged over twenty-one who were tried in a summary court for attempted suicide were given a probation order. In comparison, 20.8 per cent were given a conditional discharge and only 7.1 per cent were imprisoned.

Table 3.1 Disposal of persons aged 21 and over summarily dealt with, according to criminal statistics, England and Wales, 1953[9]

Disposal	Total no. of people	Percentage
Probation orders	335	62.6
Conditional discharge	111	20.8
Imprisonment (14 days to 6 months)	38	7.1
Absolute discharge	35	6.5
Fine	6	1.1
Otherwise dealt with	10	1.9
Total	535	100

In Scotland suicide was not illegal but attempting suicide could be prosecuted under public order legislation, such as 'breach of the peace'. Here too, defendants were mainly admonished or placed on probation. It is important to clarify, however, that across Britain many attempted suicide cases never came to the attention of the police because individuals and their families sought to keep these acts secret during a time when suicide was not only illegal and morally sinful in the eyes of the church, but also carried considerable social stigma due to its association with inherited mental illness.[10] Even when it was difficult to avoid detection by the police, for example, in cases where the attempt happened in public or the victim was sent to hospital with suspicious injuries, the police could 'turn a blind eye' or decide not to take any legal action. This was especially likely to happen if the victims had family that were willing and able to care for them. Nonetheless, while it is difficult here to account for those cases which remained outside the legal system, by using a mixture of probation and court records alongside newspaper reports, this chapter will focus on what happened in the known attempted suicide cases that were reported to the police and resulted in a people being placed on probation.

For those cases that did reach trial and resulted in a guilty verdict, the magistrate or JP had to decide whether probation was suitable for a particular individual. If probation was deemed appropriate, the magistrate or JP also had to determine what conditions should be stipulated in the probation bond, including what type of supervision was required and whether the individual should be sent for psychiatric treatment. To help make these decisions, the magistrate or JP could rely on assessments made by various professionals, including doctors, prison medical officers and probation officers. If the person was certified as insane by a doctor, he or she could be forcibly sent to an asylum. If that was not the case, there were four possible courses of action: psychiatric treatment as an in- or outpatient; supervision by a family member; supervision by a probation officer or a combination of the above. This chapter will examine these processes further, starting with psychiatric treatment, followed by supervision by a family member and finally focusing on supervision by a probation officer.

Psychiatric treatment

The majority of people who were convicted for attempting suicide were not medically certified as insane and therefore could not be forced to reside in a mental hospital. Nonetheless, doctors and prison medical officers were frequently asked to give their opinions as to whether these non-certifiable people would benefit from psychiatric treatment.[11] If treatment was considered necessary, the magistrate or JP could insert a condition in the probation bond which stipulated that the probationer was required to undergo psychiatric treatment, either in an institution or as an outpatient. In 1930, the Mental Treatment Act broadened the scope for this type of informal psychiatric treatment by allowing non-certified patients to be treated in county asylums. Probation could be used to require people to receive treatment without necessitating that they be legally certified as insane because, by agreeing to be placed on probation with this condition of treatment, they were technically volunteering to take medical treatment. Exactly how voluntary this treatment was, however, is questionable, given that the alternative to probation could have been a prison sentence of up to two years. Moreover, some people may not have been fully aware of their right to refuse probation.

The following five cases provide examples of how this system functioned and how the probation officers worked together with various medical professionals to try to rehabilitate suicidal probationers. The first case is a man named Walter B., who attempted suicide in Bristol in April 1937 by inhaling gas. According to a report in *The Western Daily Press*, this was the third attempt Walter had made to end his life due to marital problems.[12] After two weeks of medical assessment in an institution, the doctor found that Walter B. was not certifiable. The judge in the Bristol Magistrates Court therefore decided that he should be released on probation for one year 'under the condition that he attended an outpatient clinic during that time and placed himself under the supervision of a probation officer'.[13] The second example is Douglas W. who, according to the *Eastbourne Herald*, made a 'half-hearted attempt to stab himself' in 1957.[14] In this case the Eastbourne prison medical officer wrote a report describing how Douglas suffered from 'chronic anxiety' and decided that instead of being sent to hospital he should be placed on probation for two years under the supervision of a probation officer with the condition that he accept 'treatment as an out-patient'.[15]

The third, fourth and fifth cases provide examples of situations where the individual was sent for institutional treatment. In February 1920, a soldier named John M., who was suffering from shell shock after fighting in the First World War, attempted suicide by cutting his throat. An article about the case in the *Hull Daily Mail* described how the magistrate wanted to send him to a special home for shell-shocked returning soldiers but bemoaned the fact that such places did not exist and that he would therefore have to be sent to the Willerby Asylum.[16] In January 1938, twenty-five-year-old Robert W. was charged at Rotherham Police

Court of attempted suicide by drinking iodine. The magistrate released him on probation but insisted that because the defendant had previously tried many different methods of attempting suicide, he required 'proper care at a mental hospital'.[17] Similarly, in October 1947 Dorothy H. appeared at Weston Court charged with attempted suicide by taking aspirin tablets. She was found guilty and placed on probation for two years with the condition that she 'enter a home for treatment'.[18]

These cases of probation being used to *de facto* force people to undergo medical treatment, and in some cases to reside in a hospital, provide a good example of how psychiatry and the law could be used to control 'deviant' individuals. According to David Garland's concept of penal welfarism, by providing people with care and defining them as sick rather than bad, probation was part of a process which expanded the state's power to intervene into the private lives of citizens.[19] However, rather than focusing on the problems associated with this increase in social control, it is possible to look at the role of probation from another perspective: its role in providing a 'safety net' for suicidal people who needed psychiatric help. In the context of suicide prevention, probation was being used to give psychiatric treatment for people who otherwise might not have had access to much-needed sources of support and treatment. Prior to the formation of the National Health Service in 1948 and the 1959 Mental Health Act, which widened access to publicly funded psychiatric treatment, most working-class people would not have been able to afford private psychiatric care. Their main access to psychiatric treatment would have been through charitable organizations or the poor law asylum after being certified as insane under the 1890 Lunacy Act. However, the use of probation bonds with the condition of psychiatric treatment meant that affordable psychiatric treatment was made more widely available to 'nearly normal' people with mental health problems who had attempted suicide but were not certified as 'insane'.[20]

The fact that people placed on probation for attempted suicide did not need to be certified as insane to access psychiatric treatment was especially important due to the stigma surrounding insanity, particularly during the interwar period when theories of eugenics and degeneration were popular.[21] Even as these stigmas began to lessen after the Second World War, the notion that one could receive a short spell of treatment as an outpatient or as a temporary voluntary inpatient was probably preferable to the loss of control necessitated by being sectioned. This may also have made it more likely that people who were otherwise reluctant to undergo psychiatric treatment would agree to treatment, especially when refusal to accept probation could result in a prison sentence. While coercion of this nature is morally questionable, it did have the benefit of providing help for people who were at risk of committing suicide.

The full extent to which probation increased the number of people who received psychiatric treatment is difficult to gauge because the probation records do not include any systematic data about the numbers of people placed on probation for attempting suicide who were subsequently given psychiatric treatment. Nonetheless, the use of probation in this way did increase the number of people who were placed under the 'psychiatric gaze'. In this respect, it is possible to argue that probation played a role in the medicalization of suicide and the expansion of psychiatric treatment to the 'nearly normal'. Moreover, the fact that probation offered people a way to receive psychiatric outpatient care is also important in the context of discussions about the history of deinstitutionalization. For example, it is generally understood that the deinstitutionalization of psychiatric patients in Britain mainly happened after the 1960s. Despo Kritsotaki, Vicky Long, Matthew Smith, Mathew Thomson and others, however, have shown that deinstitutionalization 'had its roots in community-based services that emerged in the early twentieth century, such as mental hygiene and child guidance clinics'.[22] The use of probation to provide psychiatric treatment for people outside of institutions since at least the 1930s means that probation can be added to this list of ways in which 'care in the community' began earlier.

Supervision by the family

Not all people who were placed on probation for attempting suicide were given psychiatric treatment, however. If a probationer was not thought to require professional psychiatric treatment, the next decision to be made was whether he/she could be released into the care of family or friends. To determine this, the probation officer had to assess both the probationer and the environment into which he/she would be released. On the most basic level, the officer had to establish whether a family member was willing and able to care for the probationer. For example, in February 1939 thirty-one-year-old William E. was charged with attempting suicide after jumping off a bridge in Liverpool because, according to the report in *The Liverpool Echo*, 'his wife left him and took the children'.[23] He was placed on probation for twelve months under the supervision of his mother who 'said she would look after him'.[24] However, sixty-one-year-old John J., convicted in May 1917 at Edinburgh Burgh Court under breach of the peace legislation for attempting suicide by cutting his throat, was placed on probation for twelve months under the supervision of a probation officer and told to reside at Cornton Vale hospital in the Bridge of Allan.[25] One of the reasons for including the residence and supervision conditions in John J.'s case, but not in that of William E., was that the latter had his mother to look after him, whereas John J.'s wife had died three weeks earlier, meaning that he was 'lonely and had nobody to care for him'.[26]

The policy of releasing people on probation into the care of their family and friends continued throughout the period from 1907 to 1961 and across the country. For example, in October 1914, twenty-four-year-old James B. was charged in Preston with attempting suicide by taking poison. According to a report in *The Preston Herald*, the chief constable told the court that 'the trouble had occurred through the defendant's disappointment at a young woman for whom he had affection'.[27] James B. was discharged under the condition that he 'promised not to repeat his offence, and his father undertook to look after him'.[28] In September 1938, thirty-six-year-old Alfred B. attempted suicide by gas after his wife got a separation order from him due to persistent cruelty.[29] The court probation officer stated that the accused's mother would look after him, and he was bound over into her care and told not to visit his wife's home. In November 1940, *The Liverpool Echo* reported that seventy-four-year-old Thomas F. was released under the probation act 'under the care of his sons' after attempting suicide by gas poisoning on hearing that his company had gone bankrupt.[30] In December 1945, thirty-four-year-old Milton B. was placed on probation for attempting suicide by inhaling gas. The newspaper coverage of the trial in *The Liverpool Echo* described how Milton 'expressed his regret and said he was terribly worried. Said he had a good friend who would help him'.[31] He was subsequently placed on probation for two years under the 'care of his friend'.[32]

Not all friends and family members were considered acceptable carers, however. The probation officer had to assess the 'character' of the family and the 'social setting' in order to decide whether the environment was suitable and conducive to a healthy rehabilitation. The probation officer's assessment of an individual's motivation for attempting suicide was also important, especially if it involved problems in the domestic situation which might mean that supervision at home was not suitable. These assessments were partly based on the officers' knowledge of psychiatry and social work, but also on normative values about respectability, class, gender and religion. For example, in October 1938, a fifteen-year-old girl name Helen was placed on probation at Glasgow Sherriff Court after stealing from an Edinburgh church charity box and trying to commit suicide by drinking Lysol bleach.³³ The probation officer described how the girl's mother was 'most insolent and antagonistic and proved to be a woman without any reasoning'.³⁴ It was decided, therefore, that the girl should be sent to reside at the Guthrie's School for Girls in Edinburgh rather than with her family in Glasgow.

It was not always the family members who were blamed when a probation officer considered that the home of the probationer was not suitable, especially if the probationer himself or herself was thought to be the one causing the problems. For example, in June 1935 a sixteen-year-old girl was convicted of attempting suicide by gas poisoning in London.³⁵ During the trial it was stated that the girl had previously been brought before the court by her mother as a 'child beyond parental control', and the probation officer stated that 'the girl had been a source of trouble to the mother for some years'.³⁶ The girl was therefore placed on probation and sent to an approved school. This decision highlights how a person's age could also be important in deciding whether she/he should be placed into institutional care. The system of reformatories and industrial schools (known as approved schools after 1927) meant that it was easier and more practical to send young people to these types of institutions than it was to institutionalize adults. Moreover, the widespread use of these schools and reformatories meant that it was generally seen as more acceptable for children to be institutionalized against their will than it was for adults.

While the probation officer's judgement about the probationer and his or her home life could influence the conditions of the probation bond, this was not necessarily a one-way street. The probation officer relied on the cooperation of the probationers and their families, which meant that the family had some input into the process, even if it was only marginal. Firstly, the family had to agree to supervise a family member at home, which some refused. For example, in 1954, forty-five-year-old Eric W. was convicted of attempted suicide, but he was 'refused accommodation, financial help or any assistance whatever from his two brothers and two sisters'.³⁷ According to an article in *The Yorkshire Post*, the probation officer assigned to the case described how he had 'been round to all the relatives and all had refused to help Eric or take him in. They said this was because he would not work regularly and had ignored their advice'.³⁸ Instead of placing Eric W. on probation, the Scunthorpe magistrate therefore decided that he should be sent to prison for twenty-one days because it was 'in his best interest'.³⁹ In February 1930, twenty-seven-year-old Helen S. was placed on probation in Edinburgh for twelve months after attempting suicide by taking an overdose of opioids.⁴⁰ She was placed under the supervision of a probation officer and told to reside at home. However, when the probation officer requested that a family member come before the court in relation to the matter, both her father and husband refused.[41]

Secondly, the probationer had to agree to be looked after by a friend or family member, and some refused this option. For example, in May 1947, Patrick F. from Sunderland was convicted of attempting suicide by eating nails.[42] According to the article about the case in *The Sunderland Daily Echo*, Patrick F. had 'nowhere to go'; his stepsister offered assistance, but he 'refused to reside with her'.[43] These examples show that, after medical considerations, the domestic situation of the probationer was the next most important factor in determining what sentence he or she received. This gave the probation officer, but also the probationers and their families, some influence over the process, and this flexibility meant that there was considerable scope for individuals to shape the practical implementation of probation policy.

Supervision by a probation officer

If a probationer was thought to need more care and supervision than his or her family and friends could provide on their own, they could be placed under the supervision of a probation officer. Supervision by a probation officer was often required when a person was considered to be at risk of committing further suicide attempts and therefore in need of extra surveillance and supervision. The following three cases provide examples of this type of situation. In December 1917, twenty-nine-year-old Euphemia was convicted at Edinburgh Police Court for breach of the peace after attempting suicide by jumping into Saint Margaret's Loch in Edinburgh's Holyrood Park. After being held under observation in the Edinburgh Royal Infirmary, she was placed on probation for twelve months under the supervision of Sister Louise.[44] In April 1935, Frederick P., a forty-two-year-old unemployed tram driver from Blackpool, attempted suicide by drinking poison. The report about the trial in *The Lancashire Evening Post* described how the chief constable told the court that 'it was a most persistent case of attempting to commit suicide and for that reason he did not like to take the responsibility of allowing Mr P. to go in charge of his friends'.[45] The magistrate subsequently decided that Frederick P. should be placed on probation for six months, under the supervision of a probation officer. In December 1929, twenty-two-year-old Ralph H. from Preston was also placed under the care and supervision of a probation officer after he had tried to cut his throat with a razor. During the trial at Preston Magistrates Court, it became clear that Ralph H. needed supervision upon his release because 'he was weak physically and not right mentally' and he had made several previous attempts to take his own life.[46] Moreover, his mother told the court that 'if he does anything like this again we don't want anything to do with him', and she was less than sympathetic when she described how her son was 'only satisfied when he was being fussed over'.[47]

Surveillance and supervision were not the probation officers' only role in these situations. The officers were also meant to act like a friend to the probationers: talk with them, listen to their problems, give them advice and offer other practical help. Indeed, the motto of the probation service, 'advice, assist and befriend', fitted particularly well with their work in helping suicidal individuals. An article in *The Scotsman* newspaper in April 1925 about the duties of the Scottish probation officers provided a good description of their role in dealing with attempted suicide cases. The article explained how 'now and then there occurs an attempted suicide, breach of the peace as it is technically called, there is opportunity there to give help and guidance'.[48] It was hoped that having someone that they could talk to outside of their usual friend and family network would provide a much-needed service for people in difficult circumstances who needed someone to listen to their problems and provide advice. Prior to the establishment of the Samaritans charity in 1953 there were few places where people could get this type of help, and it is therefore fair to speculate that this service was beneficial for people who needed someone with a sympathetic ear to listen to their problems.

The type of advice and guidance that probation officers provided sometimes included offering relationship advice, particularly in cases where problems at home or disappointments in romantic affairs were thought to be the cause of a person's troubles. However, this interference in people's private lives was not necessarily welcomed and could be considered condescending. For example, in a case from Bristol in June 1937, twenty-seven-year-old Francis C. and thirty-year-old Muriel L. were placed on probation for attempting suicide after they had eloped together and ran out of money. The magistrate told Muriel that she should stop drinking and must not see Francis again.[49] Although such advice may not have always been welcomed, it was more warranted in some situations than others. For example, in December 1943, forty-five-year-old Francis A. was placed on probation in Manchester after attempting suicide. The report of the case in the *Manchester Evening News* described how Francis A. had been infatuated with a twenty-year-old woman and would not leave her alone.[50] On the occasion in question, he had pulled out a revolver, pointed it at her and then tried to turn it on himself. The magistrate told Francis A. that 'he must not go near the woman' and was reported to have told him that it was 'far from his second childhood and he should go back to his wife who is willing to take him back'.[51] The magistrate also suggested that Francis A. 'does not bring up the subject over breakfast as that is a very dangerous time'.[52] Despite the slightly flippant tone of the advice, the instruction that Francis A. should stay away from the woman whom he had threatened with a gun was certainly warranted.

If the probation officer was not able to provide all the necessary help and supervision that a probationer required, a condition within the probation bond could be used to require individuals to reside in non-medical institutions, usually reformatories or voluntary homes run by various Christian organizations. This is what happened in the following three cases. In October 1918, twenty-nine-year-old Daisy B. was charged in Boxted with attempted suicide after she was found 'lying on her back in the pond'.[53] *The Essex Newsman* described how the prison medical officer assigned to the case stated that Daisy B. had 'suffered from melancholia, but her mental condition subsequently improved'.[54] According to the report, Daisy B. did not need medical treatment, but her 'relations were not in a position to look after her'.[55] The probation officer therefore made arrangements for her to spend her twelve-month probation period at the Church Army Home. In November 1930, *The Lancashire Evening Post* reported that eighteen-year-old Nellie M. was placed on probation for three years with the condition that she should reside at the St Mary's Home in Bury after she had attempted suicide by drinking disinfectant.[56] In December 1936, Ralph H. was convicted at the Burnham on Sea Magistrates Court with attempted suicide after he had tried to drown himself in the sea. *The Western Daily Press* described how Ralph H. told the court that he had 'caused a great deal of unhappiness at home' and he 'could not face returning there'.[57] The doctor that was called to give evidence described how Ralph H. had 'recently been discharged from the Cotford Mental Home' and deemed cured. However, in his opinion,

> a man coming out of an institution like that after having everything done for him, and having been taken care of in every way, must feel completely lost and at sea when he is launched on the world without having any arrangements made to meet him, or anything of that sort, and I think that possibly may have had some bearing on his depression.[58]

For this reason, the probation officer suggested that Ralph H. be placed into the Bath Home for twelve months. Ralph H. agreed to this and gave his thanks for the way his case had been handled.[59] Probation in these cases provided people with a place in which they could reside when their usual homes were not suitable and offered an alternative to confinement in prison or an asylum. In Ralph's case at least, he seemed grateful for the opportunity to reside in a 'home'. How other people felt about this type of residential order, however, is difficult to know given the lack of sources which detail probationers' opinions – a topic which will be discussed further later.

Alcohol and attempted suicide

In cases where the individual was drunk when they attempted suicide, or they were known to have a problem with alcohol misuse, the magistrate or JP could include a condition of abstinence in the probation bond. It was hoped that stopping these individuals from drinking might also stop them from feeling suicidal or acting upon any suicidal impulses. Examples of this approach can be seen throughout the period across Britain. For example, in October 1909 thirty-two-year-old Elizabeth M. pleaded guilty to attempted suicide in Sale. The chairman told the court that 'the prisoner's position there was wholly due to drink. Drink was her failing, and she must be placed on probation, and must sign a paper not to take drink for twelve months'.[60] Similarly, in 1925, both Ivor R. and Percy S. were told by the Cardiff magistrates to abstain from intoxicating drink during the twelve-month probation bond that they had been given for attempting suicide.[61] In June 1932, thirty-nine-year-old Albert L. was convicted at Bath Police Court of attempted suicide by cutting his wrists. *The Central Somerset Gazette* described how Albert L. had 'given way to drink after being left a widower with six children'.[62] He was subsequently placed on probation for two years with 'the terms being that he signed the pledge and gave an undertaking not to go in or near a public-house nor have anything to drink of an intoxicating nature'.[63] In June 1937, thirty-one-year-old Arthur D. was convicted at Bristol Police Court for attempted suicide by poisoning. The medical officer for the case told the magistrate that 'he felt sure that D. would not do such a thing again, and also that institutional care would not be of any advantage to him'.[64] The magistrate therefore decided to put him on probation with the condition that he 'gave up alcoholic liquor'.[65] In December 1950, twenty-six-year-old John B. was found guilty at Biggleswade Magistrates Court of attempting suicide and placed on probation for two years.[66] According to the medical report, the doctor 'believed B. would not have mutilated himself had he been sober'.[67] The chairman therefore decided that the conditions of the probation bond were that B. must 'abstain from alcohol at all times and attend at the psychiatric out-patient clinic at Bedford'.[68]

There was a belief among many magistrates and probation officers that alcohol was a contributing factor behind suicidal impulses. For example, in November 1955, thirty-year-old Herbert L. was sentenced to six months in prison at Blackburn Magistrates Court for attempted suicide and breach of probation.[69] This was his third attempt to kill himself after having been placed on probation. During the trial the superintendent in charge of the case said, 'He only does this to call attention to himself and only when in drink.'[70] That probation officers made a connection between alcohol and suicide was not surprising, given the probation service's origins in the temperance movement, an organization that had long viewed suicide as one of the many social evils that could result from people drinking alcohol. As we have seen in the previous chapters, requiring probationers to abstain from alcohol was commonly included in probation bonds for other types of offences.

However, it was not only temperance supporters who saw a link between alcohol and suicide. There was both medical and popular support for the assumed connection between alcohol and suicide.[71] Moreover, this assumption can also be seen in the testimonies of the probationers and their friends or family members. For example, in September 1936 fifty-seven-year-old Laurette S. from Winsham was placed on probation for two years after attempting suicide by cutting her wrists.[72] During the trial a witness to the events described how Laurette only made the threat of wanting to 'be in the graveyard' when 'she was the worse for drink'.[73] Similarly, when thirty-two-year-old Ann M. was placed on probation in Edinburgh for twelve months in June 1919 after attempting suicide by swallowing a quantity of poison, her daughter gave her mother's intoxication as a possible cause of her actions:

> I was alone in the house when accused, my mother, came home slightly intoxicated and without saying anything she took a blue coloured glass bottle from the mantelpiece in the kitchen and which was labelled 'poison' for external use only and drank a quantity of the content of the bottle.[74]

If alcohol was contributing to people's decisions to attempt suicide, then the use of probation to enforce abstinence may well have helped to reduce the likelihood of people committing further suicide attempts. Moreover, the threat of a potential prison sentence if a probationer broke the abstinence condition made probation a more effective method for encouraging abstinence than simply relying on people to voluntarily take the pledge. Nonetheless, as we have seen in the previous chapter, abstinence orders were not easy to enforce. Without systematic records which followed up on probationers' lives after the period of probation ended, it is difficult to know exactly how successful this approach was in reducing further suicide attempts.

Material and practical help

Aside from alcohol and psychiatric illness, it was understood that there could be many other underlying reasons behind why a person might want to commit suicide. Some key underlying causes were thought to be poverty and unemployment – an assumption supported by the fact that people on trial for attempted suicide often gave unemployment as a reason for their actions. For example, in September 1910, twenty-three-year-old Edward W. explained to the Edinburgh Police Court that he attempted suicide because he was 'unemployed and had a wife and two children to support'.[75] In May 1921, a 'Middlesbrough woman' described how she attempted suicide because she was 'depressed through her husband being unemployed', and in June 1942 sixty-year-old Arthur F. from Manchester admitted that he attempted suicide 'due to being unemployed due to his sciatica'.[76] The connection was also supported by some doctors. For example, in September 1910, sixty-three-year-old Henry R. from West Ealing was charged with attempted suicide. During the trial Dr Lees told the court that 'whilst the prisoner was under the care of the Haling Cottage Hospital he did not notice any unsoundness of mind. He attributed his action to a temporary aberration, due to his being discharged from his employment. He did not think he would do it again'.[77]

Another approach that probation officers used to rehabilitate individuals who had attempted suicide due to unemployment, therefore, was to help them to find a new job. For example, in April 1935 Frederick P., a forty-two-year-old unemployed tram driver from Blackpool, attempted suicide by drinking poison.[78] He was placed on probation for six months under the supervision of a probation officer. The court testimony described how Frederick P. had become unemployed after an accident and subsequently his wife had become ill.[79] The magistrate informed Frederick P. that the 'probation officer will help him find work in some other occupation. In the meantime, he was advised to be sensible'.[80] Similarly, in Taunton during December 1937 seventeen-year-old Gertrude B. tried to commit suicide by jumping in a lake and she was subsequently placed on probation and 'taken to a home until the probation officer can find her a new situation'.[81]

The majority of unemployed probationers, regardless of the type of offence they had committed, were offered help in finding work. This was due to the probation service's long-held belief in the importance of ensuring that probationers became respectable, hard-working citizens. Such efforts could be seen in quite a cynical light that probation officers tried to help people find work to ensure that they did not become a 'burden' on the state. This interpretation certainly fits with the concepts of social control proposed by Cohen and Scull.[82] However, some probation officers may also have been influenced by psychological theories of contemporary writers, such as Cyril Burt, who stressed the psychological importance of employment because of the routine, meaning and financial independence that it could provide.[83] For people suffering from depression, especially if it was linked to their loss of employment, this approach could well have been helpful. Indeed, more recent studies by psychologists have also emphasized the importance of meaningful work for ensuring good mental health.[84] Even if the desire to work was in part an internalization of the bourgeois worth ethic, employment could nonetheless improve people's material and psychological well-being.

Furthermore, this focus on finding people employment was a practical response to the needs of the probationers who themselves pinpointed unemployment as a source of their problems. In this respect, probation officers were listening to the information provided by the probationers and responding accordingly. Three cases from 1929, a year notorious for the stock-market crash and the subsequent sharp rise in unemployment, provide examples of this.

The first case is that of William Y., a thirty-five-year-old unemployed married cabinetmaker with four children, who was placed on probation for twelve months at Edinburgh Police Court for breach of the peace after attempting suicide by drinking Lysol bleach.[85] During the trial the probation officer described how the accused had 'been out of employment and during the past three weeks has been drinking heavily'.[86] The witness who had found the accused told the court how William Y. had said 'I have ten [sic] poison, send for the doctor ... I took the Lysol as I have been worried through unemployment'.[87] The second case is that of Robert L., a fifty-one-year-old unemployed butcher, who was similarly placed on probation for twelve months at the Edinburgh Police Court after attempting suicide.[88] Robert L. described in his witness testimony that 'I am worried and downhearted as I have been unemployed for 18 months'.[89] His wife also explained to the court that her husband 'has been much depressed recently owing to a long spell of unemployment'.[90] The third case is twenty-three-year-old Sidney B., who was placed on probation for six months by the Lincoln magistrate after trying to commit suicide by cutting his throat. When charged with the offence he told the police officer that 'all I can say is I was out of work'.[91]

In addition to helping probationers find employment, probation officers also provided practical help in various other ways. Many local probation committees had access to charitable funds that they could give to probationers in difficult financial situations. For example, in 1932 the Manchester Probation Committee established a 'social welfare fund' from charitable donations to provide food, clothes and travel fares and other types of financial assistance.[92] By tending to the material needs of the probationers, probation officers were very much influenced by their philanthropic social work traditions. Although new theories about psychology were becoming more influential, many probation officers still relied on older methods of providing practical help to alleviate some of the material causes behind people's distress. While individual probation officers were unable to do anything about the larger social inequalities that caused poverty and unemployment, they at least tried to alleviate some of the immediate suffering by providing probationers with financial and practical help, something which may have brought tangible benefits and shows that the probation officers were listening to the needs of their probationers.

Probationers' resistance

As we have seen, the methods that probation officers used to rehabilitate suicidal people were influenced by their interactions with probationers. Magistrates and probation officers listened to the reasons probationers gave for wanting to kill themselves and tailored their responses accordingly. For example, if a probationer explained that he or she had attempted suicide after drinking and because of unemployment, the probation bond might include a condition of abstinence, and the probation officer would help him or her find a new job. This approach therefore relied on gaining the cooperation of the probationers and their families to divulge personal information in a thorough and truthful manner. It also relied on the probationer agreeing to the conditions of the probation bond and sticking to them.

This cooperation, however, was not always so forthcoming. Even if probation officers were trying to work in the best interest of their charges, the people placed under their care did not necessarily see it this way. For example, in November 1930, Mr P., a thirty-five-year-old fishmonger, was placed on probation for two years at Dorking Police Court for attempted suicide under the condition he should not drink alcohol.[93] Mr P. objected to that condition and questioned 'why should a respectable citizen, who has tried to do his best, be deprived of his rights?'[94] The chairman presiding over the case replied by stating that 'whatever you say will not make us alter our decision'.[95] After hesitating for some time, Mr P. said, 'Alright, I agree.'[96] In July 1942, Ann W. was put on probation for attempting suicide, but by January 1944 she had broken the condition that she should not leave the district by making a day trip to Chester and was subsequently sentenced to six months in prison. The magistrate explained that she was being sent to prison to be looked after, not to be punished.[97] Similarly, in July 1949, John J., who had been placed on probation in Cardiff for the offence of attempted suicide, absconded from the city and 'his whereabouts was unknown'.[98]

Unfortunately, another way in which people did not cooperate was by making further attempts to end their lives, and sometimes these attempts were successful. For example, in June 1932, *The West London Observer* reported on the case of a man named Robert K., who had been found drowned in the river near Putney Bridge, London.[99] At the coroner's inquest the man's widow described how the deceased had been certified as insane and confined for short periods in various hospitals. However, at the time of his death he was on probation, following his most recent attempted suicide. In October 1958, Thomas P., who had been on probation in Preston for attempting suicide, died after his second attempt to end his life.[100] Also in 1958, Donald F. committed suicide after having previously been placed on probation for twelve months in December 1957 at the Portsmouth Magistrates Court for a previous attempt.[101] That people who had previously been on probation for attempting suicide then went on to kill themselves shows that the safety net was not always sufficiently strong.

How safe was the safety net?

Assessing how successful probation was in terms of preventing suicide is very difficult because the probation committees did not keep records about probationers once their period of probation was over. However, although the probation records cannot tell us whether people went on to commit suicide after their period of probation had ended, newspaper reports can tell us more about the short-term implications of probation. For instance, there are some cases where people reported being grateful for probation officers' help. One such case was that of Sydney B., who appeared at London's Bow Street Court in February 1928 charged with attempted suicide. He was discharged under the Probation

Act and Mr Herbert, the police court missionary, 'put him in touch with people who had written to the court concerned about him and who wanted to help him'.[102] According to the article in *The Scotsman*, Sydney B. 'was very much affected and said in a broken voice, thank you very much'.[103] The judge reportedly then told him 'don't try to doctor yourself again', and he promised not to.[104] Similarly, a case from January 1929 of a fourteen-year-old girl from Widcombe who attempted suicide by drinking poison highlights how probation could offer help to vulnerable people. A newspaper article about the case described how the girl had told the bench of lady magistrates at the Bath Juvenile Court that 'I was worried so much and my parents have not been kind to me. Please let me stay here in the hospital where everyone is so very kind'.[105] The girl was subsequently placed on probation for three years under the supervision of a probation officer. However, the records also show that not everyone appreciated this intervention into their private lives, and it could cause some resentment. For example, in January 1944, a sixty-five-year-old man from Hartlepool who attempted suicide because he was suffering from rheumatism and gastritis protested that it was 'a man's privilege to commit suicide if he finds life unbearable'.[106]

Probationers' reactions to the imposition of psychiatric treatment were similarly mixed. In the majority of cases little was recorded about whether a probationer wanted psychiatric treatment. However, there were some cases where the opinion of the probationer was taken into account. For example, in October 1939 a fifty-two-year-old shopkeeper named Charles Y. was convicted at Spelthorne Petty Sessions Court for attempting suicide by coal gas poisoning. The newspaper coverage of the case described how the magistrate had consulted a medical report and the statement of a probation officer who 'had learned that the prisoner feared a recurrence of his illness'.[107] After hearing this information, the magistrate was reported to have

> considered the case sympathetically, realising that he [the accused] had had a lot of illness: He was apparently far from well at the present time, either mentally or physically, and the Bench desired to know if he would consent to go to a home and be looked after.[108]

Young agreed that he would go to live in a home and was bound over for two years. Some probationers were even enthusiastic about receiving psychological treatment. For example, a report about the Leeds probation service in 1936 described how some people were thankful for this referral for treatment:

> During the past 12 months five offenders placed on probation in Leeds accepted the advice of the probation officer to submit themselves to psychological

treatment as voluntary patients at the clinic in Wakefield and in each case the treatment had been beneficial. One probationer, charged with attempted suicide and found not to be under proper care, had received so much benefit from the treatment that his cure was regarded as certain. Another, 19 years of age, wrote to the probation officer, after treatment, saying: 'I am glad you advised me to go there – it is the finest thing that has happened to me'.[109]

However, not all probationers were so willing to undergo psychiatric treatment. For example, in Manchester in September 1939, when it was suggested that twenty-four-year-old Ronald H. should be remanded for medical observation due to his previous attempted suicide, Ronald H. shouted: 'You cannot put me in a mental hospital. I am as sane as any of you … you might as well hang me if you are going to send me to a mental hospital. It is a living death.'[110] In July 1939, twenty-two-year-old Grace H. was convicted of attempting suicide by taking liniment after the man she was having an affair with went back to his wife. The Bath magistrate sentenced her to twelve months' probation, with six months of that to be spent in a Bristol medical institution, but she said she 'preferred to go to prison'.[111] In response, the police surgeon reported that he thought the suicide attempt had been made in 'the hope of frightening the man back to her', and therefore it was decided that sending her to prison for six months would be safe.[112] Grace H.'s wish not to be sent to a medical institution was respected, but the only other option she was given in this situation was to go to prison. Her case highlights how stark the options could be for those who chose not to accept probation. While in theory the probationer had to consent to treatment, it is likely that some people only gave this consent in order to avoid a prison sentence.

Aside from doubts concerning exactly how voluntary the psychiatric treatment was, it is also possible that the use of probation in some circumstances risked adding another layer before people were given the professional psychiatric help they needed. An example of this type of scenario can be seen in the case of a seventeen-year-old boy named Derek R. who tried to kill himself twice only twenty-four hours after he had been committed for trial on a charge of attempted suicide at Shrewsbury Quarter Sessions in March 1955. Despite being found unconscious at the RAF station where he was a new entrant and having admitted that he 'was depressed' and 'I want to die', the medical officer at Shrewsbury Prison said Derek R. was 'now in normal health. It was unlikely that he would try to repeat what he had done'.[113] The judge decided that he should be placed on probation for three years but did not require him to undergo any psychiatric treatment. Given that the boy had admitted being depressed and had attempted suicide several times, it is hard not to assume that he would have benefitted from professional psychiatric help at this point. While the support, advice and guidance given by probation officers may have been helpful for some people, they were not professional psychiatrists. The fact that this system relied on magistrates to make decisions that could result in someone being placed on probation without the condition that they receive psychiatric care was therefore potentially very problematic. However, the magistrates and probation officers were reliant on the advice of the doctors and, as in Derek R.'s case, even recommendations given by doctors were sometimes wrong. Considering that the alternative to probation was to either send people to prison or do nothing, probation at least provided some support for suicidal people, even if in practice the support was sometimes inadequate.

Conclusion

The role of probation in the rehabilitation of individuals who attempted suicide was an important, yet frequently overlooked, way in which practical and psychological support was given to people who attempted suicide in Britain prior to the 1961 Suicide Act. Probation offered a way for people who required psychiatric help to receive treatment without having to be legally certified as insane, opening up opportunities for more 'nearly-normal' people to receive outpatient care. As a result, more people could receive treatment without suffering the stigma of being certified and institutionalized. In this respect, it can be argued that probation played an important role in the medicalization of suicide and helped to lay the groundwork for the deinstitutionalization of psychiatric treatment that occurred in Britain after the 1960s.

For those who did not require psychiatric treatment, but whose family or friends were not willing or able to care for them, probation provided a basic safety net of support from probation officers who offered advice, assistance and friendship. Even in situations where people were not placed under the direct supervision of a probation officer, probation officers could still help individuals tackle some of the underlying problems that had caused them to attempt suicide, such as unemployment, poverty, relationship breakdown and alcohol dependency. This type of rehabilitation corresponded more closely with older methods for caring for suicidal people that were based on traditional forms of philanthropic social work. Therefore, while suicide attempts may have increasingly been seen as resulting from psychological problems, the social causes of suicide were still considered important.

This intervention into the private lives of people who attempted suicide could be seen as another example of how the British state developed new methods of social control during the early-to-mid twentieth century. While in some respects this was true, the underlying aim of this intervention was to save lives. Moreover, the authority that probation officers wielded over the probationers was somewhat limited due to their need to cooperate with the probationers and their families, and ultimately probationers retained the right to refuse probation. This also meant that probation officers were not always able to provide an effective safety net or stop people from killing themselves. Nonetheless, even though probation officers were not able to help everyone, and there were problems associated with the potential misuses of power that could result from a system which forced people to undergo psychiatric treatment, this should not negate the value of the practical and psychological help that probation provided.

Notes

1   Hansard: HC Deb 14 July 1961 vol 644 cc.833–45, 839.
2   The Suicide Act 1961 (9 & 10 Eliz 2 c.60).
3   For studies on the history of suicide, see, for example, Olive Anderson, *Suicide in Victorian and Edwardian England* (Oxford University Press, 1987); John Weaver and David Wright (eds), *Histories of Suicide: International Perspectives on Self-Destruction in the Modern World* (University of Toronto Press, 2009); S. Chaney, 'Suicide, Mental Illness and the Asylum: The Case of Bethlem Royal Hospital 1845–1875', MA Dissertation, University College London, 2009); Barbara Gates, *Victorian Suicide: Mad Crimes and Sad Stories* (Princeton University Press, 1988); Michael MacDonald, 'The Medicalisation of Suicide in England', in Charles Rosenberg and Janet Golden (eds), *Framing Disease: Studies in Cultural History* (Rutgers University Press, 1992); Michael MacDonald and Terence Murphy, *Sleepless Souls: Suicide in Early Modern England* (Oxford University Press, 1990); Georges Minois, *History of Suicide: Voluntary Death in Western Culture* (The Johns Hopkins University Press, 1995); Andrew Scull, *Museums of Madness: Social Organisation of Insanity in Nineteenth Century England* (Penguin, 1975); Andrew Scull, *Masters of Bedlam: The Transformation of the Mad-Doctoring Trade* (Princeton University Press, 1996).
4   Chris Millar, *A History of Self-Harm in Britain: A Genealogy of Cutting and Overdosing* (Palgrave McMillan, 2015).
5   The Lunacy Act 1890 (53 Vict. c.5).
6   Elizabeth Lunbeck, *The Psychiatric Persuasion: Knowledge, Gender and Power in Modern America* (Princeton University Press, 1996).

7   Leon Radzinowicz and Roger Hood, *A History of English Criminal Law and Its Administration from 1750: Vol. 5: The Emergence of Penal Policy in Victorian and Edwardian England* (Oxford, 1990), p. 738.
8   The Royal Commission of 1878 proposed that the crime of attempted suicide should be made punishable by two years imprisonment with hard labour. For further details, see Radzinowicz and Hood, *A history of English Criminal Law*, p. 738.
9   As cited in Cyril Greenland, 'Suicide, Threatened or Attempted', *Mental Health*, 17, 2, (1958), pp. 44–9.
10 Mathew Thomson, *The Problem of Mental Deficiency: Eugenics, Democracy and Social Policy in Britain, c.1870–1959* (Clarendon, 1998).
11 Stephen Watson, The Moral Imbecile: A Study of the Relation between Penal Practice and Psychiatric Knowledge of the Habitual Offender (PhD Dissertation for the University of Lancaster, 1988), p. 2.
12 *The Western Daily Press*, 20 April 1937, p. 5.
13 Ibid.
14 *Eastbourne Herald Chronical*, 23 November 1957, p. 1.
15 Ibid.
16 *Hull Daily Mail*, 19 February 1920, p. 5.
17 *Leeds Mercury*, 21 January 1938, p. 7.
18 *The Western Daily Press*, 22 October 1947, p. 4.
19 Stanley Cohen and Andrew Scull, *Social Control and the State* (Palgrave MacMillan, 1983); Stanley Cohen, *Visions of Social Control* (Polity Press, 1985); Michel Foucault, *Discipline and Punish, The Birth of the Prison* (Penguin, 1977); Michel Foucault, *Madness and Civilisation* (Tavistock, 1967); Zola, I. K. (1972), Medicine As an Institution of Social Control. *The Sociological Review*, 20: 487–504. Nikolas Rose, *The Psychological Complex: Psychology, Politics and Society in England 1869–1939* (Routledge, 1985); David Garland, *Punishment and Welfare; A History of Penal Strategies* (Ashgate, 1985).
20 Lunbeck, *The Psychiatric Persuasion*.
21 J. Woodhouse, 'Eugenics and the Feeble-Minded, the Parliamentary Debates of 1912–14', *History of Education*, 11 (1982), pp. 127–37; John Macnicol, 'Eugenics, Medicine and Mental Deficiency', *Oxford Review of Education*, 9 (1983), pp. 177–81; Daniel Pick, *Faces of Degeneration: A European Disorder, c. 1848–c. 1918* (Cambridge University Press, 1989).
22 Despo Kritsotaki, Vicky Long and Matthew Smith (eds), *Deinstitutionalisation and after: Post-War Psychiatry in the Western World* (Palgrave MacMillan, 2016), p. 7; Mathew Thomson, *The Problem of Mental Deficiency: Eugenics, Democracy, and Social Policy in Britain c.1870–1959* (Oxford University Press, 1998); P. H. Stuart, 'Community Care and the Origins of Psychiatric Social Work', *Social Work in Health Care*, 25 (1997), pp. 25–36; Peter Bartlett and David Wright, *Outside the*

Walls of the Asylum: The History of Care in the Community, 1750–2000 (Athlone Press, 1999).
23 *The Liverpool Echo*, 11 February 1939, p. 5.
24 Ibid.
25 ECA: Edinburgh Police Court Records, May 1917.
26 Ibid.
27 *The Preston Herald*, 3 October 1914, p. 7.
28 Ibid.
29 *Western Daily Press*, 29 September 1938, p. 7.
30 *The Liverpool Echo*, 7 November 1940, p. 5.
31 *The Liverpool Echo,* 28 December 1945, p. 6.
32 Ibid.
33 The Mitchel Library, Glasgow, RU/3/4/5: Half Year Report of the Glasgow Probation Committee, 22 November 1938.
34 Ibid.
35 *Hendon & Finchley Times*, 7 June 1935, p. 7.
36 Ibid.
37 *The Yorkshire Post and Leeds Intelligencer*, 9 December 1954, p. 7.
38 Ibid.
39 Ibid.
40 ECA: Edinburgh Police Court Records, 14 February 1930.
41 Ibid.
42 *The Sunderland Daily Echo and Shipping Gazette*, 28 May 1947, p. 5.
43 Ibid.
44 Edinburgh City Archives, Edinburgh Police Court Records, 26 December 1917.
45 *The Lancashire Evening Post*, 22 April 1935, p. 3.
46 *The Lancashire Evening Post,* 23 December 1929, p. 8.
47 Ibid.
48 *The Scotsman*, 14 April 1925, p. 4.
49 *The Lancashire Evening Post*, 9 June 1937, p. 10.
50 *Manchester Evening News*, 1 December 1943, p. 4.
51 Ibid.
52 Ibid.
53 *The Essex Newsman*, 18 October 1919, p. 3.
54 Ibid.
55 Ibid.
56 *The Lancashire Evening Post,* 7 November 1930, p. 8.
57 *The Wester Daily Press*, 22 December 1936, p. 8.
58 Ibid.
59 Ibid.
60 *Alderley & Wilmslow Advertiser*, 22 October 1909, p. 11.

61 Glamorgan Archives: PSCBO/60/5: Cardiff Probation Committee Minutes, 1925.
62 *The Central Somerset Gazette*, 10 June 1932, p. 3.
63 Ibid.
64 *Wester Daily Press*, 7 June 1937, p. 5.
65 Ibid.
66 *Biggleswade Chronicle*, 8 December 1950, p. 7
67 Ibid.
68 Ibid.
69 *The Lancashire Evening Post*, 14 November 1955, p. 1.
70 Ibid.
71 Petteri Pietikainen, *Madness: A History* (Routledge, 2015), pp. 126–7.
72 *Taunton Courier, and Western Advertiser,* 12 September 1936, p. 7.
73 Ibid.
74 Edinburgh City Archives, Edinburgh Police Court Records, 27 June 1919.
75 ECA: Edinburgh Police Court Records, 10 September 1910.
76 *Sunderland Daily Echo*, 18 May 1921, p. 3; *Manchester Evening News*, 30 June 1942, p. 4.
77 *Acton Gazette,* 16 September 1910, p. 3.
78 *The Lancashire Evening Post*, 22 April 1935, p. 5.
79 Ibid.
80 Ibid.
81 *The Western Daily Press*, 16 December 1937, p. 8. N.B the phrase 'a new situation' means a new job.
82 Stanley Cohen and Andrew Scull, *Social Control and the State* (Palgrave MacMillan, 1983); Stanley Cohen, *Visions of Social Control* (Polity Press, 1985).
83 Cyril Burt, *The Young Delinquent* (London University Press, 1933), pp. 177–9.
84 McKee-Ryan et al., 'Psychological and Physical Well-Being during Unemployment: A Meta-Analytic Study', *Journal of Applied Psychology*, 90, 1 (2005), pp. 53–76; Marie Jahoda, *Employment and Unemployment: A Social Psychological Analysis* (Cambridge University Press, 1982); Peter Warr, *Work, Unemployment and Mental Health* (Oxford University Press, 1987).
85 ECA: Edinburgh Police Curt Records, 28 January 1929.
86 Ibid.
87 Ibid.
88 ECA: Edinburgh Police Court Records, 26 January 1929.
89 Ibid.
90 Ibid.
91 *The Yorkshire Post*, 14 January 1929, p. 2.
92 Manchester City Archives, GB127.M117/3/5: Manchester Probation Committee Minutes, Annual Report for 1932.
93 *The Western Daily Press,* 22 November 1930, p. 11.

94   Ibid.
95   Ibid.
96   Ibid.
97   *Liverpool Evening Express,* 24 January 1944, p. 4.
98   Glamorgan Archives, PSCBO/60/5: Cardiff Probation Committee Minutes, 27 July 1949.
99   *The West London Observer,* 3 June 1932, p. 6.
100 Lancashire Archives, PSPr/4/2: Preston Probation Committee Minutes, 8 October 1956.
101 *Hampshire Telegraph,* 17 January 1958, p. 11.
102 *The Scotsman,* February 1928, p. 13.
103 Ibid.
104 Ibid.
105 *The Western Daily Press*, 10 January 1929, p. 9.
106 *Hartlepool Northern Daily Mail,* 7 January 1944, p. 8.
107 *The Middlesex Chronicle,* 28 October 1939, p. 10.
108 Ibid.
109 *Leeds Mercury,* 25 July 1936, p. 3.
110 *Manchester Evening News*, 7 September 1939, p. 3.
111 *Western Daily Press,* 18 July 1939, p. 8.
112 Ibid.
113 *The Birmingham Daily Post*, 18 March 1955, p. 3.

4

Probation and male sexual offences: Gross indecency, indecent assault and indecent exposure

The history of how male sexuality was policed during the twentieth century in Britain has been well studied by historians focusing on subjects such as homosexuality, as well as by those looking at the history of venereal disease, sexual assault and child abuse.[1] However, less is known about the role that probation played in these policing efforts. This chapter therefore explores the different methods and motivations behind the use of probation in relation to three different types of male sexual offences: gross indecency, indecent assault and indecent exposure.

By placing men on probation, magistrates and judges could stipulate in the probation bond that men must undergo medical treatment to 'cure' their 'deviant' behaviour. The court could not force men to accept probation under these conditions, but given that the alterative to probation was imprisonment, their consent to this condition of treatment was somewhat coerced. Not all men, however, were required to undergo medical treatment, and it could be argued that in some situations, magistrates used probation in order to 'let off' men who they thought did not deserve punishment. The chapter therefore examines how the high levels of discretionary power involved in the use of probation meant that probation officers' and magistrates' attitudes towards certain types of sexual behaviour, and their opinions about the 'character' of the defendants, had considerable influence over the policing of sexual offences in Britain during the early-to-mid twentieth century. Finally, the chapter explores the extent to which the use of probation in these cases could be deemed 'successful' in changing men's sexual behaviour and considers what consequences this approach had for the men involved.

Medicalization of sexual deviancy

By the late nineteenth century sexual behaviour was gradually becoming understood in more psychological terms. The growing popularity of sexology, with its focus on the medical classification of sexual behaviours, meant that sexual deviancy was increasingly seen as biologically determined and/or caused by psychological problems.[2] This medicalized understanding of sexuality opened up the possibility that medical and psychological treatments might be able to 'cure' sexually 'deviant' behaviour, which in turn led to the use of more therapeutic approaches towards dealing with sexual deviancy.[3] Not everyone in the scientific community, however, saw all deviation from heterosexuality as necessarily being caused by an illness. For example, new psychoanalytical understandings of sexual development pioneered by Sigmund Freud called for homosexuality to be seen as a variation of sexual function, rather than an illness. Indeed, Freud himself is noted to have been sceptical about the possibility that psychoanalysis could make someone heterosexual.[4] Nonetheless, by the 1940s and 1950s, as more people within the criminal justice system started to view sexual behaviours such as homosexuality, exhibitionism and paedophilia as biologically or psychologically determined, there was a realization that sending these people to prison would not stop reoffending because it could not 'cure' the underlying problem. Sending a man to prison would only protect the public for a short period because it was likely that he would go on to commit more offences after his release. If men were required to undergo medical treatment whilst in prison or on probation, however, it was hoped that this treatment would change or subdue men's sexual desires, thus offering a much more long-term solution. The availability of medical treatment for sexual offenders in prisons was very limited due to the shortage of trained professionals working in prisons.[5] However, by using probation sentences to require men to undergo medical treatment outside of the prison, people could instead be sent to a wide range of clinical settings.

As we have seen in Chapter 3, probation provided a convenient way in which people who had attempted suicide could be required to undergo psychiatric treatment without having to be certified as insane.[6] These same powers were also used to force men who had been convicted of various sexual offences to undergo medical treatment, either as an inpatient or as an outpatient. The maximum period of probation was three years, but it was more likely that the medical treatment would be required for a shorter period, usually between three to twelve months, or according to the recommendation of the doctor. After the medical treatment was over, the probationers could still be required to report to a probation officer until the end of their probation period. The following example provides an illustration of how this process worked. In 1952, a man named as H. D. was convicted at Lancashire Quarter Sessions for gross indecency and placed on probation for two years. The Rossendale Probation Committee minutes include the following four entries about H. D.'s medical treatment and progress while he was on probation:

> 13 October 1952: H. D. placed on probation at quarter sessions for gross indecency. Went to Prestwich metal hospital, now discharged and returned to Rawtenstall. Lives with his wife, no children.
>
> 5 January 1953: H. D. Satisfactory. Working at Haslingden as labourer. Came of night work at Holland's pie works. Epileptic and night work not satisfactory for him. His wife is satisfied with his behaviour now. Not taking medical tablets now.
>
> 6 July 1953: H. D. is very conscious of his position and feels disgraced, but has made good progress, and takes tablets as and when necessary.
>
> 7 April 1954: H. D. finished probation.[7]

The actual medical treatment H. D. was given was not specified in the records. However, there is mention of H. D. taking tablets, which were most likely to have been oestrogen tablets. This method of hormone therapy was used in Britain during the late 1940s to mid-1950s after scientific studies in the 1940s showed that oestrogen could successfully reduce men's libidos, thus reducing the likelihood of them committing further offences.[8] Common side effects of oestrogen were that men could develop depression and female characteristics such as breasts, and so by the mid-1950s the use of these hormone treatments was becoming less common due to safety concerns.[9] Most infamously, oestrogen tablets were given to Dr Alan Turing, the mathematician and scientist often credited as being the 'father of theoretical computer science', who opted for medical treatment under probation rather than a prison sentence after he was convicted of gross indecency in Manchester during 1952.[10] Turing is known to have suffered from these side effects and there has been some speculation that this may have been a contributing factor in his subsequent suspected suicide in 1954.[11]

Another possible form of treatment used to 'cure' deviant sexuality was psychoanalysis. This approach relied on talking with the patient about their family background, relationships, health, employment, sexual experiences and dreams, all with the aim of developing the patient's skills in self-reflection.[12] This approach was commonly used at the Tavistock Clinic in London where, according to Claud Mullins's book *Crime and Psychology*, men convicted of sexual offences could be sent in accordance with the conditions of their probation bond. Mullins provides several examples of these types of scenarios, including the following case of a man named R. S., who was convicted of indecent assault on a boy and was subsequently sent to the Tavistock Clinic for assessment. R. S.'s medical report stated:

> I believe that his difficulties in early life at home are responsible for his condition. He was the eldest boy in the family, scared of his parents, especially of his mother, and I think that that is why he has always had a certain fear of growing up and of the responsibilities of life. He has flunked in his work. He should be in a very much better job than he has now; and, of course, he is afraid of marriage and the responsibilities of it. The result has been that he is something of a Peter Pan emotionally and so the schoolboy homo-sexual phase has persisted.[13]

R. S. was subsequently placed on probation and sent for treatment at a different clinic (name unspecified). After two months, a doctor at the clinic gave this report:

> His trouble is that of homo-sexuality. This condition can usually be greatly helped by treatment, although perfect cure is uncommon. The success of treatment, however, depends upon a real wish for cure resultant upon a sense of the discomfort and satisfactoriness of the condition. This is quite absent in his case, although several interviews have aimed at eliciting it ... He has been discharged as unsuitable for psychological treatment.[14]

Despite this apparent failure, Mullins did not want to give up on this man and so he sent him back to the Tavistock Clinic. After a few weeks' observation, a doctor at the Tavistock Clinic provided the following report:

> I still feel, as I did originally, that he is helpable, and I am fixing up treatment for him here ... At the present moment I certainly do not think he is safe, but I believe that something can be done.[15]

R. S. was admitted to two different clinics. The first assessed that he was not suitable for psychological treatment because he did not want to be cured, an important prerequisite for treatment to be successful. Nonetheless, R. S. was subsequently sent to the Tavistock Clinic for two months where they thought 'he might be fixable'.[16] The exact treatment he was given was not specified, but the Tavistock Clinic was well known for its Freudian psychoanalytic approach and it is likely that psychoanalysis was used. The Tavistock report about R. S., which pinpointed his early childhood experiences, his 'Peter Pan' type emotions and an inability to develop past the 'schoolboy homo-sexual phase' as causes for his homosexual offences are all typical examples of the Freudian explanation for why someone developed homosexual behaviour.[17]

The treatments given to the men in the two examples above reflect the fact that hormone therapy and psychoanalysis were more commonly used in Britain during the 1940s and early 1950s than the other main type of treatment, aversion therapy, which did not become a more commonplace treatment until the late 1950s and 1960s. Aversion therapy was based on classical Pavlovian conditioning techniques in which the therapist attempted to get the patient to associate his or her 'deviant' sexual feelings with pain.[18] The main method used for this was to make people look at images of the problematic sexual behaviour in question and to cause them pain at the same time. To cause the required pain the patient was either given a nausea drug to make them sick, or they were given an electric shock when they were aroused by the images. Clinics for the treatment of homosexuality were established in Birmingham, Edinburgh, Glasgow, London and Manchester, and the method of aversion therapy that was used varied throughout the country because there were no general protocols or ethical guidelines.[19]

The vagueness of the court records and newspaper reports makes it difficult to know exactly what type of treatment was given to a particular individual, especially because the type of treatment used in different institutions could vary considerably across the country. Indeed, Roger Davidson's research on the Jordanburn Nerve Hospital in Edinburgh has shown how, even within the same institution, the methods used to rehabilitate homosexual men could vary from patient to patient and in accordance with the preferences of a particular practitioner.[20] However, it can be assumed that the treatment was likely to have been one (or a mixture) of the treatments described above: psychoanalysis, hormone therapy (usually in the form of oestrogen tablets), aversion therapy. There was little proof that any of these methods were able to change a person's sexuality, and there was even less understanding of the potential long-term effects they could have. There have, however, since been studies which have shown the grave psychological harm caused by some of these methods.[21] The consequences of these medical treatments will be discussed further in the latter half of the chapter.

Gross indecency

Prior to the 1967 Sexual Offences Act, which decriminalized homosexual acts between consenting men over the age of twenty-one in England and Wales, homosexuality was mainly prosecuted under two pieces of legislation that dealt with 'gross indecency' and 'importuning for immoral purposes'.[22] Section 11 of the Criminal Law Amendment Act 1885 stipulated that

> any male person who, in public or private, commits, or is a party to the commission of, or procures, or attempts to procure the commission by any male person of, any act of gross indecency with another male person, shall be guilty of a misdemeanour, and being convicted thereof, shall be liable at the discretion of the Court to be imprisoned for any term not exceeding two years, with or without hard labour.[23]

The law did not define what gross indecency was, but it was generally understood to refer to homosexual acts that did not involve penetration. The 1898 Vagrancy Act also made it possible to prosecute 'every male person who in any public place persistently solicits or importunes for immoral purposes'.[24] During the 1950s the Act was commonly used to prosecute men who had been caught (often as part of a police undercover operation) visiting public toilets with the intent to engage in sexual acts with other men.[25] These two pieces of legislation were used to prosecute gay men more commonly than legislation relating to 'buggery' because of the difficulty in proving that intercourse had occurred. Moreover, under the Offences against the Person Act 1861, 'buggery' had a maximum sentence of life imprisonment. This meant that juries were less willing to pass guilty verdicts in 'buggery' cases because of the harshness of the sentence.[26]

While men were prosecuted for homosexual acts throughout the first half of the twentieth century, there was renewed enthusiasm for prosecuting homosexual men during the early 1950s. This was due to wider fears during this period about the threat of sexual danger and public indecency. These fears were in part linked to concerns about the corruption and blackmail of homosexual men that had been stirred up in connection to the negative publicity surrounding high-profile prosecutions of prominent public figures, such as Lord Montagu (a peer of the realm) and Peter Wildeblood (a diplomatic correspondent for *The Daily Mail*).[27] However, at the same time as there were mounting pressure to 'crack down' on male vice, some were questioning the desirability of punishing men for acting on their biological desires in cases where sex occurred in private between two consenting adults. This view was supported by new scientific studies by people such as Lindesay Neustatter, whose 1955 article 'Homosexuality: The Medical Perspective' called for the recognition of the fact that 'the invert is not a villain to be punished, but a patient to be studied'.[28] And it was not only scientists who held these views. An article that appeared in *The Birmingham Post* on 9 April 1954 suggested that these ideas about homosexuality were also being spread amongst probation officers and the public more widely. The article referred to a talk given by Dr J. Hammond to a Wolverhampton meeting of probation officers. Hammond described how 'through newspapers people were beginning to be interested and realize that questions like homosexuality were not simply acts of wickedness and that those people were suffering from a moral illness'.[29]

In 1957 the Departmental Committee on Homosexual Offences and Prostitution, which had been set up in 1954 to examine the laws relating to prostitution and homosexuality (commonly referred to as the Wolfenden Committee), recommended that homosexual acts between adults that occurred in private should not be criminalized.[30] The committee also concluded that homosexuality was not a disease, but that physicians should continue to research possible treatments for homosexuality so that men could receive effective treatment if they wanted it.[31] However, despite these recommendations it was not until the 1967 Sexual Offences Act that homosexuality was legalized in England and Wales, and not until 1980 in Scotland.[32] In the meantime, probation continued to be used as a way to allow men to avoid prison and, in some cases, as a way to ensure that men received medical treatment in a bid to 'cure' them of their homosexuality.

Examples of men being placed on probation for gross indecency and required to undergo medical treatment can be seen in the following selection of cases. In April 1944, twenty-four-year-old David M. pleaded guilty to committing an act of gross indecency and was placed on probation in Worthing with the condition he 'attended for medical attention'.[33] In August 1949, a sixteen-year-old 'Glastonbury lad' pleaded guilty to acts of gross indecency and was placed on probation for three years at Wells Juvenile Court. The magistrate agreed to place him on probation under the 'condition that the lad should submit himself to such medical treatment as may be ordered'.[34] At Derbyshire Assises in June 1952, nineteen-year-old Basil C. pleaded guilty to charges of gross indecency and was placed on probation for two years with a requirement that he resided at the Pastures Hospital for a period not exceeding twelve months.[35] In September 1954, a thirty-five-year-old former Army Major named Patrick K. who had been convicted of persistently importuning for immoral purposes had his sentence of three months' imprisonment changed to three years' probation by West Kent

Appeals Committee 'on condition that he submitted, for twelve months, to psychiatric treatment'.[36] In October 1957, a thirty-three-year-old dustman named Walter D. pleaded guilty to gross indecency at Bucks Quarter Sessions and was placed on probation for three years, during which time he was 'ordered to undergo hospital treatment'.[37] Also in 1957, twenty-three-year-old Horace P. was convicted at Warwick Assizes of committing an act of gross indecency.[38] Horace P. was placed on probation for three years, certified as a mental defective and sent to a home for psychiatric patients.

That the above examples were all from England during the 1940s and 1950s reflects how medical treatment became more commonly used during this period in England, as ideas about pathological sexuality increasingly took hold. Roger Davidson's research on homosexuality and the law in Scotland has shown that the use of probation to require men to undergo medical treatment was also fairly common in Scotland by the 1950s. His study of patient admissions to the Jordanburn Nerve Hospital (JNH) in Edinburgh revealed that during the 1950s 36 per cent of the JNH's patients were referred there 'either preceding or following criminal actions involving charges of indecency, importuning, loitering or more serious contraventions of the 1885 Criminal Law Amendment Act, Section 11'.[39] This was in part because the JNH had been designated as an approved institution that men placed on probation could be sent to under Clause 3 of the Criminal Justice (Scotland) Act 1949.

Although the use of probation to require men to undergo medical treatment only became a more common policy from the 1940s onwards in England, and from the 1950s onwards in Scotland, there were some earlier cases where the defence counsels tried to get their clients placed on probation under the proviso that they needed medical treatment. For example, in 1908 a clergyman named Douglas G. pleaded guilty to an act of gross indecency at the Central Criminal Court in London and a report about the case in *The Lakes Herald* described how his counsel made a long statement concerning his client's 'mental condition'.[40] According to the report, three medical men 'spoke as to the prisoner's psychical and mental breakdown'.[41] The judge said he would be prepared to release him under the Probation of Offenders Act, although whether Douglas G. subsequently received any medical treatment is unclear. In July 1926, a twenty-nine-year-old labourer named Harry T. was sentenced to twelve months' imprisonment for three acts of gross indecency at Derby Assizes. The report about the case in the *Nottingham Evening Post* described how the defendant 'appeared to be a neurotic' and that 'Mr Justice Acton expressed the belief that the day would come when medical science, instead of criminal law, would deal with such cases'.[42] This judge might not have yet felt able to deal with gross indecency as a medical issue, but he was aware that this approach was on the horizon.

In January 1938 there was considerable publicity surrounding the case of a prominent member of the Kincardineshire judiciary who was sentenced to two years' imprisonment at Edinburgh High Court after being found guilty of fourteen charges of committing acts of gross indecency in Edinburgh hotels. What is particularly interesting about this case is the emphasis the defence counsel placed on the man's medical condition and the fact that his lawyer requested that the judge 'might take advantage of the Probation of Offenders Act, as all the doctors who had examined the accused were of the opinion that he would benefit from institutional treatment'.[43] However, the judge refused this option, explaining that 'the main consideration to be taken into account was not what would benefit the accused, but what punishment serviced the community'.[44] He insisted that any medical treatment the accused needed would be given to him in prison.[45] Despite the fact that ideas about the medical causes of homosexuality were being voiced in courtrooms by the 1930s (and in some cases earlier), this case exemplifies how not all judges were yet willing to place men on probation instead of sending them to prison. As this judge clearly stated, there was still a belief that punishment for homosexuality was necessary for the protection of the public.

As we have seen in the previous chapters the judge, magistrate or JP had considerable discretion over what sentence was given, including whether medical treatment was required. These decisions were partly based on recommendations from doctors and probation officers, but also on the JP, magistrate or judge's own opinion about the offence and the offender. An article written by Michael Schofield in 1952, entitled *Society and the Homosexual*, emphasized how this power of discretion was particularly influential in the case of 'the homosexual offender'. He described how

> the fate of the homosexual offender now depends upon the wisdom and discretion of the magistrate. Some of them have an intelligent understanding of the nature of the disease; other are not swayed by medical opinion even when it is available and their own interpretation of the law is their only guide.[46]

While the increased medicalization of sexual deviancy meant that there was a general move towards wanting to 'cure' sexual offenders by giving them medical treatment, this opinion was not shared by all involved in the criminal justice system. Some magistrates who did not think homosexuality should be criminalized or medicalized used probation in order to avoid sending to prison men who they thought did not pose a risk to the public and did not deserve punishment. Others, however, believed that men who engaged in homosexual acts must be punished, and they were dubious about the ability of medicine to cure these men. In their opinion, homosexual men should be sent to prison in order to protect society and to deter others from committing similar offences. Anything less was a 'let off' and tantamount to condoning this type of 'dangerous' behaviour.

This punitive attitude can be seen in the views of James Adair, a former Scottish Procurator Fiscal for Edinburgh and Glasgow, who was a member of the Wolfenden Committee. Adair was very critical of psychiatrists for 'sentimentalizing' the problem of homosexuality and downplaying its dangers, especially the alleged connection to paedophilia. He was sceptical of claims that homosexuality was a disease and doubtful that doctors had the ability to 'cure' homosexuality. Instead, Adair believed that most homosexuals only sought treatment to evade a prison sentence.[47] However, Adair was also aware that not everyone in Scotland shared his scepticism about medical treatment and in the evidence that he gave to the Wolfenden Committee he described how 'some judges were very responsive to suggestions by medical men about treatment, while others agreed that these were not the concern of the judge'.[48]

This inconsistency in how different JPs, judges and magistrates utilized probation and medical treatment can be seen in the case of a man named Stephan B., who received six months' hard labour for importuning at London's Victoria Station in November 1944. During his trial it became apparent that Stephan had three previous convictions for importuning and gross indecency, and in 1937 he had been placed on probation for three years and given psychological treatment until the hospital he was staying at shut down during the Second World War. On the basis of this, his lawyer asked for a renewal of the medical and psychological treatment. The magistrate in 1944, however, refused and informed the court that 'what he had to tell Stephan B. and others like him was that if that sort of conduct was persisted in the punishment would be prison'.[49] This particular magistrate had less faith in medicine as a method for preventing reoffending than the previous magistrates who had placed Stephan B. on probation (despite his previous convictions). Considering that this was Stephan B.'s fourth conviction, it is fair to say that the magistrate was correct in his assessment that probation and medical treatment had so far been ineffective in stopping this man from reoffending. Nonetheless, his insistence that men who failed to reform should be punished highlights how this magistrate still saw homosexuality as crime worthy of punishment, rather than an illness in need of a cure.

Stephan B.'s case also illustrates how the defendant's previous conviction history played an important role in determining whether a person was deemed suitable for probation and under what conditions. That first-time offenders were more likely to be placed on probation is not surprising and fits with the larger pattern of how probation was used more generally. However, it was not only a person's record of previous convictions that could have an important influence on sentencing. Other factors such as age, class and 'character' were also very important. This can be seen in the case of two men who were convicted of committing acts of gross indecency with each other in Essex during 1943. The first man, twenty-nine-year-old Wilfred P., was a soldier with two previous convictions for theft and two for housebreaking. He had previously undergone a sentence of three years' penal servitude because of these past convictions, and on this occasion he was given an eighteen-month prison sentence. However, the second man, thirty-nine-year-old contactor's checker John G., 'a married man with two children and good character', was bound over on probation for two years.[50] Wilfred P.'s previous convictions, although for a different type of offence, probably played a part in why he received a prison sentence, whereas John G.'s status as a 'family man' with a 'good character' and no previous convictions was important in ensuring he was placed on probation without any conditions.

The importance of 'good character' in influencing sentencing decisions can be seen again in the case of a forty-year-old bacteriologist and pathologist named John L., who pleaded guilty to gross indecency at Staffordshire Quarter Sessions in October 1946. An article in the *Staffordshire Advertiser* about the case described how the defendant was 'stated to have had a distinguished career and to have been formerly senior assistant bacteriologist and pathologist to the Staffordshire County Council'.[51] The defence counsel described how John L. 'bore an excellent character' and went on to list his academic achievements at public school and Oxford University. Much was also made of the fact that on the night in question he 'had much more to drink than was usual for him' and how 'drink had a good deal to do with the offence'.[52] Even the prosecution admitted that it was a 'melancholy case because the accused was not only a first offender, but a man of distinction and attainment in his profession'.[53] This emphasis on how the offence was due to a 'temporary aberration' fits with what John Lunan has shown to be a common approach also used by probation officers when they wanted to ensure that a particular defendant was released on probation.[54]

In addition to blaming alcohol for his client's behaviour, the defence counsel was also keen to stress that it was 'safe to say it was a case in which the prosecution did not suggest that an innocent young person was corrupted – according to his information the very contrary was the case'.[55] The information they were referring to was the fact that the man with whom John L. had committed the offence was a twenty-nine-year-old soldier named Wilfred who had deserted from the army, stolen a car and previously been 'convicted of dishonesty and indecent offences'.[56] That the young soldier was portrayed as already being well versed in indecent behaviour was used as proof that John L. was not guilty of his corruption. After hearing this evidence, the judge decided to bind John L. over for two years on good behaviour because 'it was not necessary to put a man of his education on probation'.[57] Here you can see how John L.'s status as a well-educated middle-class man protected him from being sent to prison *and* from being placed on probation and having to undergo medical treatment to 'correct' his sexuality. The fact that John L. and other middle-class men like him were less likely to be required to undergo medical treatment supports the argument that social class was important in determining the provision of psychiatric treatment and thus influenced how the medicalization of sexuality occurred in practice.[58]

John L.'s case is particularly interesting as it demonstrates how factors such as age, class and respectability interacted. The newspaper made reference to the commonly held concern that older men 'corrupted' young men by encouraging them to commit incident acts and provides an example of how homosexuality was commonly erroneously associated with paedophilia during this period. As we shall see in the next section on indecent assault, men who assaulted children were dealt with more harshly than men who assaulted adults. However, in cases where sex appeared to have been consensual and both men were legally considered adults, magistrates and judges would often still give harsher sentences to older men in cases when there was a considerable age difference. This was especially true in cases where the older man was in a position of authority and the younger man was seen to have previously been of good character. This scenario can be seen in the case of forty-three-year-old John P., a miller from Aymestrey. In November 1950 he was found guilty of nine counts of gross indecency with four young men between the ages of sixteen and twenty-two.[59] John P.'s defence counsel asked the judge 'to consider sending P to an institution for treatment rather than receive a prison sentence', but the magistrate refused because John P. had

> brought into co-operation for his filthy habits men of less than half of his age. He took a serious view of the fact that he was chairman of a youth club. People thought he was a respectable, clean minded person, but instead he was following the abominable course of indulging in sexual perversions.[60]

John P. was sentenced to four years in prison, with a recommendation for medical treatment. The young men in this case were each placed on probation for twelve months.

However, not all older men who were convicted of gross indecency with young men were sent to prison. In April 1957, thirty-four-year-old Kenneth C. was convicted at West Susses Quarter Sessions of committing acts of gross indecency with a nineteen-year-old man named Raymond D. Kenneth C.'s defence counsel explained how, despite the disparity in ages, 'there was no question of corruption'. He then described how

> the tragedy of this case is the tragedy of so many homosexual cases … at a very early age he was himself corrupted, not only by fellow pupils, but by a member of staff …. Having been introduced to this type of life he was not strong enough to shake it off.[61]

The defence then made reference 'to a psychiatrist's report that Kenneth might be cured under treatment'.[62] Despite Kenneth C. having two previous convictions for a similar offence, and admitting that 'due to seniority in age, I am mainly to blame', the judge placed him on probation for two years without any conditions.[63] Unlike in the case of the youth club leader John P. described above, in Kenneth C.'s case the judge appears to have been more sympathetic about the need for probation, rather than punishment in prison. This may have partly been linked to the fact that Kenneth C. was not in an obvious position of power and influence, unlike John P.

Nonetheless, even taking these factors into account, a major theme in comparing the sentencing decisions in cases of gross indecency is the lack of consistency in how probation and medical treatment were used. Partly this was justified in cases where harsher punishment was necessary because a man had used his position of power and influence to coerce vulnerable individuals into having sex. In other situations, however, this disparity in sentencing had more to do with the judges' or magistrates' opinions about homosexuality and their judgements about the character of the offender (especially in relation to age and class). While probation officers had little influence over a judge or magistrate's attitude towards homosexuality, they could help to inform his or her perceptions of the offender. As John Lunan has shown, the social enquiries undertaken by probation officers played a crucial part in the sentencing process because the reports they made provided the judge or magistrate with key information about the defendant's 'character' and background.[64] In this way, probation officers also played a key role in determining whether probation orders were handed down, and under what conditions.

Indecent assault

Sections 52 and 62 of the Offences against the Person Act 1861 made indecent assault upon a female or male punishable by a maximum sentence of two years' imprisonment with or without hard labour.[65] The term indecent assault was used to describe sexual acts that involved forms of physical contact that did not include penetrative sex. If penetrative sex had occurred, the offence was classed as rape and dealt with under Section 48 of the 1861 Offences against the Person Act and it carried a maximum sentence of penal servitude for life. This disparity effectively meant that while men convicted of indecent assault were sometimes placed on probation, it was unlikely that men convicted of rape would be. In 1956 the Sexual Offences Act Sections 14 and 15 replaced the 1861 Act and made indecent assault on a woman or man punishable by a maximum of ten years' imprisonment.[66] Despite this increase in the maximum sentence attached to indecent assault, probation continued to be used as a sentencing option, especially in cases of first offences.

As was the case with gross indecency, men convicted of indecent assault who had been placed on probation could be required to undergo medical treatment. For example, in July 1940 forty-three-year-old Sidney F. was found guilty of indecent assault in Southend and placed on probation for two years under the condition that he would 'submit to medical treatment'.[67] Sidney F.'s defence stated that 'the accused was of good character and that this was an isolated occurrence'.[68] The report in the *Chelmsford Chronicle* about the case described how the accused tried to explain his behaviour as being down to stress because 'he looked after his father, aged 89. This matter had caused much anguish and concern'.[69] In April 1949, forty-eight-year-old William B. pleaded guilty at Plymouth Quarter Sessions to nine charges of indecently assaulting juveniles and was bound over on the sum of £5 for three years and required 'to be of good behaviour' and to 'reside where the probation officer and a psychiatrist should decide'.[70] In April 1950, an ex-prisoner of war named Fred F. was convicted of assaulting boys in the youth community club that he organized in Lincoln. He was put on probation and sent for treatment in a hospital for three years.[71] The report in *The Lincolnshire Echo* described how Fred F.'s harsh experience in the camps was to blame for his behaviour and that the Returned Prisoners of War Association was willing to give him additional help and support.[72] In June 1957, thirty-year-old bicycle dealer Dennis M. pleaded guilty at Glamorgan Quarter Sessions to two offences of indecent assault involving boys and was placed on probation for two years and 'ordered to receive medical treatment for a year'.[73]

That the above selection of cases all involved child victims is representative of a more general trend in the use of probation in cases of indecent assault. There are no judicial statistics for England, Scotland and Wales available for this period that break down sentences for indecent assault according to the age of the victim. However, from looking at a selection of cases which appeared in the probation records and in the newspapers, it appears that the majority of cases where men were placed on probation for indecent assault and were required to undergo medical treatment involved victims under sixteen. One possible practical reason for this was that under the 1908 Children Act, cases involving victims under sixteen years old could be heard by a magistrate in a court of summary justice (rather than the higher court of quarter sessions or assizes).[74] It was more common for probation officers to work with defendants tried in magistrates courts, so this may partly account for the discrepancy, but it was not the only reason because judges in higher courts could also place people on probation.

Another hypothesis is that the abuse of children was more likely to be seen as resulting from a pathological impulse symptomatic of a mental illness than was the case in assaults involving adult victims. For example, Janet Weston has shown how the medico-legal professions gave much more attention to certain sexual offences, such as those involving homosexuality and paedophilia, than to offences such as rape and assault of adult women.[75] This was because the latter offences were deemed to be caused by an excess of 'normal' sexual instincts due to poor self-control, rather than mental illness. Moreover, Carol Smart has shown how organizations such as the Association for Moral and Social Hygiene were campaigning for men who were guilty of sexually assaulting children to be categorized as a separate type of offender, one with serious mental health conditions that needed to be dealt with by medical professionals.[76] As support for this approach grew, this meant that offences against children were more likely to warrant a sentence which necessitated that the defendant be given psychiatric treatment so that they could be cured of their mental illness.

Not all men who were placed on probation for indecently assaulting children were, however, required to undergo medical treatment. For example, in February 1919 fifty-four-year-old David M. was convicted at Edinburgh Police Court for indecently assaulting a thirteen-year-old girl. David M. was described as 'mentally slow' and placed on probation for twelve months, but there was no mention of him receiving any medical treatment.[77] Similarly, in 1925 twenty-nine-year-old Lindsay M. was placed on probation for twelve months at Cardiff Police Court for an indecent assault on a child. He was required 'not to be in the company of little girls', but no requirement was made for him to undergo medical treatment.[78] The lack of medical treatment in these cases may reflect the fact that they occurred prior to the 1930s when medical treatment for sexual offences in general was still fairly uncommon, although there are some examples of men not being required to undergo medical treatment from later periods as well. For example, in May 1945 Penzance Juvenile Court found a sixteen-year-old boy guilty of indecently assaulting a six-year-old girl and gave him a three-year probation order and £4 fine, but there was no requirement to undergo medical treatment.[79] It is likely, therefore, that other factors, such as the age and character of the defendant and the victim, and the opinions of the magistrate about the effectiveness of medical treatment, also played a role.

Even as medical treatment became more common during the 1940s and 1950s, whether a man received it was dependent upon the decision of the individual magistrate or judge, and as we have seen earlier with cases of gross indecency, this decision was influenced by their attitudes towards psychiatry, sexuality, and the class and character of the defendant. A good example of how the attitude of the judge or magistrate towards psychiatry could have a strong influence on how probation was used can be seen in the case of a twenty-seven-year-old insurance agent named William J. who was convicted of gross indecency with a young person in July 1939 at Essex Quarter Sessions. A report about the case in *The Essex Newsman* described how during the first hearing of the case on 21 July 1939 the defence argued that William J. needed psychological treatment and asked whether the sentencing could be postponed until a psychological report had been made.[80] This was allowed, and William J. was subsequently sent to a psychological institute in London for testing. On 7 October 1939, William J. came to court for sentencing and *The Essex Newsman* again reported on the case. The article described how upon release from the psychological institution, William J. went to reside at a religious institution run by the Anglican church.[81] Father Potter, the man in charge of this Anglican institution, gave a witness statement about William J., detailing how he 'was helping in the garden and kitchen work and was undergoing treatment in the psychological institute'.[82] Father Potter was then reported to have said that he believed 'there was every hope of successful treatment'.[83] However, when asked for further details about William J.'s medical treatment, Father Potter told the court that 'he could not say whether William J. had been seen by a doctor, but he had visited the psychological institute' and that William J. 'had expressed a wish to become a novice in their order'.[84]

The judge in this case was understandably concerned about the prospect of William J. becoming a novice and asked Father Potter whether William J.

would be 'expected to work among young men in a celibate establishment'.[85] When Father Potter replied that he would, the judge then asked, 'Don't you think that would be very undesirable for a man with his inclinations?'[86] Father Potter apparently saw no problem with this situation, but the judge disagreed and decided that further medical treatment to be 'followed implicitly' would be a wiser course of action. He subsequently sentenced William J. to undergo six months of medical treatment.[87] The judge in this case was rightly sceptical about allowing a known child abuser to work with children in a religious institution and openly challenged Father Potter's judgement. The judge's decision to choose medical intervention over placing the accused under the care of the church played a crucial role here. Another judge or magistrate who had less faith in medicine and more trust in the ability of the church to reform this man may have made a different judgement.

The important role that perceptions about class and respectability played in sentencing decisions can also be seen in the case of forty-six-year-old ex-army officer Arthur P., who was convicted at Kent Quarter Sessions of indecently assaulting a sixteen-year-old boy at a cinema in January 1941.[88] His defence counsel described how Arthur P. had 'served in the last war and was in hospital for 18 months with shell shock and gas poisoning', and so he asked the bench to 'treat the prisoner as a man who required medical and psychological treatment'.[89] The defence also read out a report made by Colonel Reece, the consultant psychologist to the army and director of the Tavistock Clinic, which recommended that the defendant 'should be sent to the Caldecott Hall for treatment'.[90] Arthur P. was subsequently placed on probation for two years, the first year of which he was required to spend 'residing at the Caldecott Hall medical institution'.[91] Arthur P.'s medical record and his reputation as a formerly respectable ex-officer who had served his country during the First World War were clearly influential in ensuring that he was placed on probation rather than sent to prison. So, too, were his personal connections, which meant that his defence team were able to call on Colonel Reece, the consultant psychologist to the army and director of the Tavistock Clinic, to provide expert testimony to support his case.

Another example of how social class could influence sentencing can be seen in the case of the forty-six-year-old journalist and Cambridge graduate John A., who in September 1931 was convicted of indecently assaulting two girls aged nine and six.[92] He had a previous conviction for a similar offence in December 1926 for which he had received a three-month prison sentence. According to an article about the case in the *Bucks Herald*, the prison medical officer at

Oxford prison had found no evidence of gross mental disorder. However, John A.'s defence counsel successfully persuaded the magistrate that John A. was suffering from a nervous condition made worse through alcoholism and that medical treatment in an institution would be a suitable sentence. A letter was then presented to the court that had been sent by a nerve specialist called Dr Wright who said he thought John A. should be sent to a medical institution. The defence lawyer also presented a letter from Dr Kerr, the director of the Bucks Mental Hospital, who expressed his willingness to receive the defendant. Despite John A.'s previous convictions and the prison medical officer's opinion that the defendant did not have a mental disorder, the judge followed the suggestion made by John A.'s lawyer deciding that

> they had heard the advocates' remarks on the subject of mental treatment, and they had given their careful consideration and had come to the conclusion that probably it would be the wisest course to bind him over for him to reside at the Bucks Mental Hospital for twelve months.[93]

Whether the medical treatment worked is unclear because no further reports on the case exist. However, the case highlights how important wealth and social class could be in determining whether a man was sent to prison or for medical treatment. If a man could afford to hire his own expert legal counsel and get letters of recommendation from doctors (often after paying for private treatment with them), he was more likely to be successful in persuading the judge that medical treatment was the best course of action. The implications of this class-based distribution of justice will be discussed further in the final section of the chapter.

In addition to class, the age of the defendant was also a factor in determining whether probation was used in order to 'let off' men whose youth was seen to partly excuse or diminish the seriousness of their offence. For example, on 22 February 1908 *The Barking, Eastham and Ilford Advertiser* reported on the case of sixteen-year-old John H., who indecently assaulted a young woman returning home from chapel (the age of the victim was not given). The jury found him guilty but recommended him to 'mercy on account of his youth', and the judge decided to place him on probation for two years.[94] In 1953, a sixteen-year-old boy, who was convicted of indecently assaulting a five-year-old boy, was placed on probation. However, the judge at the Luton Juvenile Court was keen to point out that 'if this was an adult he would go to prison for a very long time.'[95] The importance of the age of the defendant can be seen most clearly by comparing two cases of indecent assault on a child under fourteen that were heard at the Bucks Quarter Sessions by the same judge, on the same day, in October 1940.

In the first case, a twenty-four-year-old man named Kenneth B. pleaded guilty to indecently assaulting a girl under fourteen. According to *The Buck's Herald*, the defendant made a statement to the court saying he wanted 'an operation upon himself', but the judge said that this was not admissible and sentenced him to twelve months' imprisonment.[96] The second case involved a sixteen-year-old boy named George W., who had also pleaded guilty to indecently assaulting a girl under fourteen. In this case, the mother of the defendant appealed to the magistrate, describing how the boy had run wild because there was no school place for him, but now he had been given a plot of land to work at his uncle's farm in Southport, and 'she felt this boy would do well if given a chance'.[97] The judge agreed and decided to place George W. on probation for two years, on the condition that he lived with his uncle on his farm.[98] The fate of the twenty-four-year-old man and the sixteen-year-old boy was considerably different, which reflects the more general trend of young offenders being given preference when it came to the use of probation.

Sometimes the age of the defendant could also be important at the other end of the lifecycle, with 'old men' also being treated more sympathetically if they were considered otherwise respectable and/or in ill-health. A good example of this is the case of sixty-one-year-old John B., who was convicted of gross indecency with a fifteen-year-old boy at Derbyshire Quarter Sessions in January 1952. During the trial the defence counsel stated that the defendant

> was a man suffering from a medical disorder. This was borne out by the fact that the offence happened for the first time when he was in his late 50s. The public interest would be better served if this man were rehabilitated rather than sent to prison, and on this ground, he asked for the court's leniency.[99]

To support the claim, the defence referred to a doctor's report, which stated that the defendant 'had a repressed homosexual tendency which had come out, perhaps as a result of something to do with his age'.[100] The judge appeared to be convinced by this argument and agreed to put him on probation for two years because before this offence he had 'unblemished respectability' and 'this trouble did not overtake you until your late 50s.'[101] However, the judge did require that the defendant must follow the advice of his medical advisor.[102] Old age on its own, however, was not usually enough to warrant a person being placed on probation, and, as in this case, it typically had to be combined with respectability and proof of health problems.

The age of the victim was also a crucial factor when it came to sentencing. While the youth of the victim was seen as a good reason for the defendant to receive a harsh sentence, this emphasis on age could have the reverse effect in cases where the victim was not considered by some to be 'young enough' or 'innocent enough' to qualify as a 'proper' child, despite being legally defined as such. This was especially the case in situations where the victim was a teenager and doubt was cast over the child's character. The idea that some children were more innocent than others was reflected in the legislation surrounding statutory rape.[103] In 1885 the Criminal Law Amendment Act raised the age of consent from thirteen to sixteen.[104] However, whereas sex with girls aged under thirteen was considered a felony, sex with girls aged between thirteen and sixteen was regarded as a misdemeanour. Furthermore, men accused of having sex with girls between the ages of thirteen and sixteen were entitled to plead that they did not know the girl was under sixteen (although after 1922 this defence was only allowed in cases where the defendant was under twenty-four).[105]

An example of this type of victim blaming can be seen in the case of a twenty-four-year-old farm labourer named Harvey C., who was bound over on probation without a supervision order after he was convicted of indecently assaulting a fourteen-year-old girl in January 1935. The judge at the Bucks Winter Assizes described how 'this was one of those regrettable cases where both man and girl were wrong' and that 'the girl had thrown every possible temptation in the way of the prisoner'.[106] The judge then went on to describe the girl as a 'woman of the world' arguing that this was an example of how 'girls of tender years' could act as 'accomplished prostitutes' by pestering men.[107] In another example of victim blaming from six months earlier, a twenty-six-year-old man named John A. was convicted at York Assizes of indecently assaulting a fourteen-year-old girl in July 1934. An article about the case in *The Yorkshire Post* described how Justice Humphries told the court that 'this was one of those distressing cases where a mere child of fourteen had become nothing more than a mere prostitute'.[108] He pronounced that the defendant had been 'tricked' into thinking that the girl was eighteen and therefore the defendant should be dealt with leniently.[109] John A. was subsequently placed on probation, and it was the victim who was locked up in a rescue home.

As Louise Jackson, Linda Mahood and Carol Smart have shown, sending girl victims of sexual abuse to rescue homes was a common practice that was intended to ensure that 'sexually experienced' girls would not be a danger to men or other 'innocent' girls.[110] In these types of situations, putting men on probation (especially if it was without any condition of medical treatment) can be seen as providing magistrates with a way to 'let off' men who, in their eyes, had not committed an offence serious enough to warrant a prison sentence.

Even in situations where the defendant was given a prison sentence, the rhetoric of victim blaming continued. For example, in July 1942 the *Evening Dispatch* reported on the case of a 'young girl' who had been assaulted by a soldier. The soldier was given a six-day prison sentence, and the girl was placed on probation under a care and protection order. However, rather than showing sympathy for the victim the judge at the Lewes Assizes described the girl as a 'perfect nuisance' for seducing the man and ruining the defendant's career.[111]

Even though probation could be used to 'let off' certain men, especially in situations where the man was not required to undergo medical treatment, probation was not intended to be used this way. Instead, it was hoped that medical treatments could provide a more long-term solution to stop men committing sexual assaults, or failing that, that probation officers themselves might be able to reform men without the need for medical intervention. Indeed, some of the psychiatric treatments that were provided by medical professionals, especially those relating to psychotherapy, were not too dissimilar from the methods that were used by probation officers to rehabilitate offenders. Roger Davidson, for example, has shown that some of the therapies used in the Jordanburn Nerve Hospital in Edinburgh involved more basic 'support and counselling' to help homosexual men 'readjust' their behaviour.[112] These methods were remarkably similar to those used by probation officers. For instance, both psychiatrists and probation officers provided men with advice and support which 'centred on efforts to encourage patients to regularize [his] social and work life', which in some cases meant helping men find new jobs or hobbies.[113] As we have seen in the previous chapters, probation officers' background in philanthropy and their training in social work and the behavioural sciences meant that they were able to provide a wide range of supportive services, including both practical help and a form of counselling that could be described as a lay person's version of talking-therapy.

However, before ending this section on indecent assault, it is important to point out that many of the men who were convicted of assaulting children were sent to prison and that probation (in theory at least) was only meant to be used in limited suitable cases. For example, in June 1949 thirty-three-year-old Harold G. was sent to prison for three months at Wells Magistrates Court after pleading guilty to indecently assaulting an eight-year-old boy in a cinema.[114] While the defence tried to persuade the judge to place Harold G. on probation because 'he had not previously been in trouble' and had 'had a hard life, of the institutional type', the magistrate insisted that a prison sentence was necessary because 'he was a danger to children' and that 'if treatment was required he could get it in prison'.[115] Similarly, the case of a nineteen-year-old labourer named John W., who was found guilty at East Kent Quarter Assizes of indecently assaulting an eight-year-old girl in January 1943, provides another good example of how men who assaulted children were likely to be sent to prison, even if, as in this case, the defendant was deemed to be 'mentally defective'.[116] John W. was classified by the medical superintendent at Chatham prison as a 'high grade mental defective, though not sufficiently bad to be certified. His mental age was about ten years'.[117] Nonetheless, the judge insisted that this diagnosis did not mean he could 'escape the sentence', and he was subsequently given a six-month prison sentence with hard labour.

Indecent exposure

Indecent exposure was prosecuted under Section 4 of the Vagrancy Act 1824, which made it an offence for a man to

> wilfully openly, lewdly, and obscenely expose his person in any street, road, or public highway, or in the view thereof, or in any place of public resort, with intent to insult any female.[118]

The maximum sentence was one month of hard labour. However, men could also be placed on probation. A case described by the London magistrate Claud Mullins in his book *Law and Psychology* provides a good example of how probation was used to try to rehabilitate men who had committed this offence.[119] Mullins described the case of a man named G. D. who was convicted of indecent exposure after already having two previous convictions for the same offence. Mullins wrote how 'both the probation officer and I thought that G. D. was a challenge to us', and so Mullins was determined to find out what was causing his behaviour.[120] According to Mullins, the probation office talked with G. D. and from these discussions it became clear that marital problems were the root cause. G. D. and his wife did not want more children and were therefore practising the withdrawal method which was proving unsatisfactory for G. D. This conclusion led Mullins to place G. D. on probation, and he asked the probation officer to arrange it so that G. D. would get psychological treatment from the Institute for Scientific Treatment of Delinquents as an outpatient so that he could also keep his job during this period. The probation officer was also told to give G. D.'s wife information about a gynaecology clinic where she could get help with new contraceptive methods.[121]

Requiring men convicted of indecent exposure to undergo medical treatment in this way became more common from the 1940s onwards. For example, in October 1948 twenty-three-year-old George E. pleaded guilty to indecent exposure in front of a lady in Lichfield and was sentenced to three years on probation, with the condition that he 'received medical attention'.[122] During the trial George E.'s defence solicitor told the court that he believed it was 'a case more of a medical nature and disease than a crime', and it appears that the Lichfield magistrate agreed. In January 1950, David G. was convicted in Chester of 'indecent exposure with intent to insult a female' and was placed on probation for two years, with the condition that for the first twelve months he reside in a mental home.[123] In June 1951, twenty-one-year-old Peter M. was placed on probation in Northampton for two years after he pleaded guilty to two charges of indecent exposure. The condition of his probation was that he 'enters St. Crispin Hospital as a voluntary patient for one year'.[124] In March 1952, fifty-seven-year-old Alfred R. was placed on two years' probation in Cardiff for an offence of indecent exposure, with the condition that he should attend treatment as an outpatient at Whitchurch Hospital. Later that same year in Cardiff another man, fifty-seven-year-old Arthur F., was also placed on probation for two years after being convicted of indecent exposure. The Cardiff Probation Committee minutes recorded how Arthur F. was similarly required under the condition of the probation bond 'to attend for treatment as an outpatient at Whitchurch Hospital in Cardiff'.[125] Finally, in March 1961 seventeen-year-old egg-packer John C. was convicted of two charges of indecent exposure, placed on probation at the Taunton Magistrates Court and told to 'have hospital treatment'.[126]

The records often do not clarify the exact nature of the prescribed medical treatment. However, for a more detailed description of the type of treatment that men received at these hospitals we can again turn to Claud Mullins. His book includes several examples of cases where men had been placed on probation for indecent exposure and sent for psychiatric treatment at the Tavistock Clinic. One such case was a man named as E. F. who had been found guilty of indecent exposure. Mullins deliberated about what sentence to give E. F. and decided that he would 'rather hand him over to a psychologist than inflict punishment on him, but I could only do the former if he was frank and wanted to be cured'.[127] According to Mullins, E. F. did express a willingness to go for treatment, and a subsequent assessment at the Tavistock Clinic found that he was 'very self-conscious and his behaviour was a way to compensate for his inferiority complex'.[128] The aim of the treatment, therefore, would be to help him get rid of his feelings of inferiority. Mullins consequently decided to place him on probation for a year, with the requirement that he undertook psychotherapy at the Tavistock Clinic for three months. During the year-long probation E. F. reported regularly to his probation officer, and there was apparently 'good teamwork between the probation officer, clinic, panel doctor and hospital'.[129] After his period of probation expired, E. F. continued to visit the clinic for another nine months, and in total he attended the clinic twenty-nine times. Mullins concluded that this case was a success because after six and a half years E. F. still had not reoffended.[130]

Not all magistrates, judges, JPs, probation officers and doctors took indecent exposure so seriously, however, and many men who were found guilty of this offence were not required to undergo medical treatment. For example, in April 1950 thirty-six-year-old John T. pleaded guilty at Halifax Borough Court to indecently exposing himself to a ten-year-old girl and was placed on probation for twelve months without any extra conditions.[131] In October 1952, twenty-one-year-old Peter N. was found guilty of indecent assault in Lincoln and placed on probation for two years – the only condition of his probation bond being that 'he should pull himself together'.[132] Even if a magistrate did consider the offence to be serious, they still might place men on probation without any requirements of medical treatment. For example, in November 1960 a twenty-year-old man named Bernard A. was convicted of indecently exposing himself to young girls. An article about the case in the *Taunton Courier and Western Advertiser* described how the magistrate told the defendant that 'this is a serious offence for which you should be sent to prison, and unless it stops you certainly will be'.[133] Placing a first-time offender on probation was fairly common practice. However, in this case Bernard A. had previously been on probation in 1958 after a conviction for assaulting females. Why the magistrate nevertheless gave him another chance to undergo probation is somewhat unclear, but perhaps this reflects the fact that indecent exposure was not considered as grave an offence as indecent assault.[134]

A case from the memoir of Sewell Stoke, a probation officer in London during the 1940s, provides another example of how indecent exposure was not necessarily seen as a serious offence. Stoke recalls the case of a seventy-three-year-old man named Mr Brown who had been convicted of indecent exposure. He was remanded in custody for a week and required to get a medical report to see 'what could be done to dampen down the passion roused in him by the sight of young women'.[135] When explaining the case Stokes described how 'poor Mr Brown ... was as much to be pitied ... he was the victim of his social environment ... I'm afraid my sympathy was more for him than for the young woman he'd insulted'.[136] Stokes also recalled how the doctor said that 'these old gentlemen just will do these things and really there isn't much you, or I, can do about it. But of course I'll go over Mr Brown and put something on paper for you to show your magistrate'.¹³⁷ Both the probation officer and the doctor seemed sympathetic towards Mr Brown and did not see his behaviour as dangerous. It could be argued, therefore, that probation in this case was being used as a 'let off'. However, not everyone viewed these men with pity and for repeat offenders especially, the sentence could involve imprisonment. For example, in November 1942 thirty-seven-year-old Cyril M. was found guilty of indecent exposure on a London bus. Prior to this conviction he had been charged with three similar offences and placed on probation for twelve months. Probation in this instance had clearly failed, and so the magistrate sentenced him to six weeks' imprisonment with hard labour.¹³⁸

How successful was probation?

The level of faith those within the medical establishment and the criminal justice system had in the ability of medicine to 'cure' sexual deviancy was varied. Some certainly did believe that it was possible to 'cure' these men or at least to subdue their sexual impulses. As we have seen, the Magistrate Claud Mullins was particularly optimistic about the ability of psychiatrists to cure sexual deviancy and his book *Law and Psychology* includes many examples of how psychiatric treatment was successful in a wide range of cases. For example, he described the case of a twenty-six-year-old man named T. U. who was convicted of indecent exposure and placed on probation with the requirement to undergo psychological treatment. Mullins wrote how, after several months of treatment, the doctor reported 'that there seemed to be a complete absence of desire in T. U. to repeat his offences'.¹³⁹ Mullins also noted how, at the end of the probation period, T. U. 'seemed happier and more confident. He professed gratitude for what had been done for him and even sent a message of thanks to me'.¹⁴⁰ In another example, Mullins described the case of a man named as J. K. who was convicted of soliciting for immoral purposes in a public place. According to the psychiatrist, the man was completely cured of his homosexual desire after attending a clinic for psychoanalysis sessions over a six-month period. Mullins further noted how 'J. K. tells me that there is no sort of homosexual desire or interest and that he is quite confident that it is finished'.¹⁴¹ Mullins supported this statement with the fact that '4 years later there were still no further convictions'.¹⁴²

Mullins was not the only one who trusted that psychiatry could help these men to stop offending. An example of the faith that was placed in the power of psychiatrists to 'cure' men can also be seen in a case that was recorded in the Cardiff Probation Committee minutes. In September 1953, forty-four-year-old Eric C., who had been placed on probation for indecently assaulting a boy, was declared 'cured' by the psychiatrist who was treating him as an outpatient. This diagnosis meant that his probation order was discharged, and he subsequently went on to find a new job as an organist at a church in Grimsby.[143] Considering the fact that this man was allowed to go and work in an environment where children were present, the Cardiff Probation Committee certainly placed a lot of trust in the diagnosis of the psychiatrist that he was cured. From today's perspective, placing so much faith in a diagnosis made by one expert without other safeguarding measures seems problematic.

However, despite the optimism shown by some probation officers, judges and magistrates, and a handful of examples of 'successful' cases, the extent to which probation and medical treatment were able to rehabilitate men is less clear. The probation records and newspaper reports reveal very little about the long-term effectiveness of the treatments that men were given. However, later studies have shown that treatment was often largely ineffective, and the best that most doctors hoped for was that the patient might be able to control and subdue his sexual urges. For example, a study by Smith et al. on the experiences of patients given aversion therapy during the 1960s has shown that none of the participants in the study found that the treatment had been effective or 'had any direct benefit'.[144] Moreover, the medical practitioners themselves were often doubtful about whether people who were forced to undergo treatment were good candidates for it because successful treatment relied on the patient wanting to be cured.[145] The threat of punishment did not provide a good enough motive for change.

The probation records do, however, provide various examples of 'unsuccessful cases', where men who were put on probation with medical treatment went on to commit further offences. The Cardiff Probation Case Committee minutes include several examples of men who broke their probation bonds and were subsequently sent to prison. For example, in April 1951 William M. was placed on probation for two years for an offence of indecent exposure. However, in September of that year he was sentenced to six months' imprisonment for a further offence of indecent exposure. The doctor at the Whitchurch Hospital where William M. was being treated during his probation period stated that 'no useful purpose could be served by psychiatric treatment as M. had not co-operated in the past'.[146] Similarly, thirty-two-year-old Patrick B. was placed on probation in Cardiff for three years in 1952 for an offence of indent assault. He appeared before the court again in July 1953 for the offence of distributing indecent postcards on an omnibus and was sentenced to three months' imprisonment. The probation records describe how Patrick B. was of 'weak mentality and had been unemployed for some time. He was then certified as a mental defective and the probation order was dismissed'.[147]

Examples of unsuccessful cases from other areas of the country include that of thirty-year-old Alec P., who was convicted of importuning for immoral purposes at London's Bow Street Magistrates in August 1954 and placed on probation for three years. However, in December 1955 he broke his probation bond after being found guilty of gross indecency at the Warwick Assizes and was given an eighteen-month prison sentence. The judge in this case described how Alec P. 'had his chance and he and others like him who came back to the court must be dealt with severely … You committed this horrible offence and now you must face the penalty'.[148] Similarly, in November 1953 at Luton Juvenile Borough Court a sixteen-year-old 'youth' pleaded guilty to indecently assaulting a five-year-old boy. During the trial it was reported that the defendant was currently still on probation for a similar previous offence he had committed in December 1951.[149]

In cases of gross indecency between consenting adult men, the main dangers associated with the use of probation and medical treatment were to the men themselves, who suffered from the side effects of the treatments. In particular, hormone treatment and aversion therapy could have significantly harmful physical and psychological side effects, as men were forced to repress their sexual desires and take medicines which could result in them developing feminine physical characteristics. A study by Tommy Dickenson et al. has shown that the aversion treatment received by these men was akin to torture. One man interviewed for the study described his experience in detail:

> I can still taste the vile taste of stale sick in my mouth. All I wanted was to wash my mouth out with fresh water, but I wasn't even allowed that. I remember trying to sneak out of my 'prison cell' one night to get some water, but the nurses caught me and literally threw me back in. I was not allowed out for three days. I went to the toilet in the bed; I had no basin, no toilet facilities – nothing. I had to lie in my own faeces, urine and vomit. I thought I must be dreaming at one point, it was like a barbaric torture scene by the Gestapo in Nazi Germany trying to extract information from me – I thought I was going to die.[150]

It is difficult, therefore, not to see this type of 'barbaric torture' as a form of punishment not treatment. Moreover, a study by Smith et al. that was based on interviews with men who had undergone this treatment concluded that most of the men 'were left feeling emotionally distressed'.[151] Today this type of forced medical treatment is viewed as unethical, especially in situations where it is used to try and 'cure' homosexuality, which is no longer seen as a crime or an illness. However, during the period under study homosexuality was illegal, and some saw probation with medical treatment as a more humane option than sending men to prison.

In cases of indecent assault, the fact that probation and medical treatments were unable to stop men from reoffending could have serious consequences for people other than the defendant because the public was put at risk. This was particularly worrying considering that many of these men's victims were children. For example, in October 1960 thirty-six-year-old Ernest J. was sentenced to six months' imprisonment at Birkenhead Magistrates Court after being found guilty of inciting nine-year-old girls to commit acts of gross indecency. The report about that case in the *Liverpool Echo*, however, noted that the defendant had 'five previous convictions for indecent offences and was at present on probation for one of them. He had been receiving medical treatment'.[152] Clearly then, probation and medical treatment had been ineffective, and this failure had resulted in further girls being assaulted.

Another case that highlights the dangers associated with trusting the effectiveness of probation to stop men from sexually assaulting women and children is that of a forty-four-year-old teacher named George M., from Preston who was found guilty of indecently assaulting boys between the ages of ten and twelve.[153] George M. was placed on probation for three years in October 1957, under the terms that he had to live and work where the probation officer directed and he was not allowed to take any teaching post again. During the trial it became clear that George M. had a long history of offending and that he had previously voluntarily undergone medical treatment between 1950 and 1952. However, this medical treatment had clearly not stopped him from committing further offences, and in June 1956 he was suspended from his post at a school after one of the boys made a complaint about him. A warrant was made for his arrest, but he disappeared to France until later that year, when he was found in London teaching under a new name. Prior to this, George M. had also been convicted of two other similar offences, one in Trinidad in 1942 which resulted in a three-month hard labour sentence, and another in 1944 when he was convicted in Derby for indecently assaulting a male person and sentenced to four years' penal servitude.

The condition in George M's bond that he must not work with children was in theory meant to help protect children from him. However, as Bingham et al. have shown, the system of black-listing teachers who committed sexual offences was insufficient and did not include private schools or a system which would allow for the national cross-checking of past convictions.[154] This meant that once a man's probation period had ended it would have been difficult to stop him from returning to the classroom in a private school in another part of the country. Apparently, this was exactly what George M. did, with the records showing that he had previously taught at schools in Buenos Aires, Barcelona, Tangier, Port of Spain and all over Britain despite his previous convictions. Placing George M. on probation, given his previous record, seems dangerously irresponsible. However, the fact that he had already undergone four years of penal servitude shows that imprisonment had also failed to reform him and that it was not necessarily a good long-term solution either. Crucially, however, George M. did not pose a risk to children while he was in prison.

Opinions of the probationers

As we have seen in the previous chapters, learning about the opinions and experiences of the probationers themselves is difficult due to the nature of the sources available. However, there are some fragments of information that can be gleaned from the legal records and newspaper reports relating to the court cases. Many of the lawyers who were tasked with defending men accused of gross indecency tried to persuade the judge that probation was an appropriate sentence. To support their appeals for clients to be placed on probation, lawyers often emphasized the alleged medical conditions of their clients and argued that treatment would be the best option for them and society. For example, returning to the case of sixty-one-year-old John B., who was convicted of gross indecency with a fifteen-year-old boy at Derbyshire Quarter Sessions in January 1952, John B.'s lawyer described how 'in his opinion, John B. was a man suffering from a medical disorder ... The public interest would be better served if this man were rehabilitated rather than sent to prison, and on this ground he asked for the court's leniency'.[155] Similarly, the defence lawyer in another case referred to earlier, that of Kenneth W., who was convicted of gross indecency in 1957, also asked for his client 'to be given the chance of treatment because prison often aggravates these tendencies in a man'.[156] The solicitor justified this request on the grounds that he had 'a psychiatrist's report that W. might be cured under treatment'.[157] The lawyers in these cases clearly saw probation, even if it entailed undergoing medical treatment, as a sentencing option that was preferable to prison, and presumably the defendants had agreed to this approach.

However, whether the men themselves felt probation was preferable to prison is less clear, and it is possible that some men were persuaded to agree to probation by their lawyers. This type of persuasion can be seen in the case of a man called T. U., who was convicted of indecent exposure and had agreed to undergo medical treatment as part of his probation order. In his description of the case, Mullins admits that 'the solicitor in private conversation told me that it was only with considerable difficulty that he persuaded T. U. to realize that the facts involved the necessity for treatment'.[158] Mullins saw little problem with this persuasion and justified it by the fact that 'at the end of the probation period T. U. seemed happier and more confident. He professed gratitude for what had been done for him and even sent a message of thanks to me'.[159] In Mullins's reading of the events, the end justified the means.

Mullins's enthusiasm for medical treatment may well have coloured his reading of this case. Nonetheless, there are some examples where the men themselves did appear to want to be placed on probation and 'cured'. For example, in February 1939 thirty-three-year-old Arthur W. pleaded guilty to attempting to procure the commission of an act of gross indecency after he was caught by the police in a public toilet. According to the *Essex Newsman*, Arthur W. told the police officer who arrested him that 'I don't know why I do it. I shall have to see a specialist'.[160] During the trial it was reported that Arthur W. made a statement detailing how he 'was extremely sorry, and would like to go in for some treatment'.[161] The defence also told the court that Arthur W. had previously voluntarily been to one of the 'foremost institutions for the treatment of this type of abnormality'.[162] Despite Arthur W's alleged enthusiasm for medical treatment, the chairman said that the most lenient sentence he could impose was six months of hard labour, with the promise to draw the attention of the prison commissioners to the matter of special medical treatment and observation.[163]

For men like Arthur W. who were convicted of homosexual offences involving consenting adults, agreeing to medical treatment was the only way to avoid prison. This type of reasoning can be seen in the interviews that were conducted by Tommy Dickinson et al. with men who underwent medical treatment in connection to the offence of gross indecency. In one interview, a man identified as Male 3 described how he agreed to undergo medical treatment purely to avoid a prison sentence:

> Well when I was given the option, prison or hospital, well I just thought if I go to prison … if the other inmates found out what I was in there for, well, I just thought they would kill me! I mean, I was fairly accepting of my sexuality, but in society and particularly within a prison, it was viewed in the same light as a

paedophile. No, I'm not going to prison, that is all I could think. So I just said, 'Yeah, I'll go to hospital for the aversion therapy.' It knew it was not going to make me straight, I didn't want it to, but it seemed a better option than prison.[164]

That this man did not want to be cured of homosexuality was understandable, given his acceptance of his own sexuality.

However, the situation may have been different in cases where men were convicted of assaults that caused harm to the victims, unlike in cases of consensual sex between adults. These men may have wanted to be 'cured' so that they would not be responsible for causing more harm. Indeed, the cases in which men were most enthusiastic about medical treatment were often those relating to situations where children had been assaulted. For example, twenty-four-year-old Kenneth B., who had been convicted of indecently assaulting a girl under fourteen, specifically 'suggested an operation on himself' to solve the problem.[165] However, the judge in this case said that this was not possible and sentenced him to twelve months in prison. A more detailed example can be seen in the case of thirty-one-year-old Kenneth K. from Worthing who was convicted of assaulting young boys in a choir. He too asked for an operation and his lawyer said that he had been diagnosed by Dr Smith as a 'homosexual psychopath' that needed psychiatric treatment because it was the 'last chance for him to become a respectable citizen'.[166] According to the coverage of the case in the *Worthing Herald*, Kenneth K. told the court how

> these offences have only occurred since my ill-health. If there is any treatment I can have, especially operative, I should be most willing to co-operate, as I should like to rid myself of these awful ways which sometimes prevent my being a decent citizen.[167]

The article went on to describe how prior to the trial Kenneth K. had attempted suicide 'by striking his head with a candlestick and taking two pheno-barbitone tablets'.[168] While avoiding prison was certainly a concern, the report about his testimony during the trial does suggest that he wanted to be placed on probation in order to receive medical treatment which would stop him from reoffending. The judge agreed that this would be the best course of action and placed him on probation for three years under the condition that he received psychological treatment.

Another example of a man wanting medical treatment is that of George M., a school teacher, who was found guilty at the Somerset Quarter Session in February 1957 of indecently assaulting boys at a school in Bridgewater. According to an article about the trial in the *Somerset County Herald*, George M.

was reported to have said: 'Do you realise the great unhappiness this affliction brings to a man? I would do anything in the world to co-operate and get rid of it.'[169] George M. subsequently agreed to undergo medical treatment. Similarly, in a case from December 1943, nineteen-year-old Leonard M. reported himself to an NSPCC officer and told him that he 'wanted to be sent away to be cured'.[170] The NSPCC officer, in turn, contacted a probation officer because Leonard M. had previously been sentenced to three months' imprisonment after being convicted of indecent exposure in June.[171] On that occasion Leonard M. had been assessed by a prison doctor and classified as a 'border line mental defective'.[172] Based on that assessment, the doctor determined that 'certification as a mental defective was hardly justified at this present stage' and that 'medical advice and probation supervision would enable the accused to adjust himself'.[173] However, on examining the man again in December 1943 the prison doctor concluded that he was 'certifiable as a mental defective'.[174] The magistrate therefore decided that Leonard M. should be sent to a mental institution, meaning that his wish 'to be sent away' was fulfilled.

Whether men like George M. and Leonard M. genuinely wanted the treatment in order to be 'cured' or simply to avoid prison is hard to know, given the available source material. In some situations, men may have at first accepted probation primarily to avoid prison but then become more receptive to therapy as time progressed. For example, the minutes of the Rossendale Probation Case Committee include details about the case of a thirty-six-year-old man named John C. who was placed on probation in 1953 for indecent assault. The minutes describe how 'at first C did not appreciate probation and would not report, but now reports regularly and tells me all about his troubles at home with his wife and her brother'.[175] However, without asking the men themselves it is difficult to know how they really felt about probation and medical treatment, and unfortunately there have been no interviews undertaken with people that received medical treatment as part of a sentence for indecent assault or indecent exposure.

The legal records and newspapers do, however, include some evidence which suggests that not all men were so cooperative in following the conditions of their probation bonds, and there were several examples of men refusing to undergo medical treatment. This was true in the case of David L. who was placed on probation in February 1957 for an unspecified 'homosexual offence'.[176] The minutes on the Rossendale Probation Committee described how this was his fourth conviction for 'homosexuality', and he was required to undertake treatment at Bury Hospital during his probation period. However, the doctor treating David L. told the probation committee that the patient was not responding to treatment because 'he had no desire to co-operate'.[177] Similarly, the case of twenty-five-year-old Charles T. shows how men could follow the letter of the law without necessarily committing to the rehabilitation process. In July 1950, Charles T. was convicted at Wiltshire Quarter Sessions of indecently assaulting a young boy whom he had given a lift on his bicycle and offered money.[178] During the trial the defence counsel tried to convince the judge that probation with medical treatment would be an appropriate sentence. However, as Charles T. had previously been placed on probation for three years because of a previous indecent assault conviction, the judge decided to give him a twelve-month prison sentence to 'protect children' from him.[179] During the decision-making process the probation officer was asked by the judge to detail Charles T.'s behaviour during his previous probation period. The officer admitted that Charles T. followed the rules of his probation order, but that he 'felt anxious about him, although it's difficult to give a reason why'.[180] Although Charles T. originally cooperated and received treatment, the probation officer's hunch that something was not quite right proved correct when Charles T. went on to commit another offence. Charles T.'s dismissive statement that he thought 'the treatment achieved nothing' appears to have been accurate in this case.[181]

Conclusion

The use of probation in cases of male sexual offences provides another example of how probation was used to try to change men's behaviour. As was the case with domestic violence, probation was intended as a method for curing the underlying problems that caused men's deviant behaviour, thus ensuring more long-term protection for women and children. The key difference between the approach used to rehabilitate men convicted of domestic violence and sexual offences, however, was that sexual deviancy was more medicalized. This meant that from the late 1930s onwards, men convicted of gross indecency, indecent assault and indecent exposure were increasingly likely to be required to undergo medical treatment to 'cure' their deviant sexual behaviour. For some men, especially during the 1940s and early 1950s, this treatment involved psychoanalysis and/or hormone therapy, and for other men, particularly from the late 1950s onwards, it could also involve aversion therapy. That these men were required to undergo psychiatric or medical treatment meant that the approach used to reform male sexual offenders on probation shared some similarities with the methods used to treat people who had attempted suicide. In both cases probation was used as a way to ensure people received medical treatment without necessitating that they be officially certified as insane.

While some within the criminal justice system were optimistic about the potential that probation and medical treatment had for successfully 'curing' men, others were less convinced. The limitations of the source materials mean that it is difficult to assess how successful particular treatments were in changing men's sexual behaviour and stopping them from reoffending. However, more recent research has shown that medical interventions to change men's sexuality often had poor results.[182] At best, some treatments may have been able to subdue men's libidos or taught them how not to act on their desires. At worst, it could have serious negative psychological and physiological side effects. Crucially, however, successful treatment required the cooperation of the men involved, and this was not always forthcoming. Although some men voiced their preference for probation and medical treatment in the courtroom, it is difficult to know how the men felt in private because of the types of sources available. The fact that the alternative to probation was imprisonment would certainly have played a role in their acceptance of probation with the condition of receiving treatment. However, without talking to the men themselves it is difficult to know the extent to which they really engaged with the treatments.

Not all men, however, were required to undergo medical treatment, and the use of probation without the requirement for medical treatment meant that these men endured less intervention into their private lives. In certain circumstances, therefore, probation could sometimes be used as a means to 'let off' men that were otherwise considered respectable and/or 'less guilty', perceptions of which were linked to class, age and gender prejudices surrounding the 'character' of both the defendant and the victim. Nor was it only the opinion of the JP, magistrate or judge that mattered. By undertaking 'social investigations' and providing a report about the offender's background and character, the probation officer's opinion of the offender also played an important role in this decision-making process.

The high levels of discretion in the sentencing process meant that the attitudes of individual magistrates, judges, JPs and probation officers towards psychiatry and sexuality, and their perceptions about the 'character' of the defendant and the victim, were instrumental in determining whether or not probation was used as a way to 'cure' men or to let them off. In cases of gross indecency involving consensual sex between adult men, the consequences of probation being used to 'let off' men were potentially positive from today's perspective because it meant that men could escape both prison and medical treatment, although class-based prejudice meant that working-class men were less likely to benefit from this policy. However, using probation as a 'let off' had far more serious consequences in cases of indecent assault and indecent exposure because it potentially meant the offenders faced fewer obstacles to the abuse of future victims.

Notes

1   Joanna Bourke, *Rape: A History from 1860 to the Present Day* (Virago, 2007); Alyson Brown et al., *Knowledge of Evil: Child Prostitution and Child Sexual Abuse in Twentieth Century England* (Cullompton, 2002); H. G. Cocks and Matt Houlbrook (eds), *Palgrave Advances in the Modern History of Sexuality* (Palgrave Macmillan, 2006); Roger Davidson and Gayle Davis, *The Sexual State: Sexuality and Scottish Governance* (Edinburgh University Press, 2012); Roger Davidson, *Dangerous Liaisons: A Social History of Venereal Disease in Twentieth-Century Scotland* (Amsterdam, 2000); Shanni D'Cruze, *Crimes of Outrage: Sex, Violence and Victorian Working Women* (Northern Illinois University Press, 1998); Shanni D'Cruze, 'Approaching the History of Rape and Sexual Violence: Notes towards Research', *Women's History Review*, 1 (1992), pp. 377–97; Shanni D'Cruze, 'Sexual Violence in History: A Contemporary Heritage?' in Jennifer Brown and Sandra Walklate (eds), *Handbook on Sexual Violence* (Routledge, 2012); Alkarim Jivani, *It's Not Unusual: A History of Lesbian and Gay Britain in the Twentieth Century* (Indiana University Press, 1997); Cate Haste, *Rules of Desire: Sex in Britain: World War 1 to the Present* (Vintage, 1992); Brian Lewis, *Wolfenden's Witnesses: Homosexuality in Post-War Britain* (Palgrave Macmillan, 2016); Patrick Higgins, *Heterosexual Dictatorship: Male Homosexuality in Post-War Britain* (Fourth Estate, 1996); Matt Houlbrook, *Queer London: Perils and Pleasures in the Sexual Metropolis, 1918–1957* (University of Chicago Press, 2005); Louise Jackson, 'Family, Community and the Regulation of Sexual Abuse: London 1870–1914', in A. Fletcher and S. Hussey (eds), *Childhood in Question: Children, Parents and the State* (Manchester University Press, 1999); Carol Smart, 'Reconsidering the Recent History of Child Sexual Abuse, 1910–1960', *Journal of Social Policy*, 29 (2000), pp. 55–71; Simon Watney, *Policing Desire: Pornography, Aids and the Media* (Bloomsbury, 1987); Jeffrey Weeks, *Sex. Politics and Society: The Regulation of Sexuality since 1800*, 4th edition (Routledge, 2018); Janet Weston, *Medicine, the Penal System and Sexual Crimes in England, 1919–1960s* (Bloomsbury, 2017).
2   Harry Oosterhuis, *Stepchildren of Nature*; *Krafft-Ebing, Psychiatry, and the Making of Sexual Identity* (Chicago, 2000); Anna Katharina Schaffner, *Modernism and*

Perversion: Sexual Deviance in Sexology and Literature, 1850–1930 (Basingstoke: Palgrave Macmillan, 2011).

3 Matt Cook, *A Gay History of Britain: Love and Sex between Men since the Middle Ages* (Oxford University Press, 2007).

4 Kenneth Lewes, *The Psychoanalytic Theory of Male Homosexuality* (Simona and Schuster, 1988).

5 For a more detailed discussion about the medical treatment of sexual offenders in prisons, see Weston, *Medicine, the Penal System and Sexual Crimes in England, 1919–1960s* (location 2376 kindle edition).

6 Criminal Justice Administration Act, 1914 (4 & 5 Geo. 5.).

7 Lancashire Archives, PSRd/2/2: Rossendale Probation Case Committee, Rossendale Probation Committee minutes, October 1952–April 1954.

8 F. L. Golla and R. Sessions Hodge, 'Hormone Treatment of the Sexual Offender', *The Lancet*, 11, 1 (1949).

9 Roger Davidson, 'Psychiatry and Homosexuality in Mid-Twentieth-Century Edinburgh: The View from Jordanburn Nerve Hospital', *History of Psychiatry*, 20, 4 (2009), pp. 403–24, p. 407.

10 Andrew Hodges, *Alan Turing: The Enigma, The Centenary Edition* (Princeton University Press, 2012).

11 Ibid.

12 For more on the history of psychoanalysis in Britain, see, for example, Philip Kuhn, *Psychoanalysis in Britain, 1893–1913: Histories and Historiography* (Lexington Books, 2017); R. D. Hinshelwood, 'The Organizing of Psychoanalysis in Britain', *Psychoanalysis and History*, 1, 1 (1999), pp. 87–102.

13 Claud Mullins, *Crime and Psychology* (Methuen, 1943), p. 79.

14 Ibid.

15 Mullins, *Crime and Psychology*, p. 80.

16 Ibid.

17 Chris Waters, 'Havelock Ellis, Sigmund Freud and the State: Discourses of Homosexual Identity in Interwar Britain', in Lucy Bland and Laura Doan (eds), *Sexology Culture: Labelling Bodies and Desires* (Polity Press, 1998), pp. 165–80.

18 Tommy Dickinson, Matt Cook, John Playle and Christine Hallett, 'Queer' Treatments: Giving a Voice to Former Patients who Received Treatments for Their 'Sexual Deviations', *Journal of Clinical Nursing*, 21, 9–10 (2012), pp. 1345–54.

19 Glen Smith, Michael King and Annie Bartlett, 'Treatments of Homosexuality in Britain since the 1950s – An Oral History: The Experience of Patients', *British Medical Journal* 328, 7437 (2004), pp. 1–3, p. 1; Glen Smith, Michael King and Annie Bartlett, 'Treatments of Homosexuality in Britain since the 1950s – An Oral History: The Experience of Professionals', *British Medical Journal* 328, 7437 (2004), pp. 328–429.

20 Davidson, 'Psychiatry and homosexuality'.

21 Tommy Dickinson, 'Mental Nursing and "Sexual Deviation": Exploring the Role of Nurses and the Experience of Patients, 1935–1974' (PhD Dissertation, University of Manchester, 2012).
22 The Sexual Offences Act 1967 (Eliz. II c.60). Similar provisions for Scotland were not granted until the Criminal Justice (Scotland) Act 1980 (Eliz. II c.62).
23 Criminal Law Amendment Act 1885 (48 & 49 Vict. c.69). The Act was repealed in 1956 by Section 13 of the Sexual Offences Act and for Scotland by section 21(2) of the Sexual Offences (Scotland) Act 1976.
24 Vagrancy Act 1898 (61 & 62 Vict. c.39).
25 Jeffrey Weeks, *Coming Out: Homosexual Politics in Britain from the Nineteenth Century to the Present* (Quartet, 1990).
26 The Offences against the Person Act 1861 (24 & 25 Vict. c.100).
27 For a more detailed discussion on attitudes towards homosexuality and the law during this period, see, for example, Houlbrook, *Queer London*; Jivani, *It's Not Unusual*; Jeffrey Weeks, *Sex Politics and Society: The Regulation of Sexuality since 1800* (London, 1989); Roger Davidson and Gayle Davis, 'A Field for Private Members': The Wolfenden Committee and Scottish Homosexual Law Reform, 1950-67', *Twentieth Century British History*, 15 (2004), pp. 174–201.
28 Lindesay Neustatter, 'Homosexuality: The Medical Perspective', in Tudor Rees and Harley Usill (eds), *They Stand Apart: A Critical Survey of the Problem of Homosexuality* (London, 1955).
29 *Birmingham Daily Post*, 9 April 1954, p. 7.
30 Home Office and Scottish Office, Report of the Committee on Homosexual Offences and Prostitution (1957).
31 Dickinson, 'Mental Nursing', p. 110.
32 The Sexual Offences Act 1967 (Eliz. II c.60). Similar provisions for Scotland were not granted until the Criminal Justice (Scotland) Act 1980 (Eliz. II c.62).
33 *West Sussex Gazette*, 20 April 1944, p. 3.
34 *Central Somerset Gazette*, 19 August 1949, p. 1.
35 *Ripley and Heanor News and Ilkeston Division Free Press*, 20 June 1952, p. 3.
36 *The Londonderry Sentinel*, 11 September 1954, p. 5.
37 *Buckinghamshire Examiner*, 4 October 1957, p. 10.
38 *Coventry Evening Telegraph*, 13 March 1957, p. 5.
39 Davidson, 'Psychiatry and Homosexuality', p. 405.
40 *Lakes Herald*, 13 March 1908, p. 2.
41 Ibid.
42 *Nottingham Evening Post*, 7 July 1926, p. 1.
43 *Dundee Evening Telegraph*, 28 January 1938, p. 9.
44 Ibid.
45 Ibid.

46 Michael Schofield, *Society and the Homosexual* (Dutton, 1952), p. 168.
47 Roger Davidson, *Illicit and Unnatural Practices: The Law, Sex and Society in Scotland since 1900* (Edinburgh University Press, 2018), pp. 135–6.
48 The National Archives, Public Record Office, Kew [hereafter PRO], HO345/9, Proceedings of the Wolfenden Committee on Homosexual Offences and Prostitution, Summary Record of 21st Meeting, March 1956, as cited in Davidson, *Illicit and Unnatural Practices*, p. 130.
49 *Chelsea News and General Advertiser*, 3 November 1944, p. 3.
50 *Suffolk and Essex Free Press*, 28 October 1943, p. 8.
51 *The Staffordshire Advertiser,* 12 October 1946, p. 7.
52 Ibid.
53 Ibid.
54 John Lunan, 'Probation Officers, Social Enquiry Reports, and Importuning in the 1960s', *The Historical Journal*, 56, 3 (2013), pp. 781–800.
55 Ibid.
56 Ibid.
57 Ibid.
58 For further discussion on social class and psychiatry, see Petteri Pietikainen and Jesper Vaczy Kragh (eds), *Social Class and Mental Illness in Northern Europe* (Routledge, 2019).
59 *Kington Times*, 18 November 1950, p. 3.
60 Ibid.
61 *Worthing Herald,* 12 April 1957, p. 1.
62 Ibid.
63 Ibid.
64 Lunan, 'Probation Officers, Social Enquiry Reports, and Importuning in the 1960s', p. 782.
65 Offences against the Person Act 1861 (24 & 25 Vict. c.100).
66 The Sexual Offences Act 1956 (4 & 5 Eliz.2 c.69).
67 *Chelmsford Chronicle*, 26 July 1940, p. 3.
68 Ibid.
69 Ibid.
70 *The Western Morning News*, 9 April 1949, p. 3.
71 *Lincolnshire Echo*, 18 April 1950, p. 6.
72 Ibid.
73 *Western Mail*, 28 June 1957, p. 7.
74 The Children's and Young Persons Act 1908 (Geo V. c.67).
75 Weston, *Medicine, the Penal System and Sexual Crimes in England, 1919–1960s*, p. 1052 (kindle book edition).
76 Smart, 'A History of Ambivalence and Conflict', p. 405.
77 Edinburgh City Archives, Edinburgh Police Court Records, 16 February 1919.

78 Glamorgan Archives, PSCBO/60/1: Cardiff Probation Committee Minutes, 5 October 1925.
79 *Cornishman*, 10 May 1945, p. 3.
80 *The Essex Newsman,* 22 July 1939, p. 4.
81 *The Essex Newsman*, 7 October 1939, p. 2.
82 Ibid.
83 Ibid.
84 Ibid.
85 Ibid.
86 Ibid.
87 Ibid.
88 *The Courier*, 27 January 1941, p. 5.
89 Ibid.
90 Ibid.
91 Ibid.
92 *The Bucks Herald*, 11 September 1931, p. 5.
93 Ibid.
94 *Barking, Eastham and Ilford Advertiser*, 22 February 1908, p. 3.
95 *The Luton News*, 26 November 1953, p. 4.
96 *The Bucks Herald,* 11 October 1940, p. 2.
97 Ibid.
98 Ibid.
99 *The Belper News*, 14 January 1955, p. 2.
100 Ibid.
101 Ibid.
102 Ibid.
103 For further discussion about changing attitudes towards what constituted child sexual abuse, see, for example, Carol Smart, 'A History of Ambivalence and Conflict in the Discursive Construction of the "Child Victim" of Sexual Abuse', *Social & legal studies*, 8, 3 (1999), pp. 391–409.
104 The Criminal Law Amendment Act 1885 (48 & 49 Vict. c.69).
105 Adrian Bingham, Lucy Delap, Louise Jackson and Louise Settle, 'Historical Child Sexual Abuse in England and Wales: The Role of Historians', *History of Education*, 45, 4 (2016), pp. 411–29, p. 415.
106 *The Bucks Herald*, 18 January 1935, p. 10.
107 Ibid.
108 *The Yorkshire Post,* 2 July 1934, p. 12.
109 Ibid.
110 Louise Jackson, *Child Sexual Abuse in Victorian England* (Routledge, 1999); Smart, 'A History of Ambivalence and Conflict', pp. 391–409; Linda Mahood, *Policing Gender, Class and Family, 1800–1940* (Routledge, 1995).

111 *Evening Dispatch*, 9 July 1942, p. 3.
112 Davidson, 'Psychiatry and Homosexuality', pp. 412–13.
113 Ibid.
114 *Wells Journal and Somerset and West of England Advertiser,* 17 June 1949, p. 2.
115 Ibid.
116 *The Whitstable Times and Herne Bay Herald,* 9 January 1943, p. 6.
117 Ibid.
118 The Vagrancy Act 1824 (Geo V. 4. c.83).
119 Claud Mullins, *Crime and Psychology* (London, 1943).
120 Ibid.
121 Mullins, *Crime and Psychology*, p. 92.
122 *Lichfield Mercury*, 22 October 1948, p. 8.
123 Glamorgan Archives: PSCBO/60/5: Cardiff Probation Committee Minutes, 25 January 1950.
124 *Northampton Mercury,* 15 June 1951, p. 2.
125 Glamorgan Archives: PSCBO/60/5 Cardiff Probation Committee Minutes, 26 March 1952.
126 *Taunton Courier and Western Advertiser,* 18 March 1961, p. 6.
127 Mullins, *Crime and Psychology*, p. 70.
128 Ibid., p. 71.
129 Ibid.
130 Ibid.
131 *Halifax Evening Courier*, 26 April 1950, p. 5.
132 *Louth and North Lincolnshire Advertiser,* 11 October 1952, p. 2.
133 *Taunton Courier and Western Advertiser,* 12 November 1960, p. 3
134 Ibid.
135 Sewell Stoke, *Court Circular: Experiences of a London Probation Officer* (Michael Joseph, 1950), p. 28.
136 Ibid.
137 Ibid.
138 *The Bucks Herald,* 6 November 1942, p. 8.
139 Mullins, *Crime and Psychology*, p. 90.
140 Ibid., p. 91.
141 Ibid.
142 Ibid. p. 78.
143 Glamorgan Archives: PSCBO/60/5: Cardiff Probation Committee Minutes, 23 September 1953.
144 Smith et al., 'Treatments of Homosexuality in Britain since the 1950s – An Oral History: The Experience of Patients', p. 3.
145 Davidson, 'Psychiatry and Homosexuality', p. 412.

146 Glamorgan Archives: PSCBO/60/5: Cardiff Probation Committee Minutes, 28 May 1952.
147 Glamorgan Archives: PSCBO/60/5: Cardiff Probation Committee Minutes, 22 July 1953.
148 *Coventry Evening Telegraph,* 1 December 1955, p. 2.
149 *Lunton News and Bedfordshire Telegraph,* 26 November 1953, p. 4.
150 Tommy Dickinson, Matt Cook, John Playle and Christine Hallett, 'Queer' Treatments: Giving a Voice to Former Patients who Received Treatments for Their 'Sexual Deviations', *Journal of Clinical Nursing,* 21, 9 (2012), pp. 1345–54.
151 Smith et al., 'Treatments of Homosexuality in Britain since the 1950s – An Oral History', p. 1.
152 *Liverpool Echo,* 19 October 1960, p. 20.
153 Lancashire Archives, CC/PNM/1: Lancashire Probation Committee: Minute Books, October 1957.
154 Bigham et al., 'Historical Child Sexual Abuse in England and Wales', pp. 417–18.
155 *The Bleeper News,* 14 January 1955, p. 2.
156 *Worthing Herald,* 12 April 1957, p. 1.
157 Ibid.
158 Mullins, *Crime and Psychology,* p. 90.
159 Ibid., p. 92.
160 *Essex Newsman,* 18 February 1939, p. 4.
161 Ibid.
162 Ibid.
163 *Essex Newsman,* 18 February 1939, p. 4.
164 Dickinson et al., '"Queer" treatments', p. 1349.
165 *The Bucks Herald,* 11 October 1940, p. 7.
166 *Worthing Herald,* 19 February 1954, p. 5.
167 Ibid.
168 Ibid.
169 *Somerset County Herald,* 9 February, 1957, p. 8.
170 *Rochdale Observer,* 1 December 1943, p. 2.
171 Ibid.
172 Ibid.
173 Ibid.
174 *Rochdale Observer,* 10 November 1943, p. 4.
175 Lancashire Archives, PSRd/2/2: Rossendale Probation Case Committee, July 1953.
176 Lancashire Archives, PSRd/2/2: Rossendale Probation Case Committee, February 1957.
177 Ibid.
178 *The Wiltshire Times,* 8 July 1950, p. 3.

179 Ibid.
180 Ibid.
181 Ibid.
182 Jack Drescher, 'ced*Can Sexual Orientation Be Changed?*' *Journal of Gay & Lesbian Mental Health,* 19, 1 (2015), pp. 84–93.

5

Recusing 'fallen women': Prostitution and probation

The previous chapter demonstrated the ways in which probation was used to police male 'deviant' sexual behaviour. However, it was not only men's sexual activities that were under scrutiny. Probation was also commonly used to try and reform women's sexual behaviour. In particular, probation was used to try and stop women engaging in prostitution and to save young 'good time girls' from a life of 'immorality'. It was hoped that by providing guidance and acting as a suitable role model, probation officers could steer these young women back onto the path of virtue and help them find alternative work in 'respectable' forms of employment. This chapter focuses on the use of probation in situations where women were convicted of soliciting offences and in cases of underage girls who were deemed in need of 'care and protection' under the 1908 Children Act. Whereas men placed on probation for sexual offences were increasingly given medical treatment to 'cure' their 'deviant' sexuality, women convicted of solicitation offences were more likely to be placed in a religious voluntary institution where they would receive strict supervision, moral guidance and domestic training. The chapter examines how the implementation of this system developed throughout the early to mid-twentieth century in Scotland, England and Wales, and explores the implications this had for the policing of prostitution and female sexuality.

Probation and prostitution in Scotland

Although prostitution has never been illegal anywhere in Britain, several acts and by-laws have been used to make various prostitution-related activities illegal, such as soliciting, brothel-keeping and living off the earnings of prostitution.[1] In Scotland the 1892 Burgh Police (Scotland) Act stipulated that to 'loiter about or importune for the purposes of prostitution' by a 'common prostitute or streetwalker' was an offence punishable by a fine of up to 40 shillings for each offence.² Individual cities within Scotland also had their own separate acts. For example, in Edinburgh, the 1879 Edinburgh Municipal and Police Act stated that the 'common prostitute' or 'night walker' who

> loiters or importunes passengers for the purposes of prostitution in or near any street or court, or any common stair or passage, or in any public park or garden, Holyrood park, or any other open space frequented by the public, shall be liable to a penalty not exceeding five pounds, or in the discretion of the judge or police, may, without a penalty being inflicted, be committed to prison for a period not exceeding that of 60 days.³

In Glasgow, the Glasgow Police (Further Powers) Act 1892 meant that women could be fined up to 40 shillings and be sentenced to prison for a period no longer than sixty days in default of payment.⁴ In addition to using fines and prison sentences, there was also considerable support for the use of probation to deal with the problem of prostitution in Scotland. As early as 1910 the Edinburgh Chief Constable, Roderick Ross, was calling for the further use of probation as a system for reducing prostitution. An article in *The Scotsman* newspaper described how Ross believed that

> a reformatory system of some kind by which women could be sent by the court to a home or institution would ... be far more beneficial, and have more lasting result for good, than turning them adrift again only to be re-arrested sooner or later with the same result – each arrest only hardens the woman, and makes her reformation almost hopeless.⁵

It was not only the Edinburgh Chief Constable who held this opinion. In 1913 two deputations to the Secretary for Scotland were made by representatives of Scottish local authorities in Edinburgh, Glasgow, Dundee, Aberdeen and Perth to request the Secretary to Scotland's 'help in regard to having greater powers for dealing with habitual offenders and convicted prostitutes'.⁶ However, they stressed that 'they did not mean by greater power, harsher power'.⁷ Instead, they wanted to deal with 'convicted prostitutes' in a 'more merciful way than under the existing system'.⁸ The deputation pointed out 'the futility of sending them to prison for short periods' and instead 'asked for power to detain girls who had been convicted and were under probation' so they could be placed in rescue homes.⁹ The Chief Constable of Dundee, John Carmichael, described how this approach was necessary because 'they had great difficulty in dealing with girls who had gone astray'.¹⁰

The Scottish authorities were able to follow through with their plan to send women to institutions, thanks to the 1914 Criminal Justice Administration Act which gave justices and magistrates the power to stipulate where a probationer must reside for the duration of the probation period.[11] This meant that a woman convicted of a soliciting offence could be required as part of her probation bond to reside in a rescue home. Subsequently, the practice of placing women convicted of prostitution offences on probation and then sending them to religious voluntary homes soon became common practice across Scotland. For example, in October 1914 Robina S. was required to reside at the Glasgow Magdalene Asylum under the supervision of the matron Miss Paterson and in 1921 Isabella T., Margaret L. and Marjory M. were all placed on probation for prostitution offences and required to reside at the Edinburgh Magdalene Asylum.[12]

The Magdalene Asylums in Edinburgh and Glasgow were frequently used as destinations for women placed on probation for prostitution offences. These institutions, founded in 1797 and 1864 respectively, were designed to rescue 'fallen women' and reform them into respectable citizens through good instruction, religious teaching, industrial training and hard work. During their stay the women were trained in domestic skills that would help them find respectable employment once they left. The women also worked (often with little payment other than bed, board and some clothes) in the institutions' commercial laundries which made a profit from their labour which was then used to subsidize the cost of running these charitable institutions. Conditions in the Magdalene Asylums could be harsh, with long days and strict rules that severely restricted the women's freedoms.[13] By the 1930s conditions did begin to become less repressive as new sources of entertainment, better food, work and living arrangements were introduced. Nonetheless, the women who were sent to reside in these institutions in accordance with the conditions of their probation bond could be required to stay there for periods between six months and two years. This meant they were incarcerated much longer than the maximum prison sentence for soliciting allowed (sixty days). Some women may have appreciated having food, shelter and an opportunity to avoid prison and find work outside of prostitution. However, the fact that women often ran away from these institutions suggests that being sent to one of these recuse homes was not necessarily seen as preferable to prostitution or prison.[14]

In addition to Magdalene Asylums, female probationers were also sent to other similar institution across Scotland, such as the Church of Scotland Home in Paisley, the Lochee Rescue Home in Dundee, the Seabank Home in Aberdeen, the Salvation Army house in Edinburgh and the Woodfield House in Colinton. Some women were even sent to several of these institutions, such as Mary B. who spent time at the Dalry Reformatory in 1915, followed by a stay at the Edinburgh Magdalene Asylum and the Seabank Home in Aberdeen in 1917.[15] The exact routines and methods these organizations used to reform and rehabilitate women differed slightly, but they all shared the similar aim of returning women to the domestic sphere as respectable, virtuous, hard-working citizens. Christianity played an important role in this mission, and the homes were either run directly by a particular Christian denomination or had strong affiliations with religious organizations.[16]

However, not everyone was in favour of sending women to reform homes. In 1919, the Glasgow Corporation published a report by the Special Committee on Probation of Offenders. The evidence given by various chief constables and probation officers from different divisions across the city show that attitudes towards the incarceration of women in reform homes were mixed. Some members were concerned that courts needed more power to force women to reside in institutions because they were unlikely to go there voluntarily. For example, point nine of the report described how

> probation in the case of inebriates, loose women, and habitual offenders is of little, if any, value without exercising the power to ensure residence under control. However repugnant to our ideals as to the liberty of the subject, it is abundantly evident that the exercise of such power is necessary in the interest of the individual and society, particularly for homeless women and for those who a severance from bad associations and surroundings alone affords any hope of reformation ... Whilst women of notoriously bad fame should be sent to suitable institutions, a separate home or house of detention should be provided for young offenders, particularly girls up to 21 years of age. ... such institutions should provide employment of an encouraging nature, and the remuneration, after lodging and board, should be more adequate to the work performed.[17]

The loss of liberty endured by these women was therefore couched in terms of being a necessary evil that was essential for the women's own protection and for the well-being of society. The recommendation that the institutions should pay women fairly to engage in work of an 'an encouraging nature' acted here as a sweetener to make this system of forced incarceration more palatable – although this recommendation was only for young women under twenty-one, the conditions of the institutions that older women of 'notorious bad fame' were sent were apparently of less concern. Joseph Paul, probation officer for Mary Hill division in Glasgow, agreed that 'the power to enforce residence in institutions, especially for women, is urgently needed'.[18] He was also keen to ensure that institutions are good – that they are not aimed at punishing the women as this is not helpful and they just turn back to their old ways upon release. Instead, they should offer useful employment, and certain wages could be obtained by persons working there, something in fact that would induce them to take an interest in their work, which would help them forget their past life.[19]

Similarly, Probation Officer Mrs Jessie Forbes bemoaned the fact that 'for women to be sent to homes they have to agree to be there a year and they are not paid. Women prefer to go to prison than do this'.[20] However, rather than using the law to force women to stay in these institutions, she preferred to try and encourage them to go voluntarily by making them more appealing places. In order to encourage women to voluntarily enter these homes and make probation more attractive, she suggested that women should be sent to 'a municipally controlled home where girls could earn small wages for services rendered and which had less strict rigid rules'.[21] Some contributors to the report were against the use of institutions all together, however. For example, the probation officer for Queens Park in Glasgow insisted that 'residence under control is prison not probation. Probation implies freedom for a woman to develop her life in her own way, with guidance and assistance from the probation officer'.[22] For this officer, letting women live independently was an essential element of the probation process. Incarceration, even in a well-ran, well-meaning institution like those described above, undermined this goal.

Despite the enthusiasm for the use of rescue homes shown by some, not all women placed on probation for prostitution-related offences were required to reside in institutions. Many women were instead allowed to reside at home and thus had a lot more freedom. This did not, however, mean that they escaped supervision altogether. As Linda Mahood has shown, probation could be used to discipline and control women in the home without the need for institutionalization.[23] The women on probation received regular visits from their probation officer whose role it was to ensure that the conditions of the probation bond were being followed. What is more, up until the late 1940s, most of these probation officers were working for, or associated with, religious voluntary organizations that ran rescue homes. For example, probation officers commonly named in probation orders for women convicted of soliciting in Edinburgh included Miss Stag from the National Vigilance Association, Miss Kiff from the Salvation Army, Miss Livingston from the Church of Scotland Shelter and Miss Margaret Copeland from the Edinburgh Magdalene Asylum. However, as the probation service increasingly professionalized the official ties with religious voluntary organizations lessened, and by the 1950s most officers were recruited from social work degree programmes and underwent training programmes designed by the Home Office and the Scottish Office.

One of the main tasks of the probation officer was to make detailed reports about the probationers' home life: their health and appearance, the cleanliness of their home, their behaviour, employment activities, and their relationships with friends and family. Based on these reports the probation officers could make recommendations designed to help them on their path to reformation. This could include finding them a new job and requiring them to refrain from alcohol or associating with certain people. The aim of this close surveillance and supervision was to ensure that women refrained from engaging in prostitution and instead remained in the domestic sphere as dutiful daughters, domestic workers, wives and mothers. Ideally, the impetus for this reformation would come from within, with women developing a new sense of self-restraint over their sexual behaviour as they adopted middle-class notions of respectable femininity promoted by the probation officer. However, if the probation officer believed that their charges were not heeding their advice or responding well to their supervision, then they could report them back to the magistrate who then could make another sentencing decision – potentially meaning that they could be sent to prison or another institution.

Probation and prostitution in England and Wales

Legislation related to prostitution in England and Wales was, like that in Scotland, focused on ensuring public order. In London the main acts that were used to prosecute street solicitation were the Vagrancy Act 1824, which made it an offence for a 'common prostitute to loiter or solicit in a street or public place for the purpose of prostitution', and the Metropolitan Police Act 1839, which made it an offence to solicit 'to the annoyance of inhabitants or passengers'.[24] Outside of London, the Town Police Clauses Act 1847 similarly made it an offence for 'common prostitutes' to assemble at any place of public resort.[25] The main difference between England and Wales on the one hand and Scotland on the other was the requirement in England and Wales to prove that solicitation had caused annoyance (although in practice the burden of proof in this regard was often very low).[26]

Julia Laite's research on prostitution in London between 1900 and 1960 has shown how a 'crack down' on street prostitution in London during this period resulted in women being forced to work in more clandestine and unsafe environments.[27] However, those who were against the criminalization and imprisonment of women involved in prostitution looked towards probation as a potential alternative way to police prostitution and help 'save' the women involved. For example, in 1912 an article published in the suffrage newspaper, *Common Cause*, made a plea that 'prostitutes were not the proper subjects for penal law' due to the 'futility of harrying the prostitute' who is driven to prostitution through necessity or 'evil design'.[28] The article instead promoted the use of female probation officers and rescue homes to combat prostitution.[29] It was not only feminists who supported the use of probation and rescue homes. From the very start of the probation service some English magistrates were already placing women who had been charged with solicitation offences on probation. For example, the first Bolton Probation Committee Annual Report for 1908 described how they dealt with six cases of prostitution, and in Hartlepool the 1910 crime statistics report showed that out of the seven women convicted for soliciting one was placed on probation.[30] Similarly, in 1912 a female probation officer in Sheffield described how she dealt with three prostitutes that year.[31]

Whether a woman convicted of soliciting was placed on probation depended upon the opinion of the magistrate and the probation officer as to whether she was deemed 'suitable' for probation. The cases of four different women tried at the Folkstone Magistrates Court for soliciting in 1915 provide a good example of how crucial the opinion of an individual magistrate could be in determining who was placed on probation. On 24 December 1915, the Magistrate Mr Stainer found Hettie C. guilty of soliciting for the purposes of prostitution and placed her on probation under the supervision of the police court missionary Mr Holmes, who then decided to place her in a rescue home.[32] However, later the same day, Mr Stainer sentenced Ellen S. to fourteen days in prison for the same offence. On 28 December 1915, the magistrate at Folkstone Magistrates Court for that day, Mr Swoffer, sentenced Eileen A. to twelve months' probation under Mr Holmes for a soliciting offence, but then two days later on the 30 December the same magistrate sentenced Cecilie C. to fourteen days in prison for the same soliciting offence. The newspaper reported very little about the individual circumstances of each woman, and the only clue as to why one of the women, Cecilie C., got a prison sentence rather than probation was because she had a previous conviction for a similar offence.[33]

The offender's previous conviction record was a very important factor in determining whether they were deemed suitable for probation, but it could also depend on the judge's opinion regarding things such as the woman's age and character, and whether the woman appeared willing to reform. For example, in October 1938 the magistrate in the case of eighteen-year-old Evelyn N., who had been placed on probation in London for loitering for the purposes of prostitution, decided to deal with Evelyn N. 'leniently' by placing her on probation for two years because 'she said she was very sorry and had learnt her lesson … She promised to give up her immoral life'.[34] A newspaper article about the case described how she told the magistrate that 'if I go back home I will do my best to make up for all the wrong I have done. She added she was willing to go into domestic service'.[35]

As was the case in Scotland, there was a preference for placing 'newly fallen', younger women on probation because it was assumed that they had not yet become too 'hardened' by a life of prostitution and were therefore more likely to be successfully reformed. In 1910, the Departmental Committee on the Probation of Offenders Act 1907 was tasked with reviewing the workings of the new probation service. In this report it was noted that probation was not useful for 'habitual prostitutes' because these women were deemed to be too set in their 'immoral' ways to be successfully reformed.[36] However, according to the report, the 'newly fallen prostitute' or women thought to be in danger of entering prostitution due to their 'promiscuous' behaviour were deemed prime candidates for probation because they were more susceptible to the good influence of a wise and respectable probation officer. An example of this preference for reforming the 'newly fallen' can be seen in the case of twenty-year-old Elizabeth C. who was placed on probation for twelve months and given a residence order after she was found guilty of soliciting in Marylebone, London, in February 1943. The *Marylebone Mercury* described how the Marylebone magistrate gave 'fatherly advice to the girl' telling her:

> I don't know whether you realise it, but Miss Jackson [a probation officer] and other people are anxious to help you, not punish you and push you down. There are two ways for you to choose. One of them leading to illness, worry and degradation. It may have seeming compensation at this time but later in life you will find they are terrible illusions. Miss Jackson the probation officer will also be a friend to you and if you are perplexed or in difficulties come to see her and ask her advice. She will help you. Look upon us as helpers not punishers.[37]

The statement made by the magistrate exemplifies the overall aims of probation as seen by its supporters. By offering these young women help and guidance rather than punishment it was hoped that they could be persuaded to abandon their 'immoral ways' and begin a 'respectable' life, if only they were willing to accept help.

Saving these young vulnerable women before they became too 'hardened' was considered so important that the authorities did not necessarily wait until a woman had been convicted of a soliciting offence before they intervened in her life. This approach was explained by Mr Justice Humphries who preceded over the Notts Assizes during 1934. According to the *Illustrated Police News*, Mr Justice Humphries described how

> there was a class of girls being brought up in this country in such a way that a new class of juvenile prostitute had come into existence. Young girls under 16 were shown, by evidence, time after time to be entirely beyond the control of their parents and allowed to roam the streets and act as common prostitutes. He hoped the police, who seemed to be the only people to act in such cases, would bring such girls before juvenile courts when they found these little girls acting in this dreadfully distressing way. The juvenile court had the power to send them to some home or other place where they would have a chance, before it was too late, to become decent respectable women.[38]

Justice Humphries's hope that girls should be sent to 'some sort of home' was often realized in practice. For example, in September 1919 seventeen-year-old Edith P. was charged in Canterbury with wandering and sleeping on land that belonged to the War Department and placed under the supervision of a probation officer who suggested she should be placed in a training home. While Edith P. had not been convicted for solicitation, much was made of the fact that she had run away from home and had been living off the proceeds of prostitution.[39]

That this case occurred in the context of the First World War is also important. Authorities during this time were particularly concerned about the problem of young 'amateur prostitutes' who were engaging in sexual activity with soldiers and might spread venereal disease.[40] Sending these young women to reform homes for extended periods was therefore a useful solution for stopping the spread of venereal disease, even if they had not been convicted for soliciting. For example, in April 1917 seventeen-year-olds Ada R. and Nellie M. were charged in Romford under the Defence of the Real Act with providing alcohol to soldiers undergoing hospital treatment. However, rather than focusing on the alcohol offence the magistrate highlighted how 'the girl R. bore a bad character and had been leading the life of a prostitute for some time. The way in which they behaved with soldiers was a disgrace to Romford'.[41] The magistrate decided that in the interests of the soldiers and the girls themselves they should be sent to a home.

While some of these young women had been caught breaking the law, others who had not committed any offence but were considered to be acting promiscuously could be placed on probation for their own 'care and protection' in accordance with the 1908 Children Act.[42] For example, in July 1942 a fifteen-year-old girl was brought before the Lewes Juvenile Court as being 'in need of care and protection' after she was named in the case of a soldier who was convicted of 'an offence against the girl' and given a six-day prison sentence.[43] Rather than viewing this girl as a victim of sexual abuse, the magistrate described her as a 'perfect little nuisance to men' that should be locked up to stop her from 'tempting' soldiers.[44] In a similar case, this time from York in July 1934, a fourteen-year-old girl was placed in a rescue home after she was named in the trial of a twenty-six-year-old man who was convicted of committing 'an offence against a girl'.[45] The judge at the York Assizes again blamed the girl for the man's offence, describing how the accused was 'tricked into this act' because she had lied about her age.[46]

Louise Jackson and Carol Smart's research on the history of child sexual abuse has shown how this type of victim blaming, especially in cases involving teenage girls, was very common during the early-to-mid twentieth century.[47] By furthering the idea that it was women and girls, not men, who should reform their behaviour, even in cases where the woman or girl was the victim of sexual abuse, the use of probation to control the sexual activities of young women played an important role in strengthening the sexual double moral standard and reinforcing the culture of victim blaming. Although the language of probation may have been couched in terms of protection rather than punishment, it was nonetheless women and girls' sexual behaviour that was deemed problematic, not the men who paid for sex and took advantage of women and girls.

Probation and prostitution: A timeline

As we have seen, probation was not used systematically or universally in cases of street solicitation. However, those who supported probation wanted it to be used more, and every time prostitution and its regulation came up for discussion there were proposals for furthering the use of probation.

Some of the first public discussions about the merits of using probation and rescue homes for dealing with prostitution came up in relation to Clause 3 of the Criminal Law Amendment Bill 1918. This clause proposed that powers should be given to magistrates to enable them to detain girls aged under eighteen who could be identified as 'common prostitutes' and have them placed in reform homes for up to three years. Those in favour of the clause believed these powers were necessary to rescue young women who were not capable of acting in their own best interests. They lamented the futility of fining women or sending them to prison 'because the girl would go straight back to the streets to recoup herself', but they were sceptical about claims that women would voluntarily enter rescue homes.[48] For example, an article in the *Women's Leader* described how a life on the streets meant that the young prostitute's 'will had become distorted' and it was 'as impossible for her to right herself, as it is for a lunatic to recover his mind' because her 'spiritual outlook is fogged'.[49] The power to detain women in institutions was considered necessary because they were 'too young to know [their] own mind' and were only likely to reform 'in response to firm management, patient teaching, or the influence of a magnetic personality'.[50] This 'firm management', it was argued, could best be provided by spending time at 'well-run humanistic' rescue home.[51]

However, there were many objections to the bill for a variety of reasons. Some did not like the use of the term 'common prostitute' when referring to young girls under eighteen as it was considered too harsh to label these women in such derogatory terms. Others were concerned that 'innocent' young women waiting for a friend or peering into a shop window might be seized and incarcerated unfairly. More generally, however, there was an objection to women's liberty being curtailed for periods far longer than was allowed for under laws relating to other types of similar misdemeanours.

Street Offences Committee report 1928

The issue of probation and prostitution came up again for public discussion in relation to the 1928 report of the Street Offences Committee.[52] The committee had been set up amidst concerns about the implementation of solicitation laws following the conviction of Sergeant Goddard of the Metropolitan Police for corruption offences linked to the fining of women for solicitation offences and his dealings with nightclub and brothel owners.[53] In addition to debating the morality of prostitution and the role of the law in policing it, the use of probation as a method for stopping women from becoming involved in prostitution was raised as a possible solution. During a public sitting held by the committee, Mrs Rolf from the British Social Hygiene Council proposed that women who had been involved in prostitution but wanted to leave should be given a 'sufficient period of maintenance in an institution' and Lady Emmott from the National Council of Women also 'advocated probation, women police, and, in certain cases, prolonged detention'.⁵⁴ Later during the meeting more detail on how probation might be used to deal with prostitution was provided by Mr Sempken from the National Vigilance Association who proposed that

> a thorough and comprehensive system of probation lasting up to two years should be tried; the magistrate could attach conditions, for a girl to live at home, go home to the country etc; for more serious cases, residence for six months in a voluntary home. If a girl refused consent, there should be homes helped by the state and inspected by the home office, to which the magistrate could send her, and to these homes could also be sent girls who agreed to go to a voluntary home and ran away later.⁵⁵

The proposal made by Mr Sempkin sounded like a novel idea. However, as we have seen earlier, the method of using probation in this way was already common in Scotland and some parts of England and Wales by this point. Further evidence given to the committee by Mr C. A. Macpherson, public prosecutor for Edinburgh, confirmed that 'there was often co-operation between the police and the probation officer' and women were cautioned three times before being arrested for soliciting.⁵⁶ Similarly, evidence given by Mr Stuart Deacon, the stipendiary magistrate for Liverpool, also established that probation was being used in Liverpool in cases of soliciting and that the magistrates across England were generally in favour of this practice.⁵⁷ Mr Deacon told the committee that 'the magistrates, as a broad principal, do not believe in fines as a deterrent'.⁵⁸ Instead, he advocated the method that they used in Liverpool which was to work together with voluntary organizations to reform these women. In support of this method, he provided evidence from a report which stated that 'of 44 women taken in by the Church of England Temperance Society, 37 proved satisfactory and many women became reformed characters. The probation officer had received letters of thanks from many of these girls'.⁵⁹ The use of probation, therefore, was already quite well established in many areas of the country by this point and the support shown for probation by these contributors to the Street Offences Committee further legitimized the usefulness of this approach.

The Second World War

The next point at which prostitution and probation became a topic for considerable public debate was during the Second World War. As was the case during the First World War, a moral panic emerged concerning the presence of 'amateur prostitutes' and 'good-time girls' who were behaving promiscuously with soldiers.⁶⁰ Probation was again suggested as a method for policing these women. For example, the 1942–3 Annual Report for the Manchester Probation Committee included a discussion about the problem of young girls getting tempted into prostitution and catching venereal disease.⁶¹ The report highlighted how the Emergency Powers (Defence) Act 1939 was inadequate for dealing with these women and that it was much better for them to be placed on probation so that an officer could arrange the necessary treatment for them. However, the report also emphasized that only those women who wanted to cooperate were suitable for probation. The importance of the probation officers being the ones to decide who was placed on probation was emphasized, and the report was critical of the fact that 'currently this is not always done and too many who are not suitable are being put on probation'.⁶²

It was not only in Manchester that women were increasingly placed on probation for soliciting offences during the war. An article in *The Sphere* about the London Bow Street Magistrates Court described how

> there is an increase in prostitution during the war, esp. among young women of 17 and 18. In the old days prostitutes were fined 40s. Today they are frequently bound over for the first offence or two, and the probation officers are given more responsibility in handling them.⁶³

Similarly, the *Liverpool Daily Post* described how young girls 'associating with prostitutes and undesirable men' could be placed on probation or sent to an approved school if they were under seventeen.⁶⁴ An example of this type of case can be seen in January 1945, when a twenty-year-old woman named Joyce S. was sent to 'a suitable home in Oxford for a period not less than two years' after she was found 'living the life of a prostitute and visiting American camps'.⁶⁵

At the end of the Second World War, the National Probation Officers Association asked local probation committees to provide reports about their experiences of the social work they carried out during the war. These reports were then compiled into a larger report entitled *Summary of Probation Officers Reports on Social Work during the War*.⁶⁶ This report covered many topics, but a recurring topic was the work undertaken by probation officers in relation to prostitution and promiscuity. Here too, a major preoccupation of the probation service when dealing with young women was the concern that young women were acting promiscuously with soldiers and potentially spreading venereal disease, especially with American soldiers.⁶⁷ In the introduction, which summarized the social problems caused by the war, three of the six bullet points concerned this topic. Bullet point two, for example, dealt with the issue of 'adolescents and sex problems'.⁶⁸ Under this heading the report described how the lack of parental control and school discipline, combined with high wages, too much independence and not enough wholesome entertainment, made fraternizing with soldiers particularly tempting. The report described how

> the glamour gained from being with well-paid service men, especially those from distant countries and from America, who bring into actual being a standard set by certain types of films and who must often seem like a dream come true to a girl who has taken her stand from such things. In addition, the less attractive girl, or the girl from an unhappy home, who lacks parental affection, finds that at least she is wanted and is given affection, however superfluous and fleeting, by the service man who picks her up.⁶⁹

Bullet point four linked this behaviour with the increased spread of venereal disease and bullet point five linked it with a more general breakdown of wholesome family life. According to the report, these factors had led to a five- or six-fold increase in the number of young girls involved in prostitution who needed care and protection orders since the war started.

An examination of the reports provided by the individual probation area committees shows that these beliefs about the behaviour of women were commonly held across England and Wales. For example, the Hull report described how there had been increased promiscuity between girls and American soldiers and the Shropshire report bemoaned the problem of rich American soldiers. Similarly, the Sheffield report emphasized the attraction of American soldiers who offered girls dancing and cocktails like in the movies, and the Sheffield probation officer blamed the girls 'love of pleasure at the expense of family life'.⁷⁰ To illustrate this point the report included an example of one woman 'on the game' who said she 'would not go back to a normal way of living' because she 'preferred the free existence, the thrill of living dangerously and the risk of being caught – in addition to which they earned considerable sums of money'.⁷¹

The report submitted by the Chelsea Probation Committee was equally critical of these women's behaviour, describing how they were 'without fear, entirely self-centred and apparently devoid of affection. She has no sense of need, no moral standard and no ambition'.⁷² However, the report did then clarify that the blame for this behaviour fell upon the unhappy homes from which these girls came. The author of the report, a probation officer named Bessy, described how 'of the 10 girls currently under my supervisor at Chelsea Court not one had a normal home. 1 is adopted, 3 have stepfathers, 1 has a stepmother, 3 have parents separated, 1 is illegitimate and brought up in an institution, 1 lost her mother as a child and father has a house keeper'.[73] The author also blamed the 'disgracefully low wages' that firms were paying girls aged between fourteen and eighteen. This meant that after paying their parents for board and lodgings they had 'nothing left over for cigarettes, cosmetics, or any other little extra'.[74] The Chelsea probation officer sympathized with the women's situation, lamenting that 'no wonder girls need American friends who pay for them and bring them pleasure and luxuries into their life as they think, free, but in reality, which they pay dearly'.[75]

While placing these women on probation was seen as a potential solution to this problem because officers could encourage girls to act 'respectably', the author of the Chelsea report realized that an officer's ability to influence these women was limited due to the difficult economic circumstances the women found themselves in. The officer therefore insisted that a 'minimum wage' was needed because

> no one should be expected to work under £2.50 a week. All workers are entitled to a living wage which should allow them to live decently away from home if they so wish to, without having to reply on boyfriends and run risks.[76]

The author was also keen to point out that the way in which the probation officer interacted with women was also important. She believed that girls should not be treated too harshly, and instead they needed 'care and nourishment' because if you treated them badly after they had been enjoying 'being the princesses of the American soldiers' they would not be 'ready to listen and assimilate new ideas'.[77] The author explained how the women should not be made to feel judged and instead they should be

> given complete physical rest and good nourishing food, real relaxation with time for reflection; new thoughts and surroundings conductive to thinking. For this they should each have a small, bright, attractive room for the preliminary rest, with pretty night wear, wireless headphones, magazines and handicraft. They should be brought to feel valuable ... With a wise, imaginative approach, unfailing effort and sympathetic surroundings, they can be encouraged to become happy, valuable citizens ... these girls are part of the wealth of the nation.[78]

This probation officer, at least, seemed to understand the difficulties that women faced and was sympathetic for their need to be treated kindly, fairly and with respect. Crucially, she also appreciated the importance of adequate wages so that women could be economically independent and still enjoy a few small pleasures in life. It is also significant that she was concerned about these women's happiness and that she described them as valuable citizens who were 'part of the wealth of the nation'.[79] Here she acknowledges the inherent value of ensuring women's well-being while also recognizing that this was intrinsically linked to the wider well-being of society.

It was not only the Chelsea officer who was sympathetic towards the women's difficult circumstances. The report made by the Liverpool Probation Committee also described how the conduct of these 'girls of a tender age ... should be regarded as tragic rather than criminal'.[80] The report described how the girls were 'attracted by adventure and curiosity ... [but] can't distinguish this from grave danger'.[81] The report's outline of the methods they used to help these women also highlights how concerned probation officers were with trying to improve women's future prospects. The report described how

> each case is a difficult problem and must be studied and treated individually. The home background – usually an unhappy one – must be carefully examined and very many of the girls must be removed from their homes temporarily or permanently. The girl herself must be visited in the remand home or prison – perhaps two or three times in a really difficult case – to try and establish a friendly relationship with her, to discuss plans for her own future and to try and gain her co-operation. Many of the girls have some idea of what they want to do ... generally if at all possible, and the ambition appears to be at all serious, the probation officer will make great effort to give a girl a chance in the line she asked for or at least train for it.[82]

Despite the slightly condescending tone, this focus on making friends with the women and ensuring that they were given help to find new jobs which fitted with their own ambitions shows how the probation officers were at least trying to consider the women's best interests and not simply force them into domestic service or other unsuitable employment, which had often been the case previously. Nonetheless, despite this emphasis on trying to help these women, portraying them as naive and vulnerable also made it easier to justify the moral surveillance and regulation of their behaviour.

While the majority of the local probation committees reported that their work involving young 'promiscuous' women had increased during the war, some officers argued that promiscuity had not necessarily increased all that much, especially in rural areas. The North Riding officer, for example, described how

> rural family life has remained steady during the war and the number of affiliation and maintenance orders has been extremely small. The villages and townships offer none of the anonymity of big towns for people to behave well or ill and community standards have remained steady.[83]

The Cardiff officer also pointed out that the problem of adolescent promiscuity had been prevalent even before the war and that the spread of venereal disease was not as bad as it was feared to be, especially among young people. To illustrate this, the report included figures which showed how in 1944 there were only two cases of syphilis in the age group of fourteen to seventeen and thirteen in the age ground of eighteen to twenty-one. Rather than teenagers spreading venereal disease, the report showed that it was the age group of twenty to thirty-nine that had the highest amount of venereal disease, probably, according to their interpretation, due to the large number of soldiers coming home and infecting their wives. Here, at least, the Cardiff probation officer was willing to challenge the double standard of sexual morality by attributing some of the blame to men instead of only focusing on the dangers of female sexuality, as had been the case with most of the other local probation committee reports.

The 1957 Wolfenden Committee report

After the Second World War the next time in which prostitution and probation were again widely discussed in the public arena was in relation to the Departmental Committee on Homosexual Offences and Prostitution (often referred to as the Wolfenden Committee). As noted in the previous chapter, the committee had been set up amidst concerns about the increase in arrests for homosexual offences, and it is often thought of as primarily being a committee about homosexual offences. However, another important aspect of the committee's remit was to deliberate about prostitution laws and the prevalence of street soliciting.[84]

The recommendations that the Wolfenden Committee came up with in their 1957 report were to re-interpret the role of the law in policing public morals – namely that sexual acts between consenting adults should not be subject to legal regulation if they were committed in private. In relation to homosexual offences, the report's recommendations eventually led to the 1967 Sexual Offence Act which decriminalized consensual sexual acts that happened in private between men over the age of twenty-one in England and Wales. In relation to prostitution, however, this new emphasis on prioritizing the policing of sexuality in the public sphere resulted in the passing of the 1959 Street Offences Act which increased the punishments for women who solicited on the streets.[85] The Act was somewhat successful in reducing the visibility of solicitation on the street, but it had the unintended consequence that many women were subsequently forced to work in less safe and more secluded outdoor areas, or in indoor establishments that were often very exploitative. This meant that women lost some of their independence and became more vulnerable to exploitation and abuse from those who organized indoor venues.[86]

Although the main aim of the Wolfenden Committee's recommendations in relation to prostitution was to stop street soliciting, another often-overlooked aim of the Committee's recommendations was to use the threat of imprisonment to encourage women to agree to be placed on probation. This aim was explicitly stated in the following recommendations given by the committee:

> The committee recommended that consideration should be given to the possibility of introducing more widely the more formal system of cautioning prostitutes which was in force in Edinburgh and Glasgow, and to extend the practice of referring to a moral welfare worker particulars of a prostitute cautioned for the first time. Increasing the penalties for street offences, the committee describes the present maximum fine of 40s fixed more than 100 years ago as quite inadequate ... the committee had two purposes in mind; straightforward deterrence ... equally important, however, was the reformative element in punishment. We believe that the presence of punishment may make the court anxious to try, and the individual prostitute more willing to accept, the use of probation in suitable cases. The committee attaches special importance to probation for the young prostitute, and proposes that courts be given explicit power to remand, in custody if need be, for not more than three weeks, a prostitute convicted for the first or second time of a street offence, so that a social or medical report may be obtained. They do not feel able to recommend compulsory probation for the young prostitute.[87]

As we have seen, this method of placing women on probation was already being deployed in Scotland and some parts of the England prior to the publication of this report. The Wolfenden Committee members, however, wanted to ensure this system was expanded and strengthened, and one way to do this was by increasing the incentive for women to accept probation by making the alternative less appealing. Many within the probation service were also generally in favour of this approach. For example, Mrs Elsbeth Grey, who had been a probation officer at the Marlborough Street Court in London for twenty-two years, described in an interview with a journalist from *The Evening News* how 'most of the young prostitutes who appear at Marlborough Street are never seen by a probation officer. Few girls are willing to accept probation when the maximum penalty is only 40s, and magistrates are reluctant to remand them in custody for a report for the same reason.'[88] The article explained that this was 'why Mrs Grey would like to see heavier penalties urged by the Wolfenden Committee. It would give the probation service a better chance of working on the offender'.[89]

As well as increasing the penalties for soliciting, the 1959 Street Offences Act also introduced a formal system of cautioning. A description of how this cautioning system should be implemented was given in the Home Office circular 109 in 1959.[90] The circular stated that if a woman had no previous convictions for soliciting, she should be cautioned twice before she is arrested. In order to try and prevent women and girls from 'slipping into prostitution', the officers were told that they should ask the woman if she would like to be put in touch with a moral welfare worker or probation officer. The circular ended by clarifying that they realized that many women go into prostitution 'through choice' and therefore the number that will be diverted from prostitution will be small.[91] As was the case earlier in the century, the aim of expanding the cautioning and probation system remained limited in its scope. The focus continued to be placed on trying to 'save' young women who were new to prostitution. Women who were already well-established in sex work were to be given much harsher sentences to deter them from soliciting on the street.

The Wolfenden report and the subsequent legislation are often seen as a watershed moment in the movement towards individualism and the point at which the state stepped back from attempting to regulate the sexual behaviour of consenting adults that took place in private. The committee's statement that they believed 'the great majority of prostitutes are women whose psychological make up is such that they choose this life because they find in it a style of living which is to them easier, freer and more profitable than would be provided by any other occupation' certainly attests to this. However, the committee's hope that some women might be rescued from prostitution via probation somewhat contradicts this move towards a less interventionist approach, and it suggests that there was still room for the state to play a moralistic and paternalistic role, especially in relation to young women's sexual activities. While it was agreed that women should not be forced to accept probation, increasing the penalties for soliciting was intended as a way to pressure women to choose probation. However, this focus on protecting the 'newly fallen' meant that the potential benefits associated with being placed on probation, such as avoiding prison and fines, or being given help to find new employment, were denied to women who were deemed 'hardened'. Instead, these women faced harsher penalties and were *de facto* forced into working in more secluded dangerous outdoor locations or within indoor venues which were often very exploitative.

Not everyone, however, was in favour of the extension of police powers that the 1959 Street Offences Act enabled. On 25 March 1959, an amendment to the Act was proposed in the House of Commons by Mr E. Alan Pitch to delete the penalty of up to three months' imprisonment for offenders with a previous conviction for prostitution. Mr Pitch justified the proposed amendment by warning the government that 'unless they were very careful they might drive prostitution underground and eventually be faced with worse conditions than operate at the moment'.[92] Sir Hugh Linstead agreed with Mr Pitch, stating that 'in a great majority of cases imprisonment of prostitutes was highly undesirable'.[93] However, he then pointed out that 'nonetheless, the presence of imprisonment in the law has much to be said for it. It can help persuade the beginner to place herself in the hands of the probation officers'.[94] Following on from this, Mr David Renton stated how 'probation was a way of keeping girls off the streets, but probation without the ultimate sanction of prison does not lead to effective results'.[95] Despite these objections to the Act the amendment was rejected. The desirability of deterring young women from prostitution and placing them on probation was deemed more important than the rights and safety of more established sex workers.

On 15 June 1959, another amendment was proposed, this time by Baroness Wootton in the House of Lords. The proposed amendment again sought to dispose of the three-month prison sentence for women with more than one previous conviction for soliciting because she claimed the penalty was 'extremely high for offences which were essentially those of nuisance or causing annoyance'.[96] Baroness Wootton argued that the trend of opinion 'was against the value of imprisonment' and Lord Stoneham agreed with her, adding that he 'doubted if such a term of imprisonment would have any reformative value and there was a danger of corruption by hardened prostitutes and other inmates'.[97] Replying for the government, Lord Chesham clarified that 'the government's purpose was to make it apparent to a girl on the threshold of such a life that prison was in the background; and it was hoped that a woman would be induced to accept probation and abandon prostitution'.[98] The amendment, therefore, failed again. However, the debates in both the House of Commons and the House of Lords confirm that aside from deterring street solicitation, the threat of a three-month prison sentence was intended to persuade young women to agree to probation. The government's support for the use of probation as a method for protecting young women and regulating their sexual activities shows that the state's new reluctance to intervene in the private sex lives of consenting adults did not apply to young women.

How successful was probation?

As we have seen, probation was promoted as a method for rescuing young women from prostitution and ideally, a way of stopping them from becoming involved in this type of work in the first place. However, enthusiasm for this method varied across the country and support for its use ebbed and waned over the period. What then, did this mean for those women who were placed on probation, and just how successful was this approach in practice? Both questions are difficult to answer due to the lack of source material dealing with the lives and experiences of the women involved, especially in relation to the period after their probation ended. However, the probation records and newspaper coverage of individual cases do provide some evidence about the benefits and difficulties associated with the use of probation in cases where women had been convicted of soliciting offences.

The most obvious benefit of using probation was that it reduced the number of women who were sent to prison for soliciting. An article in the *Northern Daily Mail* in July 1925 described how the increased use of probation had 'drastically cut the prison population so that a third of prisons in England and Wales have been shut down since 1914'.[99] To support this claim, the article included crime statistics that showed how during 1913–14 7,952 women had been sent to prison for soliciting offences in England and Wales, but by 1923–4 this number had decreased to 1209 women.[100] This decrease was attributed to 'social reformers' and the 'gradually working effects of probationary treatment rather than prison treatment'.[101] While this sounds somewhat plausible, there may well have been other reasons behind why the number of women sent to prison for solicitation offences declined. For example, an increase in opportunities for working in more clandestine indoor environments or for gaining employment outside of prostitution may have reduced the number of women who resorted to street solicitation or were caught importuning.

Less women being sent to prison for soliciting certainly saved the government money. It might also be assumed that women were glad to avoid imprisonment. However, whether the women themselves actually felt that probation was preferable to prison is less clear. There is evidence to suggest that at least some women were grateful that they had been placed on probation. For example, the probation records for Cardiff included references to 'letters of thanks' sent to probation officers from women who had been convicted of prostitution-related offences.[102] One of those women who wrote in 1911 was twenty-year-old May L. who was described by her probation officer as doing 'remarkably good' and that she was pleased to report that May L. 'writes regularly' and has been working as 'a nurse in a good family'.[103] The probation records for Edinburgh also include some examples of situations where probation appeared to have been successful in helping women to avoid prison and secure new types of employment. For example, in May 1916 the probation officer for twenty-five-year-old Helen M. described how 'her mother says that her conduct is quite satisfactory. I have seen her frequently and I can see she is a different girl. She has given up bad company'.[104] Similarly, in 1935 Elizabeth M's probation officer explained that Elizabeth M. 'behaved well' and that it was 'her desire to become a laundry maid'.[105] Unfortunately, however, there are no surviving letters or other sources written by the women themselves so these records still only tell us about these women's lives from the perspective of the probation officer and women's parents, rather than the women themselves.

Resisting probation

Despite the lack of written sources made by the women themselves, women's actions can tell us more about their lives and their opinions about probation. For example, the fact that several women broke their probation bonds and ran away from reform homes suggests that probation was not always successful and not all women appreciated it. Instead, some women found ways to resist the restrictions it placed on their freedom. If we turn again to Cardiff, the same probation records also documented less 'successful' cases than the one described above. For example, in September 1923 a warrant for the arrest of Lucy C. was issued because she had failed to observe the conditions of the probation order that she had been given after being found guilty of importuning earlier that year.[106] Similarly 'unsuccessful' cases were also reported to have occurred in other areas of the country. In Glasgow, several women were reported to have broken their bonds. For example, in 1914 Eliza G. was charged at Mary Hill Police Court in Glasgow for breaching her probation bond because she had again been convicted for soliciting. She was subsequently given a 10/6 fine or seven-day prison sentence.[107] In November 1919, twenty-four-year-old Margaret R., who was on probation after being convicted of a solicitation offence in Edinburgh, was sent to Glasgow Lock hospital after she behaved 'most violent' and 'gave trouble'.[108] In 1910 seventeen-year-old Davina W. was taken to reside at the Church Army home after being convicted for prostitution in Edinburgh.[109] However, the probation officer responsible for her described how Davina W. was 'a very deceitful girl ... [who] stole from her and ran away' from the home several times.[110] In London during October 1929, Margaret P. was charged at the West London Police Court with a breach of her probation bond after she admitted to continuing to live as a prostitute having failed to keep her promise that she would go into respectable employment.[111] The probation officer therefore informed the court that Margaret P. had given a false address and failed to report once a month as required by the probation recognizances.[112]

The magistrates and JPs dealing with these cases were well aware of the possibility that women might break their probation bonds. For example, in July 1938 Renee C. was charged at London's Marylebone Police Court with managing a brothel in Paddington.[113] During the trial Renee C. admitted that she had been placed on probation in December 1937 for soliciting and the probation officer reported that she had brought Renee C. before the court in March 1938 to have the probation order extended because 'she did not report regularly and she was not in work'.[114] In response to this the magistrate 'suggested that probation was a farce in this case' and the probation officer agreed that it was.[115] The magistrate informed the court that 'I strongly object to having women of this type on probation, unless they are making a genuine effort to give up this life'.[116] In consequence of her new offence and breach of probation the magistrate fined her £25 or six weeks imprisonment and told her she would not be given time in which to pay.

Some women were so reluctant to be placed on probation that they refused this sentencing option altogether. For example, in September 1917 sixteen-year-old Olive O. was charged in Folkstone with soliciting and being a common prostitute.[117] According to the *Folkstone Herald*, Miss Kirby, 'a lady enquiry officer', told the court that

> many efforts had been made to reclaim the girl. She had been sent previously to a home but had left it. There was no doubt she was a prostitute. Witnesses had formed this opinion by constant observation.[118]

On hearing this the magistrate apparently 'talk[ed] kindly to the girl', stating that 'we do not want to send you to prison' and asked Olive O. if she would 'consent to go in a home'.[119] However, Olive O. 'emphatically' replied, 'No, I would rather go to prison.'[120] When the magistrate tried to persuade Olive O. further by telling her that they were 'trying to save you, if you will help yourself', she 'firmly' replied that she 'would rather go to prison'.[121] The article then described how

> after an interval the girl was led into the court, and, with tears in her eyes, said she would agree to go into a home for three months on probation. It was

stated that at the end of that time suitable employment would probably be found for her.¹²²

Although Olive O. had been determined not to consent to being placed on probation, the threat of prison was finally enough to break her resolution. This case therefore highlights how unappealing some women saw probation and that they only consented to it under the threat of imprisonment – a fact which clearly undermined the legitimacy of their consent.

In April 1945, a twenty-year-old woman who had been convicted of stealing and was described as 'living a life of prostitution' was equally reluctant to be placed on probation and told the prison doctor 'she preferred to serve a sentence rather than be placed on probation'.¹²³ An article in *The Courier* about the case described how the defendant had had 'an institutional career since the moment she left school' and had been on probation on several previous occasions. According to the article, the probation officer who supervised this woman during her most recent period on probation had allowed her to stay with her at her own home and found her a new job, but then she ran away and stole the officer's coat. Even the probation officer's attempt to help this woman by letting her stay in her own home was not enough to encourage her to accept a probation. She instead was given a nine-month prison sentence. In a similar case from London in April 1940, twenty-seven-year-old Violet P., who had been charged with soliciting for a second time, was given the chance of probation but also declined. An article in the *West London Press* described how the magistrate asked the probation officer if she had seen the woman, and the probation officer replied that she had 'refused my assistance'.¹²⁴ Subsequently, the magistrate informed the defendant that he could 'only fine you 40s. If you wish to lead a decent life the probation officer will always help you'.¹²⁵ Despite the magistrate seeming eager for this woman to be reformed, he acknowledged there was little he could do if she did not want their help.

It was not only the women themselves who were unhappy about the use of probation in these situations, especially if it involved long stays in reform homes. In her article, *Penal Discipline*, Louisa Gordon described why she was against the policy of sending women to reform homes:

> In so far as a Home is a place of compulsory detention it is a prison. It is also a place in which an adolescent girl cannot be taught how to live, where she must learn to live – in the world. Homes are not what is needed, nor could enough ever be provided. Nor would they, on a large scale, do anything but increase the size and difficulty of the problem. Prostitution could not be touched by any small or large palliative means of the kind.¹²⁶

There was further public criticism of reform homes in November 1943 when several newspapers reported on the story of how the Independent MP for Marylebone, Captain A. S. Cunningham, criticized the probation service in the House of Commons by describing it as 'rotten' and 'soul-destroying'.[127] According to an article in the *Yorkshire Post*, Cunningham gave the case of a fifteen-year-old girl named Mary as an example of what was 'rotten' about the probation system. He described how Mary had been found drunk and incapable in the company of soldiers and placed on probation. Mary was then placed on probation and sent to do canteen work at the Land Girl's YMCA hostel in the country where she was required to undertake 'ten hours breaking drudgery a day, scrubbing floors, lavatories and dormitories'.[128] Cunningham complained that Mary was not properly supervised by a probation officer during this time and that the officer did not come to visit the girl until five weeks into her stay at the hostel. It was also reported that another girl on probation who had been working at the hostel before Mary's arrival had been dismissed from the hostel because she had contacted a venereal disease after being discovered with a lorry driver.[129]

Following Cunningham's complaint there was a discussion in the House of Commons about the problem of 'good-time girls' who came from 'broken homes' and the need to improve probation supervision to deal with this problem. Mr Osbert Peake, Home Office under secretary, spoke on behalf of the probation service in apologizing for this 'slip-up', but assured the House that this lack of adequate supervision was an isolated case that had occurred because the supervising probation officer had recently had her house bombed during the blitz. While the probation service tried to pass this case off as an exception, it does highlight how the use of long periods of institutional confinement created the potential for situations like this to occur and made women vulnerable to exploitation. For women trapped in these miserable situations, a fine or a short prison sentence may well have been preferable.

When it came to resisting the authority of the magistrates and probation officers, some women could rely on the support of their families. If we return to the case of Olive O. described earlier, one of the most interesting aspects of the case is how Olive O.'s father tried to defend his daughter's reputation in court.[130] According to the newspaper coverage, during a short break in the proceedings the stepfather shouted to Olive O.: 'Don't you go to a home.'[131] After this outburst the magistrate asked the father-in-law to speak with him and during that conversation the stepfather was reported to have stated that his stepdaughter 'is only a child. She has always been a good child. Is she forbidden to walk out with a soldier? Is it any disgrace?'[132] When the magistrate's clerk explained that the magistrate had made his decision based on the evidence of three witnesses, the stepfather rejected their interpretation that his stepdaughter's behaviour qualified as an offence by declaring that his daughter had 'never been caught in any improper act'.[133]

Similar attempts by defendants and their family members to challenge the evidence that allegedly proved the law had been broken can be seen in other cases. For example, in October 1915 a woman and her daughter were charged in Middlesex with breach of the peace, and it was insinuated that they were soliciting for the purposes of prostitution. The couple, however, hired a lawyer who argued that there was no proof of solicitation without a statement from the soldiers who they had allegedly insulted. The defendant argued that her word 'was as good as any police officer's' and that a doctor's certificate proved that her daughter was 'virgo intacta'.[134] The case of the mother was dismissed, but the daughter was placed on probation. In a similar case from Surrey in 1917, the mother of an eighteen-year-old woman who had been placed on probation after being found guilty of soliciting accused the probation officer of 'telling lies' about her daughter and insisted that there was no proof her daughter was a 'common prostitute'.[135] However, the judge decided to believe the probation officer and berated the mother, telling her that it was 'your duty to help us make a proper order and not come here and call people liars ... a girl of 18 ought to be more under the control of her mother than this girl is'.[136] The magistrate decided to remand her for a medical examination.[137]

These attempts to refute police evidence demonstrate how some women and their families tried to challenge the authorities' interpretation of their behaviour and resisted the efforts that were being made to label them as prostitutes. However, the fact that these mothers were unable to stop their daughters from being placed on probation highlights how women's scope for agency was limited and their attempts to defend themselves and their children were not always successful. The above cases also highlight how women's roles as mothers were particularly under scrutiny. Under the 1908 Children Act, children under fourteen who were found 'frequenting the company of a common prostitute or living in circumstances calculated to cause, encourage, or favour the seduction of the child' could be sent to a home or certified school for their own protection.[138] This is what happened in a case from January 1930 when an eleven-year-old boy was sent to live at a Barnardo's children's home because his mother was a 'convicted prostitute' who had been sentenced to six-months hard labour for exposing the boy to 'an environment likely to cause unnecessary suffering'.[139]

During the trial the police officer explained how he had known the woman had been working as a prostitute for four years and he had cautioned her and pointed out the risks for her son. By the 1950s it was becoming less common for children to be taken away from their mother in these types of situations. For example, in 1954 Mr Basil Henriques, an East London magistrate, gave an address to a probation officers conference in Stratford-upon-Avon which highlighted these changing attitudes. Mr Henriques told the audience of probation officers that

> the most important thing in a child's life is love ... if there was love between a mother and her children, even if she were a mother in a pigsty or a prostitute in a brothel, it was doubtful whether any court would justify taking the children away from her.[140]

Nonetheless, during the majority of the period between 1900 and 1962 women working in prostitution were at risk of having their children taken away from them if the court felt that their work was placing their children at risk. Therefore, although some women may have refused probation, broken their probation bond or run away from rescue homes, others may have accepted probation as the only alternative which allowed them to avoid prison and stay with their children.

Psychiatric treatment

The previous chapter demonstrated how probation was increasingly used as a method for providing psychiatric treatment to men convicted of various sexual offences. Women placed on probation for prostitution offences, however, were far less likely to receive psychiatric treatment. Whereas male sexual offences were increasingly seen as having psychological causes that could be cured through medical treatment, prostitution was understood more from a moral or economic perspective – a type of work that women chose or were forced into due to a mixture of social and economic factors. There are no statistics about the type of conditions that people were given as part of their probation bond. It is therefore difficult to know whether or not some women on probation for soliciting offences were sent for psychiatric treatment. However, none of the probation records or newspaper reports I have consulted have mentioned women being sent for psychiatric treatment.

If the psychology of these women *was* considered, it was usually in terms of providing a reason for why some women were able to transgress the normal moral codes that stopped other women from resorting to prostitution to make money. It was thought their willingness to engage in 'immoral' behaviour could either be due to an inherited psychological deficiency, such as 'feeble-mindedness' which meant that they had not developed a normal 'moral compass', or due to the damaging psychological effect of an early exposure to immorality. By the mid-twentieth century, there were some who considered prostitution in more psychological terms and sought to provide psychiatric treatment for women. For example, the Report on Probation Social Work during the Second World War that was referred to earlier included a section on how psychiatric help might be useful for some of the women involved in prostitution. The report described how

> a number of girls who come before the courts are mentally unstable in a very marked degree, and often one feels that a case should be dealt with under a machinery of mental hospitals or observation centres rather than by the legal system. Here is another crying need for a number of residential observation homes and hostels under qualified psychiatrists.[141]

The contribution given by the Leicester Probation Committee similarly noted how some women involved in prostitution were 'feeble-minded' and needed psychiatric help. To explain further, the Leicester Committee gave an example of a 'mentally defective' twenty-one-year-old woman with a 'mental age of a 10-year-old' who had been found living off prostitution and was placed on probation. The author of the report lamented that 'there is nothing she can do, probation or prison won't help her, but she will inevitably keep coming before the courts'.[142] Despite their concern about women's psychiatric health, both the writers of these reports appear to have seen a woman's psychological problems as justification for them not to be placed on probation in the first place, rather than seeing probation as the method in which psychiatric treatment would be made available to those women, as was the case with men convicted of sexual offences. Even in cases where psychological considerations were acknowledged as a contributing factor as to why some women became involved in prostitution, women who were placed on probation were mainly supervised by probation officers in their own homes or sent to rescue homes, where, as we have seen, hard work, religious teaching and training for jobs in domestic labour were the main methods used to reform their behaviour.

Conclusion

Across England, Scotland and Wales the aim behind placing women on probation for prostitution offences was to reform them into 'respectable' women who could then leave prostitution and return to their 'proper place' in the domestic sphere. Whether that aim was met via sending women to rescue homes or placing them under the supervision of a probation officer while she resided in her own home, the key thing was to impress upon her the rules of respectable femininity. Exactly how successful this method was in achieving this aim, however, is less clear, especially given the lack of source material which deals with women's experiences. The records do show, however, that the use of probation reduced the number of women being sent to prison for soliciting and that some women appeared grateful for this intervention. Although the fact that some women ran away from reform homes and continued their involvement in prostitution suggests that attempts to control and reform women were not always so successful, and for those who were forced to reside in rescue homes for long stretches of time, probation was not necessarily preferable to prison. Nonetheless, even though some women tried to resist probation with varying levels of success, others used probation as an opportunity to avoid prison, gain new skills and find 'respectable' work outside of prostitution. In those cases, at least, probation was successful in its aim to return women to the domestic sphere.

The previous chapters have shown how probation was used to police both men's and women's behaviour in the private sphere, including their sexual activities. However, this chapter has further emphasized how this policing differed according to gender. In cases relating to male sexual offences probation played an important role in facilitating the treatment of these behaviours as mental illnesses, but this was generally not the case when it came to policing women's sexual behaviour. For women, probation was instrumental in ensuring that their moral failings were emphasized and that the main action required to 'cure' these women was to restore them to their supposedly 'rightful' position in the domestic sphere. On the one hand, this could have been beneficial for women, as it meant they avoided having to undergo medical treatments which could have long-lasting detrimental impact on their physical and psychological health. On the other hand, it highlights how women's sexual behaviour continued to be viewed in more moralistic terms than men's was. Crucially, their incarceration in rescue homes could involve much longer lasting restriction on their freedom than was the case for men who were given medical treatment as outpatients. Nonetheless, despite these gendered differences in the methods that were used to try and reform men and women's sexual behaviour, it is clear that probation in both situations remained instrumental in facilitating the state's attempts to regulate the sexual behaviours of its citizens.

Notes

1. Louise Settle, *Sex for Sale in Scotland: Prostitution in Edinburgh and Glasgow, 1900–1939* (Edinburgh University Press, 2016).
2. The Burgh Police (Scotland) Act 1892 (55 & 56 Vict. c.55).
3. The Edinburgh Municipal and Police Act 1879 (42 & 43 Vict. c.cxxxii).
4. The Glasgow Police (Further Powers) Act 1892 (55 & 56 Vict. c.165).
5. *The Scotsman,* 21 March 1911, p. 9.
6. *The Scotsman,* 20 January 1914, p. 5.
7. Ibid.
8. Ibid.
9. Ibid.
10. Ibid.
11. Criminal Justice Administration Act 1914 (4 & 5 Geo.5. c.58).
12. Edinburgh City Archives (hereafter ECA), Edinburgh Police Court Records, 21 July 1921; ECA: Edinburgh Police Court Records, 21 April 1921; ECA: Edinburgh Police Court Records, 5 February 1921.
13. Settle, *Sex for Sale in Scotland,* see chapter 4; Linda Mahood, *The Magdalenes: Prostitution in the Nineteenth Century* (Routledge, 1990).
14. Settle, *Sex for Sale in Scotland,* chapter 4.
15. ECA: Edinburgh Police Court Records, 21 September 1921.
16. Settle, *Sex for Sale in Scotland,* chapter 4.
17. Glasgow City Archives, D.tc 14/2/15: Reports of the Corporation of Glasgow 1919–1920 vol. 9: Report by the Special Committee on Probation of Offenders and Recommendation as Approved by the Corporation.
18. Ibid., p. 82.
19. Ibid.
20. Ibid.
21. Ibid.
22. Ibid.
23. Linda Mahood, *Policing Gender, Class and Family in Britain, 1800–1945* (Routledge, 1995).
24. The Vagrancy Act 1824 (5 Geo. 4. c. 83); The Metropolitan Police Act 1839 (2 & 3 Vict. c.47).
25. The Town Police Clauses Act 1847 (10 & 11 Vict. c.89).
26. Julia Laite, *Common Prostitutes and Ordinary Citizen: Commercial Sex in London, 1885–1960* (Palgrave, 2012), p. 88.
27. Ibid.
28. *The Common Cause,* 19 September 1912, p. 417.
29. Ibid.

30 *The Bolton Evening News,* 20 January 1909, p. 3; *Hartlepool Norther Daily Mail,* 23 January 1911, p. 3.
31 *Sheffield Daily Telegraph,* 23 January 1912, p. 11.
32 *Folkstone, Hythe, Sandgate and Cheriton Herald,* 1 January 1916, p. 8.
33 Ibid.
34 *Yarmouth Independent,* 29 October 1938, p. 2.
35 Ibid.
36 The Departmental Committee on the Probation of Offenders Act 1907.
37 *Marylebone Mercury,* 6 February 1943, p. 1.
38 *Illustrated Police News,* 1 March 1934, p. 8.
39 *The Whitstable Times,* 6 September 1919, p. 3.
40 Angela Woollacott, '"Khaki Fever" and Its Control: Gender, Class, Age and Sexual Morality on the British Homefront in the First World War', *Journal of Contemporary History,* 29, 2 (1994), pp. 325–47.
41 *The Essex County Chronicle,* 13 April 1917, p. 2.
42 The Children Act 1908 (Edw. VII c. 67).
43 *Evening Despatch,* 9 July 1942, p. 1.
44 Ibid.
45 *Daily Herald,* 2 July 1934, p. 7.
46 Ibid.
47 Louise Jackson, *Child Sexual Abuse in Victorian England* (Routledge, 1999); Carol Smart, 'A History of Ambivalence and Conflict in the Discursive Construction of the "Child Victim" of Sexual Abuse', *Social & legal studies,* 8, 3 (1999), pp. 391–409.
48 *The People,* 12 May 1918, p. 5.
49 *The Woman's Leader,* 1 December 1922, p. 349.
50 Ibid.
51 Ibid.
52 For more about the Street Offences Committee, see Stefan Slater, 'Lady Astor and the Ladies of the Night: The Home Office, the Metropolitan Police and the Politics of the Street Offences Committee, 1927–28', *Law and History Review,* 30, 2 (2012), pp. 533–73.
53 Clive Emsley, 'Sergeant Goddard: The Story of the Rotten Apple, or a Diseased Orchard?' in A. Srebnick and R. Levy (eds.), *Crime and Culture a Historical Perspective* (Ashgate, 2005), pp. 85–104.
54 *The Vote,* 9 March 1928, p. 78.
55 Ibid.
56 *The Scotsman,* 28 January 1928, p. 11.
57 For further details on the methods used in Liverpool see, Samantha Caslin, *Save the Womanhood!: Vice, Urban Immorality and Social Control in Liverpool, c. 1900-1976* (Liverpool University Press, 2018).

58 *The Scotsman,* 16 January 1928, p. 13.
59 Ibid.
60 Sonya O. Rose, *Which People's War?* (Oxford University Press, 2003).
61 Manchester City Archives, GB127.M117/3/5: Manchester Probation Committee Minutes, Annual Reports for 1942–3.
62 Ibid.
63 *The Sphere,* 1 May 1943, p. 152.
64 *Liverpool Daily Post,* 27 January 1941, p. 3.
65 *The Wiltshire Times,* 13 January 1945, p. 7.
66 National Archives: H45/19505: Summary of Probation Officers' Reports on Social Work During the War.
67 Ibid.
68 Ibid.
69 Ibid.
70 Ibid.
71 Ibid.
72 Ibid.
73 Ibid.
74 Ibid.
75 Ibid.
76 Ibid.
77 Ibid.
78 Ibid.
79 Ibid.
80 Ibid.
81 Ibid.
82 Ibid.
83 Ibid.
84 For a more detailed discussion of the Wolfenden Report and prostitution, see Samantha Caslin and Julia Laite, *Wolfenden's Women: Prostitution in Post-War Britain* (Palgrave MacMillan, 2020).
85 The Street Offences Act 1959 (7 & 8 Eliz 2 c.57). Under this act the maximum punishment was: 'a fine not exceeding ten pounds or, for an offence committed after a previous conviction, to a fine not exceeding twenty-five pounds or, for an offence committed after more than one previous conviction, to a fine not exceeding twenty-five pounds or imprisonment for a period not exceeding three months or both'.
86 Laite, *Common Prostitutes and Ordinary Citizens.*
87 *The Birmingham Post,* 5 September 1957, p. 3.
88 *Evening News,* 22 November 1957, p. 14.
89 Ibid.

90 Home Office Circular 109, 1959.
91 Ibid.
92 *The Birmingham Post*, 26 March 1959, p. 7.
93 Ibid.
94 Ibid.
95 Ibid.
96 *The Birmingham Post,* 16 June 1959, p. 5.
97 Ibid.
98 Ibid.
99 *Hartlepool Northern Daily Mail,* 4 July 1925, p. 3.
100 Ibid.
101 Ibid.
102 Glamorgan Archives, PSCBO/60/1: Cardiff Probation Committee Minutes, 1919–1929.
103 ECA: Edinburgh Police Court Records, 9 October 1916.
104 ECA: Edinburgh Police Court Records, 9 May 1916.
105 ECA: Edinburgh Police Court Records, 23 August 1935.
106 Glamorgan Archives, PSCBO/60/1 Probation Committee minutes, 17 September 1923.
107 *Milngavie and Bearsden Herald,* 27 November 1914, p. 6.
108 National Records of Scotland (NRS), ED20/413: Probation Officers Reports, 1920.
109 NRS, ED20/405: Probation Officers Reports, 1910.
110 Ibid.
111 *West London Observer*, 4 October 1929, p. 12.
112 Ibid.
113 *The West London Observer*, 29 July 1938, p. 11
114 Ibid.
115 Ibid.
116 Ibid.
117 *Folkstone Herald*, 8 September 1917, p. 7.
118 Ibid.
119 Ibid.
120 Ibid.
121 Ibid.
122 Ibid.
123 *The Courier,* 20 April 1945, p. 3.
124 *West London Press*, 12 April 194, p. 4
125 Ibid
126 Louisa Gordon, *Penal discipline* (1922), p. 128.
127 *Yorkshire Post and Leeds Mercury,* 6 November 1943, p. 3.
128 Ibid.

129 Ibid.
130 *Folkstone Herald*, 8 September 1917, p. 7
131 Ibid.
132 Ibid.
133 Ibid.
134 *The Middlesex Chronicle*, 23 October 1915, p. 7.
135 *Surrey Mirror and County Post*, 14 August 1917, p. 4.
136 Ibid.
137 Ibid.
138 The Children's and Young Persons Act 1908 (Geo V. c.67).
139 *Boston Guardian,* 17 May 1930, p. 8.
140 *The Birmingham Post*, 9 October 1954, p. 7.
141 National Archives, H45/19505: Summary of Probation Officers' Reports on Social Work during the War.
142 Ibid.

6

Conclusions and reflections

Like many previous histories of probation, this book has examined how the gradual professionalization of probation during the early-to-mid twentieth century influenced the extent to which religion and the behavioural sciences shaped the methods that were used to rehabilitate probationers. Unlike previous studies, however, this book has moved beyond this introspective approach to explore how these developments in probation's history shaped the policing of specific types of offences, particularly those that occurred in the private sphere or involved interpersonal relationships. By focusing on the private sphere, it has been possible to view probation from a different perspective – one that emphasizes the importance of gender and notions of domesticity to the history of probation. Most crucially, the book has demonstrated how the home and ideas about domesticity were crucial to both the process of rehabilitation itself and the endeavour to make the home a safe environment in which these domestic ideals could come into fruition.

Central to this mission to make the domestic sphere a safe environment was the idea that, given the right material and psychological support, probation officers could stop people from reoffending by helping them to reform their own behaviour. Probation was therefore especially fitting for policing the private sphere because many of the behaviours which most threatened the viability of the home as a stable, safe and wholesome environment were difficult to police in more traditional ways. While the walls of the home could protect people from the dangers of the outside world, they could also make it easier for violence, abuse and self-harm to go on undetected. However, by penetrating the physical and psychological walls of the home and attempting to solve some of the underlying problems that were at the root of people's offending behaviours, probation had the potential to bring about real, long-lasting change. For this approach to work, however, probation officers had to rely on probationers' cooperation and willingness to follow the rules set down in probation bonds. This book has explored the extent to which probation officers were successful in gaining this cooperation, and the consequences that these successes or failures had for the individuals and families involved, and for society more widely.

How successful was probation for policing the private sphere?

Determining how successful probation was at policing the private sphere largely depends on how successful officers were in motivating people to reform their own behaviour. However, given the nature of the sources available, assessing this is very difficult, especially as there was no system in place to record whether probationers went on to reoffend after their probation period ended. The records kept by the probation officers generally showed that their efforts were fairly successful in the short term, and the statistical data they created to keep track of each probationer's progress also supported this. However, given that these calculations and assessments were made by probation officers themselves, the objectiveness of their findings can be called into question. It was in probation officers' best interests to write favourable reports which showed that they were able to successfully rehabilitate people, and they may have missed, overlooked or underreported some of the instances where probationers broke their bonds. This was not necessarily driven by self-interest but arguably by a desire to help people, especially if a negative report could result in someone being sent to prison. Probationers may also have been skilled at hiding their offending behaviour from officers.

However, if we look closely at the findings from each chapter, we can learn more about how successful probation was in specific contexts. Chapter 1 showed how one of the most time-consuming tasks undertaken by probation officers in England and Wales did not involve rehabilitating people who had committed offences but was instead linked to their involvement in marriage reconciliation. The high demand for this service, especially during the 1940s and 1950s, showed that there was considerable appetite for this type of marriage counselling from couples who were contemplating separation and divorce. Moreover, the fact that the government supported this service showed a willingness on the part of the state to intervene in the private lives of married couples due to the importance that was placed on promoting marriage stability in the interests of national stability.

The aim of marriage reconciliation was to provide couples with advice and support, and to create an environment that was conducive to listening and talking so that couples could learn how to better communicate with each other. Probation officers also tried to help solve some of the underlying practical problems that led to discontent, such as unemployment and overcrowded housing conditions. In this respect, marriage reconciliation efforts can be seen as successful in the sense that they provided a much-needed service for couples who had few alternative sources of such support. The statistics compiled by probation officers about the number of successful reconciliations they facilitated also backs up the assertion that marriage reconciliation could help to stop couples separating in the short term. However, as mentioned above, statistics compiled by the probation service should be treated with caution, especially because in this situation they only referred to whether marriage reconciliation had been successful in preventing an official separation on a particular occasion. They tell us little about the opinions of the husband and wife or about how long the reconciliation lasted.

The extent to which probation was successful in stopping domestic violence is even more ambiguous. Chapter 2 has shown how probation offered a more practical approach for dealing with violent men in situations where the imprisonment of the male breadwinner would have led to further hardship for the wife. Rather than a fine or a short prison sentence that would do little to stop men reoffending, the aim of probation was to encourage men to reform their own behaviour by promoting self-control and abstinence. The use of abstinence orders was seen as particularly helpful for those women whose husbands' violence was connected to alcohol – although this condition of abstinence did not necessarily mean that the men stopped drinking because it was impossible to keep a surveillance on their activities at all times.

By providing financial and practical support, probation officers were able to help alleviate some of the problems which contributed to domestic violence, such as bad housing and unemployment. This was especially helpful in the period prior to the welfare state. However, this approach did little to solve the wider socio-economic and gender inequalities that contributed to making an environment in which violence could occur and women were unable to leave abusive husbands. Indeed, focusing on stopping violence by prohibiting men from drinking alcohol, for example, meant that other important factors behind male violence, such as misogyny, gender inequality and the patriarchal structuring of society, were not given sufficient attention. Moreover, if men were unwilling or unable to reform their behaviour, there was a danger that probation could allow men to go on committing violence with impunity. This put women at risk and belittled the seriousness of domestic violence. However, the alternative of a prison sentence did not necessarily make the long-term situation any safer for women, especially because sentences were often woefully short. Unless the underlying causes that were underpinning men's violent and misogynist behaviour on both the individual and societal levels were dealt with, these men would continue to pose a threat to women. The aim of encouraging long-term changes in men's behaviour was therefore well-intentioned, but unfortunately in practice this aim was not always successfully carried out.

Chapter 3 has similarly shown discrepancies between the aims of probation policy and its results. It was hoped that placing people who attempted suicide on probation would provide them with a 'safety net' of support that they may otherwise have lacked. In some situations, this could include people being sent for psychiatric treatment at a hospital as an in- or outpatient, which meant that they could gain access to free psychiatric treatment without having to suffer the stigma of being certified as insane. In other situations, the safety net consisted of practical and emotional help. This could involve a form of 'layperson talking therapy' provided by probation officers, or help in dealing with more practical issues, such as finding employment and housing. However, the chapter has shown how this safety net often had many holes and not everyone received sufficient help, especially in situations where people were released into the care of their family without being given psychiatric treatment or a supervision order. Nonetheless, given that the alterative to probation was to do nothing or send people to prison, a safety net with holes was better than none at all.

The question of whether probation was successful in the context of policing male sexual offences is a particularly difficult topic to address. Chapter 4 has shown how probation was increasingly used as a way to ensure that men were given psychiatric treatment to 'cure' behaviours which were deemed sexually deviant. In situations where men had sexually assaulted women, children and other men, this approach may have been warranted if it could ensure that these men no longer posed a threat to future victims. Hormone treatments which reduced a man's libido were somewhat capable of achieving this aim, although there is little evidence to show exactly how effective medical interventions were in stopping abusive behaviour in the long term. If this treatment failed, however, the men continued to pose a risk to the public. In situations where men had been convicted of gross indecency with consenting adult men, the use of probation to force men to undergo psychiatric treatments was much more problematic because we now understand that homosexuality is not an illness or something which should be criminalized. There were no victims to protect; yet, the men who underwent these treatments suffered from side effects which could have long-term impacts on their psychological and physical health. What is more, these treatments were largely unsuccessful in their misguided aim of converting men to heterosexuality.

Chapter 5 has shown how efforts to stop women soliciting for the purposes of prostitution were somewhat more successful than attempts to police male sexual offences. Rather than being required to undergo psychiatric treatment, women were more likely to be sent to institutions run by religious voluntary organizations, where the aim was to rehabilitate them back into the private sphere by teaching them domestic skills. In some cases, these efforts proved successful, and there are examples of women being able to leave prostitution and find new employment, thanks to the support of probation officers and voluntary institutions that gave them practical and material aid. However, the rehabilitation process depended upon the women's cooperation and a desire to exit prostitution. For those who did not have this motivation, probation was unlikely to be effective and many women broke their probation bonds and ran away from voluntary institutions. Moreover, probation was only intended to be used for women who were considered 'newly fallen' and thus more likely to be receptive to the rehabilitation methods used in voluntary reform homes and by probation officers. Those considered 'hardened' prostitutes were unlikely to be placed on probation, which meant that the scope and effectiveness of this approach were somewhat limited. Making distinctions in this way also reinforced imagined distinctions between 'virtuous' and 'immoral' women and had serious consequences for the policing of female sexuality and the moral surveillance of women in the public sphere.

Experiences of probation

How the probationers themselves viewed probation, and whether they deemed it successful, is especially difficult to establish. On the most basic level, it is fair to assume that probation as an alternative to imprisonment was viewed favourably by those who were facing the prospect of a prison sentence. Moreover, for those who wanted to stop their offending behaviour, probation offered a much better chance of achieving that goal than imprisonment. The advice, friendship and assistance that probation officers gave people, and the provision of financial aid, psychiatric therapy and help with finding employment and new housing, could have a significant impact on probationers' lives and make it easier for them to desist from offending behaviour. However, whether this impact was viewed positively depended upon individual circumstances, and the lack of extant sources by the probationers themselves means it is very difficult to know how they experienced probation. There are a small number of documents which were written by probationers, such as letters to probation officers, but in the main we have to rely on documents that were not produced by the probationers themselves. In these documents there are instances in which probationers appeared to respond well to rehabilitation efforts and seemed thankful for the opportunities that probation provided. For example, men who sexually assaulted children were often keen to be placed on probation so that they could receive medical treatment that would hopefully 'cure' them. However, given that these records were compiled by the probation service, evidence of positive experiences was arguably more likely to be kept than documents referring to complaints or bad experiences.

If we look at the actions of probationers, the fact that a considerable number of people broke their bonds or left the voluntary and medical institutions to which they had been sent suggests that not everyone responded well to probation or felt that it was preferable to prison. These acts of resistance also remind us that probation was based on cooperation, which meant that probationers had some input in the process. While the extent of their agency was limited by the fact that breaking a probation bond could result in a prison sentence, the probation officers' powers of surveillance were limited, and probationers could have considerable influence over everyday practices of probation. Nonetheless, while this book has provided some examples of how probation impacted the lives of probationers in the short term, a fuller understanding of their experiences and the long-term impact that probation had on their lives would require an in-depth oral history study.

Was probation a let off?

A recurring theme throughout this book and the history of probation more generally has been the debate about whether probation was a lenient sentence. Supporters of probation and the rehabilitative ideal were keen to defend probation against the commonly made assumption that probation was a 'let off'. They were aware that many people did not fully understand the aims and methods of probation, especially in relation to the types of rules and conditions that probationers had to follow. Rather than a method of individualized rehabilitation that was aimed at helping people to desist from offending in the long term, it was feared that many people saw probation simply as a means to avoid sending young and/or petty first-time offenders to prison. However, this book has shown that probation was used to rehabilitate adults in a wide range of situations and could sometimes result in much higher levels of intervention into people's private lives than would have resulted from a fine or short prison sentence. This was especially the case when probationers were required to reside in institutions or undergo medical treatment. For example, Chapter 5 has shown how women sent to voluntary reform homes after being found guilty of soliciting could have their freedom restricted for far longer periods than if they had been given the maximum prison sentence for soliciting. Similarly, Chapter 4 has shown how men convicted of indecent exposure could be required to undergo medical treatment, either as an in- or an outpatient, which potentially had much more far-reaching consequences than the alternative fine or short prison sentence. However, it was not only situations in which people were sent to institutions or required to undergo medical treatment that probation could result in intensive interventions into people's everyday lives. Probationers were expected to meet regularly with their probation officers and to allow them into their homes to inspect things such as their cleanliness, domestic skills and spending habits. Probationers could also be required to follow certain conditions, such as abstaining from alcohol, finding and retaining employment and not associating with certain people, all of which could involve considerable intervention into their private lives.

However, not all probationers were subject to such intense levels of intervention into their private lives, and in some situations, probation *was* used as a lenient sentencing option. The attitude of the probation officer, magistrate, JP or judge towards the offence and the offender was crucial in determining whether probation was used as a 'let off' because these individuals determined the remit of the probation bond, especially whether an individual was placed under supervision and given certain conditions to follow. For example, Chapter 2 has shown how the JP, magistrate or judge's assessment of whether a man had been 'provoked' into assaulting his wife could determine whether he was required to be placed under supervision. That assessment, in turn, was based on judgements about what constituted reasonable and acceptable behaviour of men and women within marriage. For instance, a man who assaulted his wife after he found out about her adultery might be treated more sympathetically than a man who assaulted his wife who was known to be 'faithful' and 'dutiful'. Attitudes towards factors such as age, sexuality, ethnicity, class and gender were therefore very important. Similarly, social enquiry reports made by probation officers that assessed the home environment, including whether alcohol, unemployment or other social factors played a role in causing violence, could influence a judge's opinions about the character of the husband and wife which could determine whether conditions such as abstinence were included in the bond.

The importance of attitudes towards class, gender and sexuality for shaping probation practices can be seen especially clearly in Chapter 4, which dealt with male sexual offences. This chapter showed that men from respectable middle-class backgrounds who had been placed on probation for homosexual offences with consenting adult men were less likely to be placed under supervision or required to follow certain conditions, such as undergoing medical treatment, than men from working-class backgrounds. However, it was not only opinions about the 'character' of the offender that were important. Chapter 4 showed how assessments made about the character of the victims of sexual assaults could also influence the conditions of the probation bond, including whether the accused was required to be placed under supervision and/or receive psychiatric treatment. For example, in situations where a man had assaulted a teenage girl or woman whose 'virtue' prior to the assault had been called into question, it was less likely that the man would be placed under supervision or be required to undergo medical treatment. In those situations, probation *was* sometimes used as a 'let off' by judges who believed that the man had not committed an offence that warranted a harsh sentence because the victim was blamed for provoking the assault through her own 'immoral' behaviour. The high levels of discretion involved in the probation system could therefore result in prejudices surrounding class, age, gender and sexuality having a serious impact on the everyday practices of probation.

Influence of local differences, Christianity and psychiatry

The high levels of discretion involved in the probation system also meant that probation practice could vary a lot between different locations. The considerable discrepancies between the types of records available for each probation committee area have meant that a like-with-like comparison has not been possible. However, by looking at practices in different towns and cities across the UK, this book has highlighted how important local environments were for shaping probation practices. Most notably, the different legislation and legal practices in Scotland, compared to those of England and Wales, resulted in some important differences in probation policy and practice. For example, in Scotland there was no official involvement of probation officers in marriage reconciliation and attempted suicide was not illegal. There were also important variations in probation-specific legislation, procedures, rules and training programmes. However, despite these considerable differences, the book has shown that there were also some important similarities and examples of policy exchange. For example, the practice of placing women convicted of soliciting offences on probation and sending them to reform homes was a policy that England and Wales adopted from Scotland.

The book has also illustrated how there could be more differences between areas *within* the same country than there were *between* countries. This can be seen most prominently in the role that local conditions and individual personalities had on the ways in which religion and the behavioural sciences influenced probation practices. For example, the attitude of a particular JP, magistrate or judge towards psychiatry could have a decisive impact on whether probationers were given conditions stipulating that they undergo psychiatric treatment as part of their probation order. Even though the acceptance of psychiatric interventions generally increased from the 1930s onwards as probation became increasingly professionalized, the rate at which individuals embraced these new approaches differed considerably. For example, some probation officers and magistrates, such as magistrate Claud Mullins in London, were extremely enthusiastic about psychology whereas others, such as Mary Wilkinson, a probation officer in Bedfordshire between 1939 and 1972, continued to emphasize the importance of religious faith throughout her career and remained sceptical of psychiatry. The local availability of treatment facilities was also important. For example, in large cities with easy access to psychiatric institutions and outpatient clinics it was easier for JPs, magistrates and judges to find suitable places to send probationers for treatment than in smaller towns or rural areas with few psychiatric services nearby. Conversely, in areas with strong religious missionary traditions and an active voluntary sector, it was more likely that probationers would be placed under the supervision of people affiliated with religious organizations or sent to institutions run by voluntary organizations. The likelihood that a probationer would undergo medical treatment or be sent to a voluntary institution could therefore vary considerably in different parts of the country, or even within the same city, depending upon the services available and the inclinations of a particular magistrate, JP or judge.

The extent to which religion and the behavioural sciences shaped probation policy also depended on the particular offence in question. For example, in the case of domestic violence, the influence of the Christian temperance movement remained significant due to the emphasis that was placed on giving men abstinence orders (although rather than relying on men to voluntarily sign the pledge, probation officers now had the power of the law to enforce abstinence orders). In policing attempted suicide, however, the influence of the behavioural sciences on probation practice can be seen more strongly. Indeed, Chapter 3 has shown that the use of probation in cases of attempted suicide enabled more people to receive psychiatric treatment as an inpatient or an outpatient without needing to be certified as insane. This meant that more people were able to access psychiatric treatment who otherwise might not have been eligible for free treatment or may have been reluctant to seek help due to the stigma of being certified and institutionalized. In this respect, probation played an important role in both the medicalization of suicide and in paving the way towards the deinstitutionalization of psychiatric care that occurred after the 1960s. However, this did not mean that the religious philanthropic approach no longer played a role in helping suicidal people. The emphasis that was placed on helping probationers deal with some of the material problems that had contributed to suicidal behaviour, by helping them to find employment or new homes, for example, still resembled older philanthropic approaches to helping suicidal people. Similarly, probation officers' attempts to provide their own version of lay counselling by sympathetically listening to people's problems and offering friendly advice also resembled older approaches based on the motto 'advise, assist, befriend'. Clearly then, both science and religion had an influence on shaping the methods that probation officers used, and these two approaches could often complement each other.

The complexities involved in disentangling the ways in which both science and religion influenced probation practice can be seen most clearly in the work of probation officers involved in marriage reconciliation. Here we can again see how officers used methods inspired by both psychiatry and Christianity, and in many instances developed their own unique methods that incorporated elements of both. For example, the advice given to couples was often heavily influenced by Christian ideas about the sanctity of marriage and the gender norms that accompanied those traditions. However, the type of counselling provided by probation officers could closely resemble that offered by professional therapists, and often incorporated theories inspired by their education in psychology and new concepts of mutual love and the companionate marriage.

Gender and the penal welfare complex

The book has shown how a good relationship based on cooperation between the probation officer and probationer was essential for the rehabilitation process to work. To encourage this cooperation, probationers were provided with practical and material help, along with the offer of friendship and emotional support. Crucial to ensuring people cooperated, however, was the fact that successful cooperation with the probation officer enabled people to avoid imprisonment. Probation, therefore, is the perfect example of a form of social control that is best described by David Garland in his concept of the penal welfare complex. A major criticism of this penal welfare approach has been its propensity to be used as a way to force middle-class ideologies about domesticity, gender and sexuality onto working-class homes – something which this book has shown could be especially problematic when probation was used to police the private sphere. However, the book has shown how the type of social control envisioned by Garland and others was not necessarily achieved so completely as one might expect. Probation relied on cooperation, and if the people placed on probation were unwilling to cooperate, there were many ways in which they could undermine the effectiveness of probation as a form of social control. Their attempts to avoid cooperating with probation officers may not always have been successful, especially as breeching the conditions of a probation bond could result in a prison sentence, but these attempts remind us that there were limits to the level of control that probation officers had over their charges.

From another perspective, the book has shown how focusing too narrowly on the negative aspects of probation's propensity for social control risks obscuring some of the more positive aspects of how probation was used to protect people from domestic violence, sexual abuse and self-harm. This book has therefore sought to shed light on some of the ways in which probation was used to help families who were affected by various types of offending behaviours that occurred in the private sphere which were not easily stopped through more traditional criminal justice approaches. Although probation was not always successful in stopping people from reoffending, by trying to tailor the rehabilitation methods to the individual needs and circumstances of each probationer, probation at least had the potential to offer a new approach that was more effective than fines and short prison sentences.

Another criticism often levelled at probation is in relation to the gendered expectations that were placed on women to live up to idealized notions of respectable femininity which prioritized motherhood, domesticity and sexual purity. This is certainly a fair argument, and Chapters 2 and 5 have shown how this criticism was especially relevant in relation to the policing of domestic violence and prostitution. However, the book has shown that it was not only women who were expected to follow certain gendered standards of behaviour. Men were also expected to live up to specific notions of domesticated respectable masculinity that required them to fulfil the role of a caring and responsible husband, father and breadwinner. This expectation that both men and women were responsible for ensuring a happy domestic environment can be seen most clearly in Chapter 1, which showed how both husband and wife were expected to change their behaviour in order to live up to specific gender roles within marriage that were, in theory at least, separate but equal.

Nonetheless, despite both men and women being expected to conform with separate sphere ideologies, the methods used to encourage them to do so could differ immensely. For example, Chapter 4 has shown how men convicted of various sexual offences could be sent for medical treatment to 'cure' their sexually 'deviant' behaviour. By subduing men's libidos through the use of hormone therapies or converting them to heterosexuality through conversion therapies and psychoanalysis, it was hoped that medical interventions would re-align these men's transgressive behaviours so that they fitted better with heteronormative concepts of masculinity. Chapter 5, however, has demonstrated how women who were convicted of soliciting for the purposes of prostitution were unlikely to receive any psychiatric treatment and were instead more likely to be sent to religious voluntary organizations to be rehabilitated through hard work and religious piety. By policing female sexuality in this way, the legacy of probation's origins in Christian missionary work thus continued to have much more of an influence over the methods used to police women's sexuality than psychiatry did. These discrepancies between the methods used to rehabilitate men and women demonstrate how gender could have an important impact on shaping the ways in which science and religion influenced probation practices.

To understand why gender had such a strong influence on how probation was practised requires a better understanding of the ways in which notions of what constituted a mental illness (and who needed psychiatric treatment) were connected to concepts of masculinity and femininity. For example, one explanation for why men who committed sexual offences against children or with other men were more likely to get medical treatment is because homosexuality and paedophilia were regarded as such an abhorrent threat to masculinity that it was easier (and possibly even necessary for some people) to conceive of these men as being psychologically ill. Female prostitution, however, was more likely to be seen as a form of economic activity in which women engaged in out of material necessity, rather than because of mental illness. Therefore, while supposedly men needed medical treatment to cure their illness, women could instead be helped through training in domestic skills so that they could get married or find employment in other, more respectable occupations. This explanation would also account for why men convicted of sexually assaulting adult women were less likely to be required to undergo psychiatric treatment, because an assault on an adult woman was seen as an excess of normal heterosexual male desire, rather than a sign of mental illness. This type of behaviour could therefore be rectified by encouraging more self-control. Similarly, men who physically assaulted their wives were also unlikely to be sent for psychiatric treatment because their behaviour was again considered an excess of normal male aggression, which in some instances was seen as an understandable reaction by men who were apparently 'provoked' by the 'errant' behaviour of their wives. While violence was generally not viewed as acceptable, the way to stop it was not by giving men therapy, but by promoting self-control and abstinence. The only situation in which both men and women were likely to receive psychiatric treatment was when somebody had attempted suicide because the desire to kill yourself was strongly connected with psychological illness. Even then, however, gender could still influence the likelihood that a man or woman would receive psychiatric treatment in any given situation.

Concluding thoughts and reflections

This book has not provided an exhaustive policy history of probation – that aim has already been achieved by others.[1] Instead, the book has focused on probation's contribution to the policing of particular offences that occurred in the private sphere and on what these contributions can tell us about British social history. Similarly, the aim of this final section is not to offer detailed probation policy advice, that is not a historian's task. Instead, the intention here is to reflect on some of the wider social issues relating to probation, gender and the policing of the private sphere that have been raised in the book and still have relevance today.

The book has shown how probation policy and practice in the period 1907–62 were both shaped by domestic sphere ideologies and helped to endorse them. The aim of making the domestic sphere a safer environment was well intentioned and, when successful, these policies can be credited with protecting people from abuse that was otherwise difficult to police. However, this preoccupation with domesticity could also have dangerous implications. For example, Chapters 1 and 2 highlighted how couples were sometimes encouraged to stay together in situations of domestic violence in the hope that men could be helped to change their behaviour. Not only could this leave women vulnerable to future abuse if probation failed to reform men, but this focus on the behaviour of individual men and women drew attention away from wider socio-economic inequalities and social attitudes that underpinned the prevalence of violence against women. Similarly, Chapters 4 and 5 demonstrated how probation officers' adherence to patriarchal ideologies that valued women's sexual purity contributed to a culture of victim-blaming. In some instances, this could even result in probation being used to give lenient sentences to men who assaulted women and girls that did not conform with these defined gender roles.

Today, men who are convicted of domestic violence and sexual assault are more likely to be given prison sentences than those in the period covered by this book (although that is not necessarily always the case, and the problems of underreporting and low conviction rates remain serious). The imposition of long prison sentences is important for protecting women and signalling the seriousness with which sexual assault and domestic violence are taken by society and the criminal justice system. However, recent studies have shown that persistent offenders account for a large percentage of all reported cases of domestic violence.[2] Therefore, unless these men are kept in prison for the rest of their lives, probation can play an important role in ensuring that men do not commit further offences upon their release. The emphasis that was placed on trying to get men to undergo sustained personal change in the early-to-mid twentieth century is therefore just as relevant for the twenty-first century.

Probation policy and practices are now much better informed when it comes to recognizing and addressing the attitudes and societal structures which underpin gender-based violence. Indeed, feminist theories have been central to many of the rehabilitation programmes that have been developed over the past twenty years to tackle domestic violence and the underlying gendered belief systems that contribute to its continued prevalence in society.[3] However, the problem of insufficient time and funding to carry out these policies and programmes can undermine their effectiveness, especially if time is not given for developing close individual relationships between supervisor and supervisee.[4] As we have seen throughout the book, if probation is to be successful, proper funding and training are essential, and so too are personal relationships. In addition to this, there are new methods which could be used to protect women that were not utilized in the early-to-mid twentieth century. For example, it was established in Chapter 2 how men who committed domestic violence during the early-to-mid twentieth century were unlikely to receive psychiatric treatment. However, recent studies have shown that a significant proportion of male perpetrators of domestic violence display evidence of psychological disorders.[5] Addressing men's underlying mental health problems could therefore be a helpful approach in suitable cases. Initiatives in the late twentieth century did see the introduction of programmes aimed at reducing male violence through the use of cognitive behavioural therapies.[6] The evidence about their success rates is mixed, but some studies have suggested that they were helpful in reducing reoffending in certain contexts.[7] Further research and funding are therefore needed to continue developing and improving these programmes.

All these initiatives, however, were put under threat in England and Wales when the English and Welsh probation service was part-privatized in 2014 and the responsibility for domestic abuse programmes was given to privately owned community rehabilitation companies (CRCs). The devastating results of this policy can be seen most starkly in the report made by HM Inspectorate of Probation in 2018 about the work of CRCs in relation to domestic violence.[8] The report concluded that there were no overall coordinated strategies in place to ensure good standards and that contractual targets were prioritized over good-quality and safe practice. Moreover, many of the practitioners were given unmanageable workloads and needed more training, support and oversight. Most worryingly, the report found that there was not enough contact between practitioners and people under their supervision and that work to protect victims was of grave concern. Fortunately, in May 2019 the UK government announced that all offenders in England and Wales will be monitored by the National Probation Service from December 2020, ending the role of CRCs in supervising low- and medium-risk offenders. Nonetheless, the speed at which good practices were undermined between 2014 and 2019 highlights the importance of not taking for granted the expertise and experience that had taken years to develop.

Domestic violence and sexual abuse committed by men remain a serious problem, but probation and criminal justice policies alone are not enough to protect people from these threats. As David Morran and others have shown, it is difficult for men to truly change their behaviour if they continue to live in a patriarchal society.[9] Indeed, this book reminds us that one of the reasons why it is so difficult to end domestic violence is because the attitudes and social structures which underpin gender inequality and misogyny are so deeply ingrained in British society and history. Education is one of the key ways in which these wider social and cultural attitudes could be reversed. However, although there has been marked progress in this respect, including the introduction in 2020 of statutory requirements to provide school children with relationship, sex and health education, not enough time and resources are dedicated to it. Chapters 1 and 3 highlighted how the probation service used to be involved in activities that were not strictly related to supervising people who had committed offences, but instead revolved around providing relationship advice and support for people who were facing marital breakdown or had attempted suicide. It may not be suitable or feasible to suggest that the probation service adopts these types of roles again. However, these chapters did highlight the fact that there once was more appetite for government funding of such initiatives. Perhaps, then, it is time to dedicate more resources to developing proper services that can provide the type of high-quality education and counselling needed to tackle the underlying cultural attitudes that underpin persistently high levels of domestic violence in British society.

The book has also demonstrated how the practical and financial help which probation officers and voluntary organizations gave women during the early-to-mid twentieth century was essential for helping them to escape from domestic violence. However, this type of integrated approach was undermined by the Conservative UK government's austerity policies, which began in 2009 and resulted in the de-funding of refuges for women and less economic support for low-income families, especially those headed by single mothers. All of this, in turn, made it less feasible for women to leave abusive partners safely. If we are to be serious about tackling domestic violence, then proper funding is needed to provide high-quality services for victims as well as effective rehabilitation programmes for perpetrators. The book has demonstrated how collaboration with voluntary organizations could be helpful for providing these types of services. However, the collaboration needs to happen under the guidance of professionals with high levels of relevant training and in the context of a properly resourced social security system that provides adequate welfare support for families who need it.

Even with the best services, some perpetrators will nevertheless still reoffend. This has been recognized in the context of sexual abuse and was one of the reasons behind the creation of the Violent and Sexual Offenders Register in Britain in 1997. However, there is currently nothing similar in the context of domestic violence. This is why organizations such as Paladin National Stalking Advocacy Service are campaigning for the creation of a register for serial stalkers and domestic violence perpetrators that can be incorporated into the existing framework for sex offenders. This type of register would help the probation service to protect people from domestic violence. Providing officers with tools like this is important because, as we have seen throughout this book, probation officers of the early-to-mid twentieth century were, like their modern-day counterparts, bound by existing laws and regulations and relied on support from others within the criminal justice system.

These reflections have primarily focused on the policing of domestic violence and sexual assault, but the arguments about the importance of adequate funding and training are equally valid to the wider context of probation, regardless of the specific type of offence in question. Crucially, the book has illustrated how important the relationship between the probation officer and the probationer was – especially in relation to how successfully officers were able to help motivate people to change, something which is still identified as a main factor in determining whether or not programmes are successful in stopping people from reoffending.[10] Building and sustaining these relationships needs skilled professionalism and time to develop. None of this can be done effectively 'on the cheap' for profit. Probation experts and practitioners already knew this to be true, and it was one of the many reasons why the majority of them so vehemently objected to the part-privatization of probation that occurred in England and Wales in 2014. It was also the reason why the part-privatization of probation failed and should not be allowed to happen again.

Notes

1. See, for example, Dorothy Bochel, *Probation and After-Care: Its Development in England and Wales* (Scottish Academic Press, 1976); Raymond Gard, *Probation and Rehabilitation in England and Wales, 1876–1962* (Bloomsbury Academic, 2014); George Mair and Lol Burke, *Redemption, Rehabilitation and Risk Management: A History of Probation* (Routledge, 2012); Maurice Vanstone, *Supervising Offenders in the Community: A History of Probation Theory and Practice* (Ashgate, 2004); Philip Whitehead and Roger Statham, *The History of Probation: Politics, Power and Cultural Change 1876–2005* (Crayford, 2006).
2. Amanda Robinson, 'Serial Domestic Abuse in Wales: An Exploratory Study into Its Definition, Prevalence, Correlates, and Management', *Victims & Offenders*, 12, 5 (2017), pp. 643–62.
3. Will Hughes, 'Lessons from the Integrated Domestic Abuse Programme, for the Implementation of Building Better Relationships', *Probation Journal*, 64, 2 (2017), pp. 129–45.

4   Alyson Rees, 'Let a Hundred Flowers Bloom, Let a Hundred Schools of Thought Contend': Towards a Variety in Programmes for Perpetrators of Domestic Violence', *Probation Journal*, 52, 3 (2005), pp. 277–88.
5   Edward Gondolf, *Batterer Intervention Systems* (Sage, 2002).
6   David Morran, 'Re-Education or Recovery? Re-Thinking Some Aspects of Domestic Violence Perpetrator Programmes', *Probation Journal*, 58, 1 (2010), pp. 23–36.
7   R. Emerson Dobash, Russel P. Dobash, Kate Cavanagh and Ruth Lewis, *Research Evaluation of Programmes for Violent Men* (The Scottish Office Central Research Unit, 1996).
8   Vivienne Raine, *Domestic Abuse: The Work Undertaken by Community Rehabilitation Companies (CRCs)* (HM Inspectorate of Probation, 2018).
9   Morran, 'Re-Education or Recovery?', p. 31.
10 Will Hughes, 'Lessons from the Integrated Domestic Abuse Programme, for the Implementation of Building Better Relationships', *Probation Journal*, 64, 2 (2017), pp. 129–45.

Bibliography

Archive Sources

Bristol Archives:

Jmag/adm/4/2: Bristol Probation Committee Minutes, 1937–69.
Pamphlet/1383: Missionaries to Managers. Memories of the Probation Service in the Bristol Area, 1907–87.

Edinburgh City Archives (ECA):

Edinburgh Police Court Records, 1909–35.

Glamorgan Archives:

PSCBO/60/1: Cardiff Probation Committee Minutes, 1919–29.
PSCBO/60/5: Cardiff Probation Committee Minutes, 1948–56.
Q/A/M/7/2/1 Cardiff Probation Committee Agendas, Officers Reports and Related Papers, 1936–56.

Lancashire Archives:

CC/PNM/1: Lancashire Probation Committees: Minute Books, 1949–59.
PSRd/2/2: Rossendale Probation Case Committee, 1952–8.
PSPr/4/2: Preston Probation Committee Minutes, 1943–62.

Liverpool City Archives:

347 MAG/1/6: Liverpool Probation Committee Minutes, 1931–74.

London Metropolitan Archives:

PS/SWE/ COL: London South Western Police Court, Newspaper Cuttings Collection.

Manchester City Archives:

GB127.M117/3/5: Manchester Probation Committee Minutes, 1926–65.

Modern Records Centre, University of Warwick, WISEArchive:

The Cohen Interviews, edited by Tim Cook and Harry Marsh.

National Records of Scotland (NRS):

ED20/2: Minutes of the Special Committee on Probation Guardianship of Criminal Offenders, 7 June 1905.

ED20/3: Probation of Offenders Draft Bill, 1906: Newspaper Cutting from *Dundee Country and Municipal Record*, 20 June 1905.

ED20/130: Matrimonial Conciliation by Probation Officers 1949–50: Home Office Memorandum on the Principles and Practice in the Work of Matrimonial Conciliation in Magistrates Courts, 1948.

ED20/130: The 1936 Report of The Departmental Committee on the Social Services in Courts of Summary Jurisdiction.

ED20/400–416: Probation Officers Reports, 1908–23.

ED20/417–485: Probation Officers Returns, 1908–35.

Scottish Catholic Archives:

SCA/DE/120/4: Minutes of the Scottish Catholic Probation Officers Association.

The Mitchel Library, Glasgow:

D.tc 14/2/15: Reports of the Corporation of Glasgow vol. 9, 1919–20.
RU/3/4/5: Half Year Report of the Glasgow Probation Committee, 1938.

The National Archives:

H45/19505: 10th Meetings of the Probation Training Board, July 1939.

H45/19505: Summary of Probation Officers' Reports on Social Work during the War.

HO 330/9: Probation and After Care Department, Criminal Statistics: Indictable Offences Known to the Police 1950–9.

HO 345/9: Proceedings of the Wolfenden Committee on Homosexual Offences and Prostitution.

West Glamorgan Archives:

P/60/CW/152: The Moral Welfare Council, *The Threshold of Marriage*.
S/TC4/Probation/1: Probation Committee Minutes, 1940–73.

Newspapers

Aberdeen Evening Express
Acton Gazette
Alderley & Wilmslow Advertiser
Barking, East Ham & Ilford Advertiser
Bath Chronical and Weekly Gazette
Biggleswade Chronicle
Birmingham Daily Post
Boston Guardian
Buckinghamshire Examiner
Chelmsford Chronicle
Chelsea News and General Advertiser
Cornishman
Coventry Evening Telegraph
Daily Herald
Derby Evening Telegraph
Dundee Evening Telegraph
Eastbourne Chronical
Essex Newsman
Folkstone, Hythe, Sandgate and Cheriton Herald
Halifax Evening Courier
Hampshire Telegraph
Hartlepool Norther Daily Mail
Hendon & Finchley Times, 7 June 1935, 7
Hull Daily Mail
Illustrated Police News
Kington Times
Lakes Herald
Leeds Mercury
Lichfield Mercury
Lincolnshire Echo
Liverpool Daily Post
Liverpool Echo
Liverpool Evening Express
Louth and North Lincolnshire Advertiser
Manchester Evening News
Marylebone Mercury
Milngavie and Bearsden Herald
Motherwell Times
Northampton Mercury
Northern Daily Mail

Nottingham Evening Post
Ripley and Heanor News and Ilkeston Division Free Press
Rochdale Observer
Sheffield Daily Telegraph
Somerset County Herald
Suffolk and Essex Free Press
Sunderland Daily Echo and Shipping Gazette
Surrey Mirror and County Post
Taunton Courier and Western Advertiser
Thanet Advertiser
The Bleeper News
The Bolton Evening News
The Bucks Herald
The Central Somerset Gazette
The Citizen
The Common Cause
The Courier
The Eastbourne Herald
The Essex County Chronicle
The Essex Newsman
The Herald and News
The Lancashire Evening Post
The Londonderry Sentinel
The Luton News and Bedfordshire Chronicle
The Mid Sussex Times
The Middlesex Chronicle
The People
The Preston Herald
The Scotsman
The Sphere
The Staffordshire Advertiser
The Vote
The West London Observer
The Western Daily Press
The Western Gazette
The Western Morning News
The Whitstable Times
The Woman's Leader
The Worthing Herald
The Yorkshire Post and Leeds Intelligencer
The Yorkshire Post and Leeds Mercury
Wells Journal and Somerset and West of England Advertiser

West London Press
West Sussex Gazette
Western Mail
Wishaw Press
Yarmouth Independent

Acts

The 1857 Matrimonial Clauses Act (20 & 21 Vict. C.85).
The Burgh Police (Scotland) Act 1892 (55 & 56 Vict.c.55).
The Children Act 1908 (Geo V. c.67).
The Children and Young Persons Act 1933 (23 & 24 Geo.5 c.12).
The Criminal Justice (Scotland) Act 1949 (12, 13 & 14 Geo.6 c.94).
The Criminal Justice (Scotland) Act 1980 (Eliz. II c.62).
The Criminal Justice Act 1948 (11 & 12 Geo 6 c.58).
The Criminal Justice Administration Act 1914 (4 & 5 Geo.5.).
The Criminal Law Amendment Act 1885 (48 & 49 Vict. c.69).
The Edinburgh Municipal and Police Act 1879 (42 & 43 Vict. c.cxxxii).
The Family Allowances Act 1945 (8 & 9 Go. VI c.41).
The Glasgow Police (Further Powers) Act 1892 (55 & 56 Vict. c.165).
The Lunacy Act 1890 (53 Vict. c.5).
The Matrimonial Clauses Act 1878 (41 & 42 Vict. c.19).
The Metropolitan Police Act 1839 (2 & 3 Vict. c.47).
The Offences Against the Person Act 1861 (24 & 25 Vict. c.100).
The Probation of First Time Offenders Act 1887 (50 & 51 Vict. c.25).
The Probation of Offenders Act 1907(3 Edw. 7, c.25).
The Sexual Offences (Scotland) Act 1976.
The Sexual Offences Act 1956 (4 & 5 Eliz.2 c.69).
The Sexual Offences Act 1967 (Eliz. II c.60).
The Street Offences Act 1959 (7 & 8 Eliz 2 c.57).
The Suicide Act 1961 (9 & 10 Eliz 2 c.60).
The Town Police Clauses Act 1847 (10 & 11 Vict. c.89).
The Vagrancy Act 1824 (Geo V. 4, c.83).
The Vagrancy Act 1898 (61 & 62 Vict. c.39).

Published Books

Anderson, Olive. *Suicide in Victorian and Edwardian England*. Oxford: Oxford University Press, 1987.

Bailey, Victor. *Delinquency and Citizenship: Reclaiming the Young Offender, 1914–48.* Oxford: Clarendon Press, 1987.

Bailey, Victor. *The Rise and Fall of the Rehabilitative Ideal, 1895–1970.* London: Routledge, 2019.

Bartlett, Peter and David Wright. *Outside the Walls of the Asylum: The History of Care in the Community, 1750–2000.* New Brunswick: Athlone Press, 1999.

Bingham, Adrian. *Family Newspapers? Sex, Private Life, and the British Popular Press, 1918–1978.* Oxford: Oxford University Press, 2009.

Bochel, Dorothy. *Probation and After-care: Its Development in England and Wales.* Edinburgh: Scottish Academic Press, 1976.

Bourke, Joanna. *Rape: A History from 1860 to the Present Day.* London: Virago, 2007.

Brown, Alyson, David Barrett and Ian Sparks. *Knowledge of Evil: Child Prostitution and Child Sexual Abuse in Twentieth Century England.* Cullompton: Villan, 2002.

Brown, Calum. *The Death of Christian Britain: Understanding Secularisation 1800–2000.* London: Routledge, 2001.

Brown, Jennifer and Sandra Walklate (Eds). *Handbook on Sexual Violence.* London: Routledge, 2012.

Burt, Cyril. *The Young Delinquent.* London: London University Press, 1933.

Caslin, Samantha. *Save the Womanhood!: Vice, Urban Immorality and Social Control in Liverpool, c. 1900–1976.* Liverpool: Liverpool University Press, 2018.

Caslin, Samantha and Julia Laite. *Wolfenden's Women: Prostitution in Post-War Britain.* London: Palgrave MacMillan, 2020.

City of Glasgow Probation Area Committee. *Brief Survey of Fifty Years of the Probation Service of the City of Glasgow 1905–1955.* Glasgow: Glasgow Corporation, 1955.

Cocks, H. G. and Matt Houlbrook (Eds). *Palgrave Advances in the Modern History of Sexuality.* Basingstoke: Palgrave Macmillan, 2006.

Cohen, Debora. *Family Secrets, the Things We Tried to Hide.* London: Penguin Books, 2014.

Cohen, Stanley and Andrew Scull. *Social Control and the State.* London: Palgrave MacMillan, 1983.

Cohen, Stanley. *Visions of Social Control.* Cambridge: Polity Press, 1985.

Collins, Marcus. *Modern Love: An Intimate History of Men and Women in Twentieth Century Britain* London: Atlantic Books, 2003.

Collins, Marcus (ed). *The Permissive Society and Its Enemies: Sixties British Culture.* London: Rivers Oram Press, 2007.

Cook, Matt. *A Gay History of Britain: Love and Sex between Men since the Middle Ages.* Oxford: Oxford University Press, 2007.

Cox, Pamela. *Bad Girls in Britain, Gender, Justice and Welfare, 1900-1950.* New York: Palgrave, 2003.

D'Cruze, Shani. *Crimes of Outrage: Sex, Violence and Victorian Working Women.* Illinois: Northern Illinois University Press, 1998.

Davidson, Roger. *Dangerous Liaisons: A Social History of Venereal Disease in Twentieth-Century Scotland.* Amsterdam: Rodopi, 2000.

Davidson, Roger. *Illicit and Unnatural Practices: The Law, Sex and Society in Scotland since 1900*. Edinburg: Edinburgh University Press, 2020.

Davidson, Roger and Gayle Davis. *The Sexual State: Sexuality and Scottish Governance*. Edinburgh: Edinburgh University Press, 2012.

Delap, Lucy, Ben Griffin and Abigail Wills (Eds). *The Politics of Domestic Authority in Britain since 1800*. Basingstoke: Palgrave Macmillian, 2009.

Doggett, Maeve E. *Marriage, Wife-Beating and the Law in Victorian England*. South Carolina: University of South Carolina Press, 1993.

Donzelot, Jacques. *The Policing of Families*. Baltimore: The Johns Hopkins University Press, 1997.

Elias, Norbert. *The Civilizing Process: The History of Manners*. New York: Urizen Books, 1978.

Fisher, Kate and Simon Szreter. *Sex before the Sexual Revolution: Intimate Life in England 1918–1963*. Cambridge: Cambridge University Press, 2010.

Foucault, Michel. *Madness and Civilisation*. London: Tavistock, 1967.

Foucault, Michel. *Discipline and Punish*. Harmondsworth: Penguin Books, 1977.

Foucault, Michel. *The History of Sexuality. Volume 1*. Harmondsworth: Penguin Books, 1990.

Gard, Raymond. *Probation and Rehabilitation in England and Wales, 1876–1962*. London: Bloomsbury Academic, 2014.

Garland, David. *Punishment and Welfare: A History of Penal Strategies*. Farnham: Ashgate, 1985.

Garland, David. *The Culture of Control: Crime and Social Order in Contemporary Society*. Oxford: Oxford University Press, 2001.

Gates, Barbara. *Victorian Suicide: Mad Crimes and Sad Stories*. Princeton: Princeton University Press, 1988.

Gondolf, Edward. *Batterer Intervention Systems*. Thousand Oaks: Sage, 2002.

Gordon, Linda. *Heroes of Their Own Lives: The Politics and History of Family Violence*. New York: Viking, 1988.

Gordon, Louisa. *Penal Discipline*. New York: E. Dutton & Co., 1922.

Hammerton, James. *Cruelty and Companionship: Conflict in Nineteenth Century Married Life*. London: Routledge, 1992.

Harris, Jo. *Probation: A Sheaf of Memories*. Suffolk: M.F. Robinson, 1937.

Haste, Cate. *Rules of Desire: Sex in Britain: World War 1 to the Present*. London: Vintage, 1992.

Higgins, Patrick. *Heterosexual Dictatorship: Male Homosexuality in Post-War Britain*. London: Fourth Estate, 1996.

Hodges, Andrew. *Alan Turing: The Enigma, The Centenary Edition*. Princeton: Princeton University Press, 2012.

Houlbrook, Matt. *Queer London: Perils and Pleasures in the Sexual Metropolis, 1918–1957*. Chicago: University of Chicago Press, 2005.

Jackson, Louise. *Child Sexual Abuse in Victorian England*. London: Routledge, 1999.

Jahoda, Marie. *Employment and Unemployment: A Social Psychological Analysis*. Cambridge: Cambridge University Press, 1982.

Jivani, Alkarim. *It's Not Unusual: A History of Lesbian and Gay Britain in the Twentieth Century*. Bloomington: Indiana University Press, 1997.

Kritsotaki, Despo, Vicky Long and Matthew Smith (Eds). *Deinstitutionalisation and after Post-War Psychiatry in the Western World*. London: Palgrave MacMillan, 2016.

Kuhn, Philip. *Psychoanalysis in Britain, 1893–1913: Histories and Historiography*. Lanham: Lexington Books, 2017.

Laite, Julia. *Common Prostitutes and Ordinary Citizen: Commercial Sex in London, 1885–1960*. London: Palgrave Macmillan, 2012.

Langhamer, Claire. *The English in Love: The Intimate Story of an Emotional Revolution*. Oxford: Oxford University Press, 2013.

Lewes, Kenneth. *The Psychoanalytic Theory of Male Homosexuality*. New York: Simona and Schuster, 1988.

Lewis, Brian. *Wolfenden's Witnesses: Homosexuality in Post-war Britain*. Basingstoke: Palgrave Macmillan, 2016.

Lewis, Jane. *Whom God Hath Joined Together: Work of Marriage Guidance*. London: Routledge, 1991.

Lunbeck, Elizabeth. *The Psychiatric Persuasion: Knowledge, Gender and Power in Modern America*. Princeton: Princeton University Press, 1996.

MacDonald, Michael and Terence Murphy. *Sleepless Souls: Suicide in Early Modern England*. Oxford: Oxford University Press, 1990.

Mahood, Linda. *Policing Gender, Class and Family: Britain, 1850–1940*. London: Routledge, 1995.

Mahood, Linda. *The Magdalenes: Prostitution in the Nineteenth Century*. London: Routledge, 1990.

Mair, George and Lol Burke. *Redemption, Rehabilitation and Risk Management: A History of Probation*. London: Routledge, 2012.

McLeod, Hugh. *The Decline of Christendom in Western Europe 1750–2000*. Cambridge: Cambridge University Press, 2003.

Millar, Chris. *A History of Self-Harm in Britain: A Genealogy of Cutting and Overdosing*. London: Palgrave MacMillan, 2015.

Minois, Georges. *History of Suicide: Voluntary Death in Western Culture*. Baltimore: The Johns Hopkins University Press, 1995.

Mullins, Claud. *Wife vs Husband in the Courts*. London: George Allen & Unwin, Ltd., 1935.

Mullins, Claud. *Crime and Psychology*. North Yorkshire: Methuen, 1943.

Norwood East, W. *The Adolescent Criminal: A Medico-Sociological Study of 4,000 Male Adolescent*. London: J. & A. Churchill, 1942.

Olsen, Stephanie. *Juvenile Nation: Youth, Emotions and the Making of the Modern British Citizen, 1880–1914*. London: Bloomsbury Academic, 2015.

Oosterhuis, Harry. *Stepchildren of Nature; Krafft-Ebing, Psychiatry, and the Making of Sexual Identity*. Chicago: Chicago University Press, 2000.

Page, Martin. *Crimefighters of London: A History of the Origins and Development of the Probation and Aftercare Service*. London: London Action Trust, 1972.

Pick, Daniel. *Faces of Degeneration: A European Disorder, c. 1848–c. 1918*. Cambridge: Cambridge University Press, 1989.

Pietikainen, Petteri and Jesper Vaczy Kragh (Eds). *Social Class and Mental Illness in Northern Europe*. London: Routledge, 2019.

Pietikainen, Petteri. *Madness: A History*. London: Routledge, 2015.

Priestley, Philip and Maurice Vanstone (Eds). *Offenders or Citizens? A Reader in Rehabilitation*. London: Routledge, 2010.

Radzinowicz, Leon and Roger Hood. *A history of English Criminal Law and Its Administration from 1750: Vol. 5: The Emergence of Penal Policy in Victorian and Edwardian England*. Oxford: Oxford Press, 1990.

Rimmer, Joyce. *Changing Lives, An Oral History of Probation*. London: National Association of Probation Officers, 2007.

Rose, Nikolas. *The Psychological Complex: Psychology, Politics and Society in England, 1869–1939*. London: Routledge, 1985.

Rose, Nikolas. *Governing the Soul: The Shaping of the Private Self*. London: Routledge, 1990.

Rose, Sonya O. *Which People's War?* Oxford: Oxford University Press, 2003.

Schaffner, Anna Katharina. *Modernism and Perversion: Sexual Deviance in Sexology and Literature, 1850–1930*. Basingstoke: Palgrave Macmillan, 2011.

Schofield, Michael. *Society and the Homosexual*. Westport: Greenwood Press, 1952.

Scott, James. *Weapons of the Weak: Everyday Forms of Peasant Resistance*. Yale: Yale University Press, 1985.

Scull, Andrew. *Museums of Madness: Social Organisation of Insanity in Nineteenth Century England*. London: Penguin Books, 1975.

Scull, Andrew. *Masters of Bedlam: The Transformation of the Mad-Doctoring Trade*. Princeton: Princeton University Press, 1996.

Settle, Louise. *Sex for Sale in Scotland: Prostitution in Edinburgh and Glasgow*. Edinburgh:Edinburgh University Press, 2016.

Stanton, Walter. *Sidelights on Police Court Mission Work*. Worcester: Trinity Press, 1935.

Stoke, Sewell. *Court Circular: Experiences of a London Probation Officer*. London: Michael Joseph, 1950.

Thane, Pat and Tanya Evans. *Sinners? Scroungers? Saints? Unmarried Motherhood in Twentieth-Century England*. Oxford: Oxford University Press, 2012.

Thomson, Mathew. *The Problem of Mental Deficiency: Eugenics, Democracy and Social Policy in Britain, c. 1870–1959*. Oxford: Clarendon Press, 1998.

Vanstone, Maurice. *Supervising Offenders in the Community: A History of Probation Theory and Practice*. Farnham: Ashgate, 2004.

Vanstone, Maurice and Philip Priestley (Eds). *Probation and Politics: Academic Reflections from Former Practitioners*. Basingstoke: Palgrave Macmillan, 2016.

Warr, Peter. *Work, Unemployment and Mental Health*. Oxford: Oxford University Press, 1987.

Watney, Simon. *Policing Desire: Pornography, Aids and the Media*. London: Bloomsbury, 1987.

Weaver, John and David Wright (Eds). *Histories of Suicide: International Perspectives on Self-Destruction in the Modern World*. Toronto: University of Toronto Press, 2009.

Weeks, Jeffery. *Sex Politics and Society: The Regulation of Sexuality since 1800*. London: Longman, 1989.

Weeks, Jeffery. *Coming Out: Homosexual Politics in Britain from the Nineteenth Century to the Present*. London: Quartet, 1990.

Weiner, Martin. *Men of Blood: Violence, Manliness, and Criminal Justice in Victorian England*. Cambridge: Cambridge University Press, 2004.

Whitehead, Philip and Roger Statham. *The History of Probation: Politics, Power and Cultural Change 1876-2005*. Crayford: Shaw, 2006.

Wood, John Carter. *Violence and Crime in Nineteenth-Century England: The Shadow of Our Refinement*. London: Routledge, 2004.

Book Chapters

Ayers, Pat and Jan Lambertz. 'Marriage Relations, Money and Domestic Violence in Working-Class Liverpool, 1919-39'. In *Labour and Love: Women's Experience of Home and Family 1850-1940*, edited by Jane Lewis. Hoboken: Blackwell, 1986.

Emsley, Clive. 'Sergeant Goddard: The Story of the Rotten Apple, or a Diseased Orchard?' In *Crime and Culture a Historical Perspective*, edited by Amy Srebnick and René Levy, 85-104. Farnham: Ashgate, 2005.

Garland, David. 'Of Crimes and Criminals: The Development of Criminology in Britain'. In *The Oxford Handbook of Criminology*, 3rd edition, edited by Mike Maguire et al, 7-50. Oxford: Oxford University Press, 2002.

Jackson, Louise. 'Family, Community and the Regulation of Sexual Abuse: London 1870-1914'. In *Childhood in Question: Children, Parents and the State*, edited by Anthony Fletcher and Stephen Hussey, 133-51. Manchester: Manchester University Press, 1999.

MacDonald, Michael. 'The Medicalisation of Suicide in England'. In *Framing Disease: Studies in Cultural History*, edited by Charles Rosenberg and Janet Golden, 85-103. New Jersey: Rutgers University Press, 1992.

Neustatter, Lindesay. 'Homosexuality: The Medical Perspective'. In *They Stand Apart: A Critical Survey of the Problem of Homosexuality*, edited by Tudor Rees and Harley Usill. London: Heinemann, 1955.

Waters, Chris. 'Havelock Ellis, Sigmund Freud and the State: Discourses of Homosexual Identity in Interwar Britain'. In *Sexology in Culture: Labelling Bodies and Desires*, edited by Lucy Bland and Laura Doan, 165-80. Cambridge: Polity Press, 1998.

Articles

Annison, Jill. 'A Gendered Review of Change within the Probation Service'. *The Howard Journal of Criminal Justice* 46, no. 2 (2007): 145–61.

Annison, Jill. 'Delving into the Probation Journal: Portrayals of Women Probation Officers and Women Offenders'. *Probation Journal* 56, no. 4 (2009): 435–50.

Auerbach, Sascha. 'Beyond the Pale of Mercy: Victorian Penal Culture, Police Court Missionaries, and the Origins of Probation in England'. *Law and History Review* 33, no. 3 (2015): 621–63.

Behlmer, George. 'Summary Justice and Working-Class Marriage in England, 1870–1940'. *Law and History Review* 12, no. 2 (1994): 229–75.

Bingham, Adrian, Lucy Delap, Louise Jackson and Louise Settle. 'Historical Child Sexual Abuse in England and Wales: The Role of Historians'. *History of Education* 45 (2016): 411–29.

Brooke, Stephan. 'Gender and Working-class Identity in Britain during the 1950s'. *Journal of Social History* 35 (2001): 773–95.

Clark, J. C. D. 'Secularization and Modernisation: The Failure of the Grand Narrative'. *The Historical Journal* 55, no. 1 (2012): 161–94.

D'Cruze, Shanni. 'Approaching the History of Rape and Sexual Violence: Notes towards Research'. *Women's History Review* 1 (1992): 377–97.

Davidson, Roger and Gayle Davis. 'A field for Private Members: The Wolfenden Committee and Scottish Homosexual Law Reform, 1950–67'. *Twentieth Century British History* 15 (2004): 174–201.

Davidson, Roger. 'Psychiatry and Homosexuality in Mid-twentieth-century Edinburgh: The View from the Jordanburn Nerve Hospital'. *History of Psychiatry* 20, no. 4 (2009): 403–24.

Davis, Jennifer. 'A Poor Man's System of Justice: The London Police Courts in the Second Half of the Nineteenth Century'. *Historical Journal* 27 (1984): 309–35.

Dickinson, Tommy, Matt Cook, John Playle and Christine Hallett. 'Queer' Treatments: Giving a Voice to Former Patients Who Received Treatments for Their 'Sexual Deviations'. *Journal of Clinical Nursing* 21, no. 9–10 (2021): 1345–54.

Drescher, Jack. 'Can Sexual Orientation Be Changed?' *Journal of Gay & Lesbian Mental Health* 19, no. 1 (2015): 84–93.

Francis, Martin. 'The Domestication of the Male? Recent Research on Nineteenth and Twentieth-Century British Masculinity'. *History Workshop Journal* 45, no. 3 (2002): 637–52.

Golla, F. L. and R. Sessions Hodge. 'Hormone Treatment of the Sexual Offender'. *The Lancet* 253, no. 6563 (1949): 1006–7.

Greenland, Cyril. 'Suicide, Threatened or Attempted'. *Mental Health* 17, no. 2 (1958): 44–9.

Harrison, Grace. 'The Case Load of the Probation Officer'. *Probation* 1, no. 13 (1932): 201–2.

Hinshelwood, R. D. 'The Organizing of Psychoanalysis in Britain'. *Psychoanalysis and History* 1, no. 1 (1999).

Hughes, Annmarie. 'The "Non-Criminal" Class: Wife-beating in Scotland (c. 1800-1949)'. *Crime History & Society* 14, no. 2 (2010): 31–54.

Hughes, Will. 'Lessons from the Integrated Domestic Abuse Programme, for the Implementation of Building Better Relationships'. *Probation Journal* 64, no. 2 (2017): 129–45.

Hunt, Margaret. 'Wife-beating, Domesticity and Women's Independence in Eighteenth and Nineteenth Century London'. *Gender and History* 4 (1992): 10–33.

Kelly, Christine. 'Probation Officers for Young Offenders in 1920's Scotland'. *European Journal of Probation* 9, no. 2 (2017): 169–91.

King, Peter. 'Punishing Assault: The Transformation of Attitudes in the English Courts'. *Journal of Interdisciplinary History* 27 (1996): 43–74.

Lunan, John. 'Probation Officers, Social Enquiry Reports, and Importuning in the 1960s'. *The Historical Journal* 56, no. 3 (2013): 781–800.

Mace, David R. 'A Marriage Welfare Service'. *Probation* 5, no. 7 (1947): 86.

Macnicol, John. 'Eugenics, Medicine and Mental Deficiency: An Introduction'. *Oxford Review of Education* 9 (1983): 177–81.

Mahood, Linda and Barbara Littlewood. 'The "Vicious" Girl and the "Street-Corner" Boy: Sexuality and the Gendered Delinquent in the Scottish Child-Saving Movement, 1850–1940'. *Journal of History of Sexuality* 4, no. 4 (1994): 549–78.

Martinson, R. 'What Works? Questions and Answers about Prison Reform'. *The Public Interest* 5 (1974): 22–54.

McKee-Ryan, Frances, Zhaoli Song, Connie Wanberg and Angelo Kinicki. 'Psychological and Physical Well-Being during Unemployment: A Meta-Analytic Study'. *The Journal of Applied Psychology* 90, no. 1 (2005): 53–76.

McNeill, Fergus. 'Remembering Probation in Scotland'. *Probation Journal* 52, no. 1 (2005): 23–38.

McWilliams, William. 'The Mission to the English Police Courts 1876–1936'. *The Howard Journal of Criminal Justice* 22, no. 1–3 (1983): 129–47.

McWilliams, William. 'The Mission Transformed: Professionalisation of Probation Between the Wars'. *The Howard Journal of Criminal Justice* 24, no. 4 (1985): 7–274.

McWilliams, William. 'The English Probation System and the Diagnostic Ideal'. *The Howard Journal of Criminal Justice* 25, no. 4 (1986): 241–60.

McWilliams, William. 'Probation, Pragmatism and Policy'. *The Howard Journal of Criminal Justice* 26, no. 2 (1987): 97–121.

Mogey, John. 'Marriage Counselling and Family Life Education in England'. *Marriage and Family Living* 23, no. 2 (1961): 146–54.

Morran, David. 'Re-Education or Recovery? Re-Thinking Some Aspects of Domestic Violence Perpetrator Programmes'. *Probation Journal* 58, no. 1 (2010): 23–36.

Mullins, Claud. 'The Matrimonial Work of the Courts'. *Probation* 3, no. 1 (1938): 4–7.

Mullins, Claud. 'Probation Officers and Postwar Problems'. *Probation* 4, no. 3 (1943): 59.

Nash, David. 'Reconnecting Religion with Social and Cultural History: Secularization's Failure as a Master Narrative'. *Cultural and Social History* 1 (2004): 302–25.
Norman, H. E. 'Family Unity and Probation'. *Probation* 1, no. 14 (1933): 213.
Norman, H. E. 'Matrimonial Conciliation'. *Probation* 3, no. 4 (1939): 60.
Pollard, Beatrice E. 'Research in Matrimonial Work'. *Probation* 7, no. 2 (1954): 51.
Pollard, Beatrice E. 'Marriage and Divorce: Report of the Royal Commission'. *Probation* 8, no. 2 (1956): 27–30.
Pollard, Beatrice E. 'The Distinctive Nature of Probation Work'. *Probation* 9, no. 2 (1959): 22–4.
Rees, Alyson. 'Let a Hundred Flowers Bloom, let a Hundred Schools of Thought Contend': Towards a Variety in Programmes for Perpetrators of Domestic Violence'. *Probation Journal* 52, no. 3 (2005): 277–88.
Robertson, Stephen. 'What's Law Got to Do with It? Legal Records and Sexual Histories'. *Journal of the History of Sexuality* 14, no. 1/2 (2005): 161–85.
Robinson, Amanda. 'Serial Domestic Abuse in Wales: An Exploratory Study into Its Definition, Prevalence, Correlates, and Management'. *Victims & Offenders* 12, no. 5 (2017): 643–62.
Roloff, M. A. 'Matrimonial Courts: How Can the Probation Officer Best Help?' *Probation* 4, no. 7 (1944): 82–5.
Rose, Sonya O. 'Girls and GIs: Race, Sex, and Diplomacy in Second World War Britain'. *The International History Review* 19, no. 1 (1997): 146–60.
Slater, Stefan. 'Lady Astor and the Ladies of the Night: The Home Office, the Metropolitan Police and the Politics of the Street Offences Committee, 1927–28'. *Law and History Review* 30, no. 2 (2012): 533–73.
Smart, Carol. 'A History of Ambivalence and Conflict in the Discursive Construction of the "Child Victim" of Sexual Abuse', *Social & Legal Studies* 8, no. 3 (1999): 391–409.
Smart, Carol. 'Reconsidering the Recent History of Child Sexual Abuse, 1910–1960'. *Journal of Social Policy* 29 (2000): 55–71.
Smith, Glenn, Annie Bartlett and Michael King. 'Treatments of Homosexuality in Britain since the 1950s – An Oral History: The Experience of Patients'. *British Medical Journal* 328, 7437 (2004): 427.
Smith, Glenn, Annie Bartlett and Michael King. 'Treatments of Homosexuality in Britain since the 1950s – An Oral History: The Experience of Professionals'. *British Medical Journal* 328, 7437 (2004), pp. 328–429.
Stanley, C. H. 'The Probation Officer and Conciliation'. *Probation* 8, no. 1 (1956): 4.
Stanley, C. H. 'The Probation Officer and Conciliation'. *Probation* 8, no. 1 (1956): 6.
Stuart, H. 'Community Care and the Origins of Psychiatric Social Work'. *Social Work in Health Care* 25 (1997): 25–36.
Tomes, Nancy. 'A "Torrent of Abuse": Crimes of Violence between Working-Class Men and Women in London, 1840–1875'. *Journal of Social History* 11 (1978): 328–45.
Tyrer, A. E. 'A Probation Officer at Work'. *Probation* 2, no. 4 (1936): 58.

Vanstone, Maurice. 'A History of the Use of Groups in Probation Work: Part One – From "Clubbing the Unclubbables" to Therapeutic Intervention'. *The Howard Journal of Crime and Justice* 42, no. 1 (2003): 69–86.

Westbury, A. J. 'Questionnaire Survey into Reconciliation Work'. *Probation* 3, no. 4 (1939): 60–2.

Woodhouse, J. 'Eugenics and the Feeble-Minded, the Parliamentary Debates of 1912–14'. *History of Education* 11 (1982): 127–37.

Woollacott, Angela. '"Khaki Fever" and Its Control: Gender, Class, Age and Sexual Morality on the British Homefront in the First World War'. *Journal of Contemporary History* 29, no. 2 (1994): 325–47.

Zola, Irving Kenneth. 'Medicine as an Institution of Social Control'. *The Sociological Review* 20, no. 4 (1972): 487–504.

Unpublished Theses

Chaney, S. 'Suicide, Mental Illness and the Asylum: The Case of Bethlem Royal Hospital 1845–1875'. MA diss., University College London, 2009.

Dickinson, Tommy. 'Mental Nursing and "Sexual Deviation": Exploring the Role of Nurses and the Experience of Patients, 1935–1974'. PhD diss., University of Manchester, 2012.

Watson, Stephen. 'The Moral Imbecile: A Study of the Relation between Penal Practice and Psychiatric Knowledge of the Habitual Offender'. PhD diss., The University of Lancaster, 1988.

Poems

Houseman, A. E. *Last Poems, XII, The Laws of God the Laws of Man*, 1922.

Index

Aberdeen Evening Express 89–91
abstinence 8, 16, 76, 78–81, 86, 93, 98, 99, 116–18, 120, 209, 214, 216, 219
Adair, J. 140
age 5, 15, 112, 123, 136, 142, 143, 145, 146, 148–50, 189
agency 34, 35, 46, 48, 87, 198, 212
alcohol 5, 8, 13, 148
    and attempted suicide 116–18
    consumption 71, 74, 79, 95, 209
    and domestic violence 78–80, 86
aversion therapy 135, 156, 157, 161, 163

Barking, Eastham and Ilford Advertiser, The 148
Bath Chronical and Weekly Gazette 94–5
Behlmer, G. 88
Birmingham Post, The 137
Bochel, D. 17
Bolton Probation Committee Annual Report 179
Bow Street Magistrates Court 121, 157, 185
Bristol Probation Committee 46, 51–4
broken homes 30–2, 49, 197
Bucks Herald 147–9
Burgh Police (Scotland) Act 1892 173
Burke, L. 17
Burt, C. 7, 21, 31–2

Cardiff Probation Committee 31, 37, 49, 54, 87, 153, 156
Central Somerset Gazette, The 116
character 3, 15, 16, 62, 84, 90, 111, 131, 141–4, 146, 150, 164, 179, 181, 184, 214
Chelmsford Chronicle 144
Chelsea Probation Committee 186
Children Act 1908 145, 173, 182, 198
Christianity 8, 23, 43, 176, 216
Church of England Temperance Society (CETS) 4, 15–16, 21, 42, 184
civilizing process 72–4

class
    attitudes 214
    middle 5, 6, 35, 87, 88, 142, 178, 217
    and respectability 147
    social 142, 147, 148
    working 5, 6, 35, 43, 44, 55, 73, 87, 88, 98, 109, 165, 214, 217
Clause 3 of the Criminal Justice (Scotland) Act 1949 138
Clause 3 of the Criminal Law Amendment Bill 1918 182
Cohen, D. 35–6
Collins, M. 39
Common Cause 179
community rehabilitation companies (CRCs) 24, 221
Corporation of Glasgow Special Committee on Probation of Offenders Report 75, 176
Courier, The 196
Criminal Justice Act
    1925 19–20
    1948 22
    1967 23
Criminal Justice (Scotland) Act 1949 22
Criminal Justice Administration Act 1914 18–19, 174–5
criminal justice system 2, 15, 17, 23, 132, 139, 155, 164, 220, 223
Criminal Law Amendment Act 1885 136, 138, 150
Cunningham, A. S. 197

Davidson, R. 135, 138, 151
Davies, J. 42, 88
Defence of the Real Act 181
delinquency 18, 21, 31, 32, 89
Denning Committee 48, 59
Departmental Committee on Homosexual Offences and Prostitution 137, 189
Departmental Committee on the Probation of Offenders Act 1907 180

Departmental Committee on the Social
    Services in Courts of Summary
    Jurisdiction 32, 33, 44, 59
deviancy 132–5, 139, 155, 163
Dickinson, T. 157, 160
divorce 22, 30, 31, 33, 36, 43, 44, 46, 48,
    49, 53, 59, 73, 208
Divorce Reform Act 1969 49
domestic violence 57, 59, 64, 71–80, 86,
    87, 91, 96, 98, 99, 163, 209, 216–18,
    220–3
Donzelot, J. 6

Eastbourne Herald, The 30, 108
Edinburgh Municipal and Police Act 1879
    174
Edinburgh Police Court 71, 77, 84, 85, 93,
    96, 113, 118, 119, 145
education 17, 21, 38, 72, 142, 216, 221–2
Elias, N. 72
Emergency Powers (Defence) Act 1939
    185
emotions 4, 5, 7, 12, 21, 29, 30, 36, 38–40,
    62, 63, 72, 76, 89, 97, 105, 134, 135,
    210, 217
Essex Newsman 83, 115, 146, 160
Essex Quarter Sessions 77, 146
Evening Dispatch 151
Evening News, The 190
experience
    of marriage 40
    of probation 11, 15, 21, 39, 159, 211–12
    of reconciliation 64
    sexual 150
    of social work 185
    women 193, 201

family
    and friendship 35
    keeping families together 76, 88–91,
        94, 97, 98
    life 2, 39, 186, 188
    low-income 222
    nuclear 80
    relationship 21, 22, 32, 62
    stability 13, 22, 30
    supervision 107, 110–13
    working-class 87, 88, 98
Family Allowance Act 1945 76, 88, 98
femininity 178, 201, 217, 218

feminism 179, 220
First World War 18, 78, 108, 147, 181, 184
Fiscal Depute 82–3
Folkstone Herald 195
Folkstone Magistrates Court 179
Foucault, M. 6
Freud, S. 21, 132, 135

Gard, R. 7, 9, 17, 19, 21, 23, 40
Garland, D. 6, 87, 109, 217
gender
    attitudes 214
    differences 201
    and domesticity 207
    inequality 98, 209, 221
    norms 80, 216
    and penal welfare complex 217–19
    relations 5, 13, 30, 80
    roles 30, 39, 63, 84–6, 218, 220
    standards 85
    violence 220
Glasgow Corporation 176
Glasgow Police (Further Powers) Act 1892
    174
good character 84, 97, 141, 142, 144
Gordon, L. 80
Govan Police Superintendent Mackinnon
    93
gross indecency 133, 136–44, 146, 149,
    157–60, 163, 164, 210

Hammerton, J. 73
heterosexuality 132, 211, 218
Home Office Memorandum on the
    Principles and Practice in the Work
    of Matrimonial Conciliation in
    Magistrates Courts 37, 46
homosexual acts 136, 137, 140
homosexuality 8, 131, 132, 135–40, 142,
    143, 145, 149, 151, 155, 158, 160–2,
    189, 210, 214, 218
homosexual offences 135, 160, 162, 189,
    214
homosexual offender 139
hormone therapy 133, 135, 163
Houseman, A. E. 1–2
Howard, M. 24
Hughes, A. 72–4, 95
Hull Daily Mail 108
Hull report 186

Illustrated Police News 181
indecent assault 134, 142, 144–52, 154, 158, 162, 163, 165
indecent exposure 152–6, 160, 162, 163, 213

Jordanburn Nerve Hospital (JNH) 138
Justice of the Peace (JP) 6, 7, 15, 18, 73, 76, 82, 86, 89, 90, 93, 107, 108, 116, 139, 164, 213, 215

Kelly, C. 4
Kilbrandon Report 23

Laite, J. 178–9
Lakes Herald, The 138
Lancashire Evening Post, The 113, 115
Legal Aid and Advice Act 1949 43, 44, 48
Leicester Probation Committee 200
Lincolnshire Echo, The 144
Liverpool Daily Post 185
Liverpool Echo, The 110, 111, 158
Liverpool Probation Committee 32, 37, 39, 42, 45, 46, 51, 56, 76, 87, 188
Lunacy Act 1890 105, 109
Lunan, J. 141, 143
Lunbeck, E. 106
Luton Juvenile Court 148, 157

Mace, D. 35
McNeil, F. 4
McWilliams, W. 21, 22
Magdalene Asylums
 Edinburgh 175–7
 Glasgow 175
Mahood, L. 6, 87, 150, 177
Mair, G. 17
male sexual offences 14–15, 131, 163–5, 201, 210, 211, 214
Manchester Evening News 114
Manchester Probation Committee 32, 43, 50, 52, 53, 56, 57, 87, 89, 120, 185
Marriage Guidance Council 34–5
marriage reconciliation 29–30, 208–9
 counselling service 34–8
 couples opinion 55–62
 emotional support and mutual love 38–40
 legal advice and practical help 43–6

methods 33–5
 religion and psychological approach 40–3
 Second World War 46–9
 separation and maintenance orders 30–3
 success 49–55
Martinson, R. 23
Marylebone Mercury 180
masculinity 72, 73, 81, 84, 218
Matrimonial Clauses Act
 1857 30
 1878 32–3
 1937 30, 42
Matrimonial Summary Jurisdiction (Domestic Proceedings) Act 1937 12, 29, 32
medicalization 8, 14, 110, 124, 132–5, 139–40, 142, 216
Mental Health Act 1959 109
Mental Treatment Act 1930 108
Metropolitan Police Act 1839 178
Middlesex Probation Committee 31
Millar, C. 105
Mogey, J. 55
Moral Welfare Council 31
Morran, D. 221
Morrison Committee 23
Morrison Report 9
Mullins, C. 31–2, 44, 134, 152–6, 160, 215
mutual love 38–40, 63, 216

National Assistance Act 1948 76, 98
National Association of Probation Officers 20–3, 36
National Council on Family Relations 52
National Health Service 8, 109
National Marriage Guidance Council (NMGC) 34
National Probation Service (NPS) 24
National Vigilance Association 177, 184
Neustatter, L. 137
Norman, H. E. 31, 35, 36
Northern Daily Mail 193
Norwood East, W. 21
Nottingham Evening Post 138

Offences against the Person Act 1861 136, 144

paedophilia 140, 142, 145, 218
Paladin National Stalking Advocacy
    Service 222
patriarchy 38, 73, 209, 220, 221
Penal Discipline 196
penal welfare 6, 109, 217–19
Police Court Missionaries 17, 42, 72, 76, 98
policing 6
    attempted suicide 216
    of domestic violence 223
    female sexuality 218
    men's private lives 80–6
    private sphere 208–11
    sexual behaviour 131, 189, 201, 223
power
    discretionary 14, 15, 131, 139
    exercise 176
    and influence 143
    relationships 3, 11
    and social control 6
    of surveillance 5, 212
practical help
    and financial help 87–8
    legal advice and 6, 43–6, 114
    material and 118–20
Preston Heard, The 111
Preston Probation Committee 96
private sphere 4, 5, 7, 9, 30, 62, 80, 98, 201, 207–11, 217, 219
privatization 24, 223
probation 74–6
    aims and historiography 3–5
    experiences of 211–12
    methods and sources 8–11
    policy 18, 23, 113, 210, 215, 216, 219, 220
    and psychology 7–8
    resisting 194–9
    and social control 5–7
    success 91–6, 155–9, 193–4, 208–11
probation officers
    alcohol and domestic violence 78
    alcohol and suicide 117
    and doctors 154–5
    in England and Wales 21, 23
    judgement 112
    legal knowledge 44–5
    in marriage reconciliation 34, 64
    men's private lives 81–4

    and opinions 159–63
    powers of surveillance 5
    probationer and 11, 19, 20, 112
    reconciliation efforts of 54
    role 2, 6, 14, 33, 36, 37, 177
    Scottish 29
    supervision of 71, 74, 79, 84, 85, 93, 94, 107, 108, 111–16, 122, 124, 196, 197
Probation of First Offenders Act 1887 16
Probation of Offenders Act
    1907 3, 9, 13, 16–18, 138, 139, 180
    1919 75, 77
    1931 9, 10, 19, 20
Probation Social Work Report 37, 200
professionalization 4, 8, 19, 20, 22, 40, 41, 177, 207, 215
prostitution 15, 137, 173, 200–1, 211, 218
    in England and Wales 178–82
    in London 178–9
    probation success 193–4
    and promiscuity 185
    psychiatric treatment 199–200
    resisting probation 194–9
    in Scotland 173–8
    Second World War 184–9
    Street Offences Committee 183–4
    time 182–3
    Wolfenden Committee 189–92
psychiatric gaze 110
psychiatric treatment 7, 8, 10, 14, 18, 90, 91, 105–10, 122–5, 132, 138, 142, 145, 151, 153, 155, 156, 161, 199–200, 210, 211, 214–16, 218, 219, 221
psychiatry 14, 19, 40–3, 88–91, 109, 111, 146, 155, 164, 215, 216, 218
psychoanalysis 14, 21, 40, 41, 132, 133–5, 155, 163, 218
psychology 4, 7–8, 19, 21–3, 40, 41, 43, 72, 89, 120, 199, 215, 216

recidivism 2, 4, 93
reconciliation. *See* marriage reconciliation
rehabilitation 2–4, 8, 9, 11, 12, 23, 24, 98, 111, 124, 163, 207, 208, 211–13, 217, 220–2
relationships 2–4, 12, 13, 17, 19, 20–2, 29, 30, 32, 33, 38, 59, 61–3, 82, 86, 89, 114, 124, 133, 178, 188, 207, 217, 220, 222, 223

religion 4, 8, 23, 40–3, 207, 215, 216, 218
resistance 120–1, 212
respectability 5, 14, 111, 142, 147, 149
Rose, N. 6
Rossendale Probation Committee 96, 133, 162
Royal Commission 126 n.8
Royal Commission on Marriage and Divorce 48

safety net 14, 105, 109, 124, 125, 210
Samaritans charity 114
Schofield, M. 139
Scotsman, The 39, 114, 122, 174
Scottish Catholic Probation Officers Association 88
Scottish National Society for Prevention of Cruelty to Children (SNSPCC) 71, 86
Second World War 10, 21–2, 29, 36, 37, 39, 45–9, 55, 59, 88, 109, 140, 184–9, 200
sexual abuse 150, 182, 221, 222
sexual behaviour 15, 131, 132, 135, 163, 164, 173, 178, 182, 191, 201
sexual deviancy 132–5, 139, 155, 163
sexuality 14, 43, 131–5, 138, 142, 146, 160, 161, 164, 173, 189, 211, 213, 214, 217, 218
sexual offences 15, 18, 24, 173, 199, 200, 218. *See also* male sexual offences
Sexual Offences Act
  1956 144
  1967 136, 137
sexual offenders 15, 132, 139, 163
Sheffield Daily Telegraph 36, 49, 97
Short History of the Bristol Probation Service 34
Smart, C. 145, 150
sobriety 76–80
social class 142, 147–8
social control 5–7, 109, 119, 125, 217
social work 2, 4, 7–10, 14, 20, 23, 29, 30, 36, 37, 40, 43, 45–7, 72, 80, 97, 111, 120, 124, 151, 178, 185
Social Work (Scotland) Act 1968 9
Society and the Homosexual (Schofield) 139
Somerset County Herald 161–2
Sphere, The 185

Staffordshire Advertiser 141
Stanley, C. H. 32, 36, 40, 41, 60
Street Offences Act 1959 189–92, 204 n.85
Street Offences Committee 183–4, 189
Suicide Act 1961 13, 105, 106, 124
suicide attempt 8, 13–14, 105–6, 124–5, 132, 161, 164, 210, 215, 216, 219, 222
  alcohol and 116–18
  family supervision 110–13
  and the law 106–7
  material and practical help 118–20
  probationers' resistance 120–1
  probation officer supervision 113–16
  psychiatric treatment 107–10
  safety 121–4
  in Scotland 107
Summary of Probation Officers' Reports on Social Work during the War 47, 185
Sunderland Daily Echo, The 113
Swansea Probation Committee 37–8

Taunton Courier and Western Advertiser 154
Tavistock Clinic 134, 135, 147, 153, 154
temperance 8, 42, 71, 72, 74, 76–8, 80, 98, 117, 184, 216
therapy
  aversion 135, 156, 157, 161, 163
  cognitive behavioural 221
  conversion 8, 218
  hormone 133, 135, 163, 218
  psychiatric 8, 99, 105, 211
  talking 40, 41, 43, 210
Town Police Clauses Act 1847 178

unemployment 118–20

Vagrancy Act
  1824 152, 178
  1898 136
Vanstone, M. 4, 6, 17, 19, 21, 41
victims 84, 86, 96, 107, 145, 146, 148–51, 154, 158, 161, 164, 165, 182, 210, 214, 220–2
Violent and Sexual Offenders Register 222

welfare state 7, 76, 88–91, 97, 98, 209
Western Daily Press, The 108, 115
Western Gazette, The 97

West London Observer, The 121
West London Press 196
West Sussex Probation Committee 54
wife assaults 13, 39, 72–5, 77–9, 84, 85, 87, 90–4, 96
Wolfenden Committee 137, 140, 189–92
women. *See also* prostitution
    to domestic violence 71–81, 84, 88–90, 94–9, 209
    economic dependence 75
    economic realities 97
    fallen 175
    liberty 176
    in marriage 63
    promiscuous 188
    in prostitution 200
    psychiatric health 200
    psychology of 199–200
    sexuality 191, 201, 218, 220
Women's Leader 183
Wootton, B. 192
Worthing Herald 88–9, 161

Yorkshire Post, The 112, 150, 197

www.ingramcontent.com/pod-product-compliance
Lightning Source LLC
Chambersburg PA
CBHW062136300426
44115CB00012BA/1946